Statelessness in Public Law

Ius, Lex et Res Publica
Studies in Law, Philosophy and Political Cultures

Edited by Barbara Janusz-Pohl and Anna Jaron

Volume 26

Dorota Pudzianowska

Statelessness in Public Law

PETER LANG

Lausanne · Berlin · Bruxelles · Chennai · New York · Oxford

Bibliographic Information published by the Deutsche Nationalbibliothek
The Deutsche Nationalbibliothek lists this publication
in the Deutsche Nationalbibliografie; detailed bibliographic
data is available online at http://dnb.d-nb.de.

Library of Congress Cataloging-in-Publication Data
A CIP catalog record for this book has been applied for at the
Library of Congress.

This publication is financially supported by National Science Centre (Poland),
project no. 2017/27/B/HS5/02083.

ISSN 2191-3250
ISBN 978-3-631-86072-4 (Print)
E-ISBN 978-3-631-90704-7 (E-Book)
E-ISBN 978-3-631-90705-4 (E-PUB)
DOI 10.3726/b21117

Published by Peter Lang GmbH, Berlin, Deutschland

info@peterlang.com - www.peterlang.com

This publication has been peer - reviewed.

To Piotr, Wiktor and Teodor

Contents

List of Abbreviations

Legislation

CEDAW — Convention on the Elimination of All Forms of Discrimination against Women, adopted in New York on 18 December 1979, United Nations General Assembly, UN Treaty Series (UNTS), vol. 1249, p. 13.
ECN — European Convention on Nationality, signed in Strasbourg on 6 November 1997, Council of Europe, European Treaty Series (ETS) No. 166.
ECHR — Convention for the Protection of Human Rights and Fundamental Freedoms, done at Rome on 4 November 1950, amended by Protocols 3, 5 and 8 and supplemented by Protocol 2, ETS 5.
Charter of the United Nations (UN Charter) — Charter of the United Nations, Statute of the International Court of Justice and agreement establishing the United Nations Preparatory Commission, 24 October 1945, 1 UNTS XVI.
Constitution of the Republic of Poland (Polish Constitution) — Constitution of the Republic of Poland of 2 April 1997 (Polish Journal of Laws: Dz.U.78.483, as rectified and amended).
The 1951 Geneva Convention (1951 RC) — Convention Relating to the Status of Refugees, done at Geneva on 28 July 1951 (UNTS, vol. 189, p. 137).
The 1930 Hague Convention (1930 HC) — Convention on Certain Questions Relating to the Conflict of Nationality Law, signed on 13 April 1930 in the Hague, League of Nations Treaty Series, vol. 179, p. 89, No. 4137.
The 1954 Convention — Convention Relating to the Status of Stateless Persons, adopted on 28 September 1954 by a Conference of Plenipotentiaries convened by Economic and Social Council Resolution 526 A (XVII) of 26 April 1954, UNTS, vol. 360, p. 117.
The 1957 Convention — Convention of the Nationality of Married Women, opened for signature in New York on 20 February 1957, United Nations General Assembly, A/RES/1040.
The 1961 Convention — Convention on the Reduction of Statelessness, adopted on 30 August 1961 by a Conference of Plenipotentiaries in pursuance of General Assembly Resolution no. 896 (IX) of 4 December 1954, UNTS, vol. 989, p. 175.
CRC — Convention on the Rights of the Child, adopted by the United Nations General Assembly, UNTS, vol. 1577, p. 3.
ICCPR — International Covenant on Civil and Political Rights, opened for signature in New York on 19 December 1966, UNTS, vol. 999, p. 171.

UDHR — Universal Declaration of Human Rights, adopted by General Assembly Resolution 217 A(III) on 10 December 1948 in Paris, 217 A (III).
Act on Polish Citizenship — Act of 2 April 2009 on Polish Citizenship (Polish Journal of Laws: Dz.U.2018.1829).

Official journals and periodicals

Dz.U. — Polish Journal of Laws
ETS — European Treaty Series

Other

CCPR — Centre for Civil and Political Rights
ECtHR — European Court of Human Rights
FAC (Switzerland) — Federal Administrative Court of Switzerland
OAR — Spanish Asylum and Refugee Office
OSCE — Organization for Security and Co-operation in Europe
OFPRA — French Office for the Protection of Refugees and Stateless Persons (*Office français de protection de réfugiés et apatrides*)
UN — United Nations
SIP — statelessness-identification procedures
SDP — statelessness-determination procedures
ECOSOC — United Nations Economic and Social Council
SEM — Swiss Secretariat of State for Migrations (*Secrétariat d'Etat aux migrations*)
FSC (Switzerland) — Federal Supreme Court of Switzerland
CJEU — Court of Justice of the European Union
UNHCR — United Nations High Commissioner for Refugees

Introduction

For a long time, topics relating to statelessness in public law had remained an area of neglect, to experience a reawakening of interest only in the last decade.[1] To this date, statelessness continues to be an important legal category. This is the consequence of how, despite efforts undertaken since the 20s of the 20th century, its elimination has never been achieved, whilst legal protection offered to stateless persons by the general human-rights system has not been fully effective.

The purpose of this book is twofold. Firstly, it is to offer an introduction to the problems of statelessness and an analysis of the fundamental problems pertaining to the legal dogmatics of the public law in this area, such as the definition of statelessness, the legal definition of a stateless person, the regulatory framework of statelessness, or the status of a stateless person. These will be discussed on selected examples from domestic legislations in the context of the standard established by international law.

This research goal is warranted by how available literature on the subject emphasizes the aspects pertaining to international law. By contrast, thus far, the topic of statelessness has not been able to claim its rightful place in analysis done from the perspective of domestic provisions. Accordingly, some authors explicitly remark that research efforts in the area of statelessness should focus on domestic aspects in a greater degree.[2]

1 Not among Polish writers, however. Polish publications touching on the public aspects of problems relating to statelessness are few and far between. Other than articles authored or co-authored by myself, mentioned in the bibliography at the end of this book, there are practically no contemporary academic studies into statelessness from the perspective of public law. One could only note C. Mik, *Analiza stopnia implementacji postanowień konwencji dotyczących bezpaństwowców z 1954 r. i 1961 r. w prawie polskim*, Zeszyty Prawnicze Biura Analiz Sejmowych 2018/3(59), which is essentially a practical study. In older literature, attention to the problems of statelessness in public law was paid by J. Litwin in *Pozbawienie obywatelstwa z przyczyn politycznych w ustawodawstwie powojennej Europy*, Palestra 1934/9, p. 570, and Palestra 1934/10, p. 635.

2 W.E. Conklin, *Statelessness. The enigma of an international community*, London 2014, p. 20.

Another novelty in this approach is that my analysis is not limited to aspects of counteraction of statelessness[3] but extends to the protection of stateless persons. Throughout the last several decades, the already scant attention paid by the global subject literature to statelessness focused largely on the counteraction of statelessness (and that mainly in international law). The matter of a protection status for stateless persons in domestic legislation has remained completely in the margins, for which reason a need for studies in this area has been suggested.[4]

The second of the principal goals of this work is to prove a thesis born of several years of my studies into statelessness. My attention has been drawn primarily to how the analysis of statelessness in available studies is often done *en bloc*, as though all cases were similar. For example, it is often simply remarked that stateless persons are particularly vulnerable individuals in need of protection.[5] Not infrequently, that is indeed the case. In my professional practice, I have assisted stateless persons, often children, finding themselves in an outright Catch-22 situation due to the lack of a comprehensive regulatory framework for statelessness in Poland's domestic legal system.[6] Certain cases, however, do not fit under this umbrella. Several preliminary observations led to the formulation of thesis of this book.

---

3 Different terms are employed to describe the elimination of the phaenomenon of statelessness. Those include 'reduction' (title of the 1961 Convention), 'elimination' (e.g. the Draft Convention on the Elimination of Future Statelessness), 'avoidance' (e.g. Article 4(b) ECN), 'prevention' (see. e.g. the report of the UNHCR Executive Committee titled Prevention and Reduction of Statelessness and the Protection of Stateless Persons no. 78 (XLVI) – 1995, 20 Executive Committee 46th session, October 1995). Because, however, there is no consistency in their use, this book uses the umbrella term 'counteraction' or the corresponding verb.

4 G. Gyulai, *Nationality Unknown? An overview of the safeguards and gaps related to the prevention of statelessness at birth in Hungary*, Hungarian Helsinki Committee, Budapest 2014, p. 116.

5 See e.g. UNHCR, *Note on UNHCR and Stateless Persons*, 2 June 1995, EC/1995/SCP/CRP.2 (*statelessness itself creates vulnerability*); UNHCR, *Text of the 1954 Convention relating to the Status of Stateless Persons with an Introductory Note by the Office of the United Nations High Commissioner for Refugees*, Geneva 2014, p. 3 (*profound vulnerability that affects people who are stateless*); K. Bianchini, *Protecting stateless persons: The Implementation of the Convention Relating to the Status of Stateless Persons across EU States*, Leiden–Boston 2018, p. 1 ('stateless persons are among the most vulnerable in the world').

6 Concerning such type of cases see footnotes 196 and 599 in this book.

The first indication that the *en bloc* approach might not be an appropriate theoretical and regulatory perspective came from the observation that the analysis of statelessness done in this manner consigns to the margins the question of whether states' obligations to counteract statelessness and protect stateless persons are applicable to all persons in the same degree. For example, the problem emerges whether states are required to offer equal treatment to those who are voluntarily stateless persons as to those whose statelessness is not voluntary (e.g. caused by having been deprived of one's original nationality[7] with no hope of recovering it).

Another indication that the *en bloc* approach might not be appropriate came from reflection on W.E. Conklin's thesis of the ineffectiveness of international regulation in the area of statelessness. In his opinion, the continued existence of statelessness despite the international community's efforts to eliminate it poses an enigma.[8] In this general perspective, however, Conklin's thesis fails to account for the circumstance that with regard to certain groups of stateless persons such regulation has proved its effectiveness. For example, the statelessness of women due to the conflict of nationality laws has been eradicated successfully.

The third and last clue was the observation that failure to appreciate the differences among the various cases of statelessness leads to recommending one-size-fits-all solutions for all of its types. The predominant approach is that statelessness ought to be reduced as a matter of principle, meaning that a stateless person should eventually be granted the nationality of some state or other. Not only does this approach ignore the already mentioned fact that not all stateless persons may wish to obtain the nationality of any state, it also leads to a lack of complex thinking about the different mechanisms for the regulation of statelessness in all of its different types.

The above clues have prompted the concentration of my efforts on the study of the regulatory frameworks for statelessness in international law and in domestic

---

7 Throughout this book, I use the term 'nationality' (as the preferred term) in the same sense in which it is used in international treaties and other documents dealing with statelessness, i.e. in the sense of citizenship and not of ethnicity. Thus, one's 'state of nationality' is synonymous with their 'state of citizenship', i.e. the state of which the individual is a citizen. References to 'citizenship' or a 'citizen' have the same meaning. See UNHCR, Handbook on Protection of Stateless Persons, Geneva 2014, paragraph 52 (on p. 21). Discussion of topics such as nationality without citizenship, citizenship without nationality or the downsides or dangers of conflating the two terms fall outside the scope of this book.

8 W.E. Conklin, *Statelessness...*, 2014, pp. 1–2.

legal systems in juxtaposition with the various types (categories) of statelessness. I was particularly interested in tracing the manifestations of a regulatory approach that was looking through the lens of the different categories of individuals who can be stateless persons. My research hypothesis was that the provisions of international law and domestic legal systems reflect not an *en bloc* approach to statelessness but rather one that could be termed 'categorial' — consisting in the delineation of categories of individuals to which a specially adapted regulatory approach is taken. Closer analysis has revealed that existing legal frameworks of statelessness in international law and in domestic jurisdictions do to a certain extent categorize statelessness into different cases or scenarios.

In the above light, the overarching thesis of my book is that, firstly, an approach to statelessness from the perspective of the different categories of individuals is already present in statelessness regulation, and, secondly, that it constitutes a useful theoretical and practical perspective. The idea of this paradigm — which, for the sake of brevity, I will refer to as the 'categorial approach' — is not only that, in the simplest terms possible, there are different categories of statelessness persons, such as voluntarily stateless persons as opposed those whose statelessness results from a situation forced on them. It is also that the different situations in which different persons find themselves may be viewed differently for the purposes of e.g. statelessness-prevention mechanisms. For example, as I will illustrate with some examples, deprivation of nationality resulting in statelessness is an available sanction for perpetrators of specific criminal offences in some countries.

For reasons of analytical structure demanded by the thesis, this book is divided in two parts. In the first part, I demonstrate that inherent to statelessness as an area of research is its internal diversification in all of its various cases. Analysis of the general considerations of statelessness reveals traces of a categorial approach in the legislation touching on this problem area.

Chapter I offers a general introduction to the problem of statelessness. There, I explain the meaning of the concept of statelessness (which is not synonymous with a stateless person) and define the scope of the problem area of statelessness. I discuss the legal nature of the concept of statelessness, as well as its underlying causes. What follows is an overview of the preliminary issues relating to the regulation of statelessness in international law, whether in general instruments for the protection of human rights or specific instruments dealing with statelessness. The chapter ends with the identification of two core legal mechanisms for the regulation of statelessness — instruments counteracting statelessness *versus* instruments protecting stateless persons — which provide the axis of later discussion in this book.

Chapter II concerns itself with the definition of a stateless person. There, I identify and discuss the various meanings of a stateless person in legislation and in the literature of international law since the end of World War II, noting the distinction between *de facto* and *de iure* statelessness. Afterwards, I analyse the definition of a stateless person provided by Article 1(1) of the 1954 Convention and discuss the interpretative problems surfacing in modern debate. I also identify problems relating to the definition of a stateless person in the various states' domestic legislation.

Chapter III provides a synthetic overview of topics relating to statelessness-counteraction mechanisms. It discusses on the one hand the instruments for the prevention of statelessness adopted in international law and in domestic legal systems, and on the other hand instruments for the reduction of statelessness. Chapter IV deals with topics of protection of stateless persons, focusing on statelessness-determination procedures and the status of a stateless person.

The second part of the book revisits some of the aspects identified in the first part and aims to provide a detailed analysis of mechanisms for the counteraction of statelessness and protection of stateless persons with regard to sample categories of individuals. I distinguish four categories of individuals as lens for the analysis of the statelessness-counteraction and stateless-protection mechanisms in international law and selected domestic jurisdictions identified in the first part:

(1) 'women',
(2) 'children',[9]
(3) individuals distinguished on the grounds of protection of the public interest,
(4) individuals distinguished on the grounds of being 'voluntarily stateless'.

The demarcation of the above-identified categories for separate analysis is not based on a set of uniform criteria (nor are they disjoint categories). I distinguish the first two due to the existence (at present or in the past) of a consensus, in principle, as to the need for special treatment of those individuals from the perspective of counteracting statelessness. The international community has endeavoured to eliminate the statelessness of these categories of individuals since the 20s of the 20th century. As regards the category of 'women', the distinction is primarily of historical significance, for in the past conflicts of laws leaving women stateless in connection with marriage or divorce were the single most important cause of statelessness. The decision

9 The reason for the use of quotation marks is that the categories of women and children are construed not on the basis of the constitutive characteristics of a woman or a child as a concept but rather on the basis of the cases of statelessness characteristic of them. I discuss the exact meaning of these two categories in their corresponding chapters.

to make this category of individuals the subject of more in-depth analysis is also prompted by the question of how this erstwhile predominant cause of statelessness in women has been eliminated successfully.

With respect to the other distinguished category, i.e. 'children' (the individuals concerned are usually minors),[10] it must be noted that statelessness arising at birth in connection with specific parent-child configurations is given special treatment by international law and domestic legal systems. The reason is an aspiration not to perpetuate statelessness arising at birth. The statelessness of children is an interesting case due to how — in defiance of all the efforts undertaken on the international level in the course of several decades until the present — we are still contending with statelessness derived from the circumstances of one's birth. The causes of this situation will be the subject of closer analysis.

By contrast, the reason for distinguishing the latter two categories is that preliminary findings demonstrate the absence of a consensus as to the necessity of counteracting statelessness and offering protection to certain categories of persons. Concerning the category of individuals distinguished on the grounds of public interest, the analysis accomplished thus far reveals that with regard to this category of persons statelessness-counteraction and statelessness-prevention mechanisms are not infrequently excluded. One particularly interesting question is what individuals can be counted in this group and what the specific reasons for their exclusion from the legal framework addressing statelessness might be. After all, the category of persons distinguished on the basis of the 'voluntarity' of their statelessness illustrates the specificity of aspects relating to statelessness in the context of, for example, matters of refugee protection. It is possible for an individual to be a stateless person voluntarily, and being so can give rise to different treatment for the purposes of reduction and protection mechanisms. Here, too, the criteria adopted in international law and in domestic legal systems for the legal classification of voluntary statelessness will be analysed.

For the most part, analysis of topics relating to statelessness in the light of aspects (or categorizations) pertaining to international law called for the use of research methods proper to legal sciences (the dogmatic, historical and comparative methods). I analysed the various instruments and selected legal provisions and other norms of domestic and international law in three areas: (i) the origin of statelessness, (ii) counteraction of statelessness, and (iii) protection of stateless persons. My studies encompassed both historical and contemporary instruments and norms. I selected the 20th century as the cut-off point, because that is when the first legal frameworks

10 As to how the category of 'children' should be understood, see footnotes 207 and 456.

devised to counteract statelessness made their appearance in domestic jurisdictions, and the first international instruments relating to statelessness began to emerge. For the study of modern domestic legal systems from the perspective of counteraction of statelessness and protection of stateless persons, I relied on the comparative method, involving the analysis of selected legal instruments and available subject literature. To that end, among other instruments used in my research, I incorporated the aids I had co-designed myself as a national expert initially (from 2009 onward) in the EUDO CITIZENSHIP programme and thereafter for the purposes of GLOBALCIT (from 2017)[11] and of the *Statelessness Index Survey*[12].

It will be necessary to make several methodological caveats. Firstly, systematic study was restricted to European legal systems due to the existence of proximate migration-related problems. The discussed solutions from domestic jurisdictions provide fitting examples to highlight the diversity of the frameworks adopted in European countries. From time to time, I invoke examples from non-European countries, for example when their specific regulatory frameworks are the reason for the statelessness of migrants residing in Europe (the most prominent example is of former US citizens surrendering American citizenship and settling in Europe). Secondly, because of the migration context of this study of statelessness, I do not consider in great detail the situation of *in situ* stateless persons or those whose statelessness is the result of e.g. the succession of states.[13] Thirdly, although the analysis of the international law standard encompasses a broad convention spectrum, its focus is on the 1930 Hague Convention, the 1961 Convention and the regional instrument that is the European Convention on Nationality (ECN) with regard to the detailed characteristics of the various legal frameworks designed for the counteraction of statelessness and protection of stateless persons.

The first version of this book was published in Polish in 2019 by Wolters Kluwer. This version, as well as my research into statelessness, were made possible by the financial support of Polish National Science Centre in the form of a research grant.[14]

---

11 See: https://globalcit.eu/ (accessed 2 January 2023).

12 See: https://index.statelessness.eu (accessed 2 January 2023).

13 Accordingly, I do not embark on a detailed analysis of frameworks dealing with the situation of e.g. 'non-citizens' in Latvia or Estonia. See footnote 52.

14 Research grant for project no. 2017/27/B/HS5/02083 *Bezpaństwowość w prawie publicznym* [*Statelessness in public law*], approved for financing through the OPUS 14 competition.

Part I

Chapter I Statelessness: Introduction to the Problem

1. The evolution of the legal concept of statelessness

Statelessness is not a novel problem. In the eyes of some authors, it is as old as society itself, dating back to the first migrations.[15] However, it appears to be more appropriate to link the origins of the phaenomenon of statelessness to the formation of the modern system of nation states and introduction of modern legislation dealing with nationality (appearing almost simultaneously in several European states *ca.* AD 1800). The enactment of the first legislative provisions governing citizenship established a groundwork for inclusion into and exclusion from the civic community, with statelessness as a side-effect of the system.[16]

For a long time, the existence of statelessness used to be denied or ignored in legal studies. The reason probably came down to its problematic nature from the perspective of classic concepts of international law grounded in the interstate order. In a world founded upon belonging to a state, the condition of statelessness was seen as an anomaly. According to M. Vichniac, some jurists outright denied its legal existence, insisting that international law permitted a change of nationality but not the lack of any nationality at all. From the literature of the turn of the 19th and 20th centuries, he quotes opinions such as that a situation of not holding any nationality was 'wholly and absolutely impossible'[17] (V.M. Hessen) or that the problem was of no great significance, with stateless persons being 'international vagabonds'[18] (D. de Folleville)[19]. During that period the courts, too, were reluctant to recognize the status of statelessness. According to the Supreme

15 M. Vichniac, *Le statut international des apatrides*, Recueil des Cours 1933-I/43, p. 119. Among other considerations, it is noted that statelessness was known already to Roman law, with a category of individuals designated as *peregrini sine civitate* (p. 121). This observation is cited by subsequent writers. See e.g. C. Wihtol de Wenden, *La question migratoire au XXI siècle. Migrants, réfugiés et relations internationales*, Paris 2017, p. 140. In my own opinion, due to the different concept of citizenship in Old Rome, a search for the origins of statelessness in the Roman Empire is of not much informative value.

16 Having multiple nationalities was another such side effect.

17 *Complètement et absolument impossible.*

18 *Vagabonds internationaux.*

19 M. Vichniac, *Le statut...*, p. 127.

Court of the United States in *United States v. Wong Kim Ark*, 169 (US) 649, 1898, 'the existence of a man without a country [was] not recognized.'[20] Similarly, as discussed by R. Graupner, English and French courts saw a difficulty in recognizing the existence of any such status in law — 'French courts for a long time regarded statelessness as a legal impossibility until they hesitantly changed their view after the last war.'[21]

Statelessness has been recognized as a valid problem since the end of the First World War due to the enormous number of apatrides (another name for a stateless person) during that period. The situation of statelessness, however, was viewed primarily through the lens of conflicts it could trigger among states. Rather than focusing on the protection of stateless persons, frameworks adopted at the time focused on the counteraction of statelessness (the common term I use for prevention and reduction). The first provisions addressing statelessness dealt with it as a consequence of a conflict of laws, especially in the cases of children and married women. In this context, it will be appropriate to begin with the provisions of the 1930 Hague Convention. In the 20s of the 20th century, the first steps to counteract statelessness were also taken by individual states (e.g. Poland[22] and the US[23]). Nevertheless, only the experience of the Second World War era, especially the mass denationalizations of Jews by the Nazis in Germany and fascists in Italy, inspired the intensification of efforts to protect stateless persons and devise a more comprehensive framework for the counteraction of statelessness.

2. The concept of statelessness and the law of statelessness

Statelessness is the situation of not holding the nationality of any state. It is a negative condition (situation) constituting the opposite of the legal status of

20 Available at https://supreme.justia.com/cases/federal/us/169/649/case.html (accessed 2 January 2023).

21 R. Graupner, *Statelessness as a consequence of the change of sovereignty over territory after the last war* [in:] British Section of the World Jewish Congress, *The Problem of Statelessness*, London 1944, p. 28.

22 The Act of 20 January 1920 on the Citizenship of the Polish State (Dz.U.7.44, as amended) already included provisions to protect female Polish nationals marrying foreigners (including stateless persons) from becoming stateless. For a more extensive discussion see Chapter V.

23 So-called The Cable Act (Married Woman's Act) 1922. For a more extensive discussion see Chapter V.

nationality.[24] Although statelessness is usually defined by reference to the concept of a stateless person (and its definition in international law),[25] its denotation is broader and is not limited to a class of existing individuals capable of being termed stateless persons.

To appreciate of the difference in scope of the terms 'statelessness' and 'stateless person' is of key importance to the problem area of statelessness. The need for reference to be made to the broader meaning of the concept of statelessness becomes all the more pronounced whenever the discussion touches upon statelessness-prevention mechanisms intended, as will be discussed later, to prevent cases of statelessness from arising (i.e. to prevent the number of stateless persons from increasing). Therefore, the problem area of statelessness extends to legal frameworks dealing with stateless persons (with the goal being to protect them or to allow them to acquire a nationality) but also complex frameworks for statelessness prevention (i.e. designed to prevent statelessness from arising).

The need to recognize the extensive denotation of the term 'statelessness' is also of fundamental importance from the perspective of appreciating the importance of this topic range as a subject of academic interest and research. As the topic range of statelessness is not limited to the situation of stateless persons but also includes the analysis of legal frameworks for statelessness prevention and reduction, it will not be appropriate to judge the importance of the problem of statelessness through the lens of the number of stateless persons globally or in individual states. Depending on the perspective taken, the number of ca. 10 million stateless persons worldwide can be viewed as either considerable or relatively insignificant.[26] Similarly, the number of stateless persons in individual

---

24 I do not employ the term 'negative status', even though it can be found in the subject literature (R. Graupner, *Statelessness...*, p. 28), because in the tradition created by G. Jellinek it is usually referred to freedom rights — *status negativus* (*libertatis*); see G. Jellinek, *System der subjektiven öffentlichen Rechte*, Tübingen 1905, p. 81ff, after: J. Kostrubiec, *Georg Jellinek — klasyk niemieckiej nauki o państwie (w 95. rocznicę śmierci)*, 7 Studia Iuridica Lublinensia 2006, p. 61.

25 Concerning the definition of a stateless person provided in Article 1(1) of the 1954 Convention see Chapter II.

26 For example, D. Owen, writing about the activities of the Office of the United Nations High Commissioner for Refugees in the field of statelessness, noted that the activities continue to be undertaken even though the number of *de iure* stateless persons is 'only' a little more than 0.001% of the global population, which exceeds 7 billion; see D. Owen, *Citizenship and Human Rights* [in:] A. Shachar, R. Bauböck, I. Bloemraad and M. Vink (eds.), *The Oxford Handbook of Citizenship*, Oxford 2017, p. 248.

states can provide the incentive to perceive the importance of the problem of statelessness through that lens. Aside from the obvious difficulty of thinking about human rights solely in a context of numbers, it will become necessary here to emphasize that, whatever our opinion of it might be, the current number of stateless persons is something we owe to the gradual adoption of frameworks for the prevention and reduction of statelessness since the 20s of the 20th century.

Statelessness frameworks include provisions belonging to the scope of traditionally understood law of foreigners (aspects of protection) and nationality law (prevention and reduction of statelessness). Regulations aiming to counteract statelessness can also be found in civil-registration law. Examination of these instruments and provisions through the prism of statelessness makes it possible to discern the existence of a 'law of statelessness' (not only 'international law of statelessness') as a separate field of interest within public law.[27]

3. The legal essence of statelessness

Defining statelessness as a 'negative condition' does not tell as much about its essence. Before we can take a closer look on this matter, it will become necessary to discuss the nature of nationality, which will then allow us to identify the legal nature of statelessness.

Nationality establishes a legal relationship between an individual and a state. From the perspective of its legal nature, this relationship can be viewed in a dual domestic and international light. This is the consequence of the dual role of nationality, which defines, firstly, the individual's position in society (citizenship under domestic law) and, secondly, the link between the individual and the state in the sphere of international law. In reference to this dual relationship created by nationality,[28] the legal character of statelessness can be encapsulated as the absence of a legal relationship between an individual and any state in these two aspects: domestic and international.

In the domestic dimension, statelessness means that the individual is not entitled in any state to the enjoyment of the fullest extent of rights reserved to nationals.[29] Although in modern states numerous rights are extended to

---

27 A. Edwards, L. van Waas, *Introduction* [in:] A. Edwards and L. van Waas (eds.), *Nationality and Statelessness under International Law*, Cambridge 2014, p. 1.

28 For a more extensive discussion see D. Pudzianowska, *Obywatelstwo w procesie zmian*, Warszawa 2013, pp. 34–52.

29 On the domestic level, the institution of citizenship establishes a relationship expressed by the mutual rights and obligations of the individual and of the state. Citizenship is

foreigners, there continues to exist a category of rights historically linked to nationality and closed to foreigners (e.g. the right to practise certain professions, right to diplomatic assistance or electoral rights on the national tier). The list of the specific rights differs from one state to the next, but what is of the essence is that stateless persons do not have access to the most extensive list in any state in the world.

The discussion of the definition of nationality is relevant to the definition of the legal nature of statelessness. The core issue at hand is whether there exist any such rights as might constitute the contents of nationality. In other words, is nationality solely a formal legal construct,[30] or is it substantive to some extent. Debate is ongoing as to the possibility of identifying any rights necessarily linked to nationality (constituting its contents). My own opinion is that the right to enter the country and take up residence in it is a right constitutive to nationality.[31] Some authors also include the right to diplomatic assistance.[32]

The debate on what rights should be recognized as the content of nationality has direct consequences for how we define a stateless person. For this, I will provide two examples. On the one hand, we can imagine a situation when an individual does formally hold the nationality of a state but, for example, they cannot enter the state of nationality and are not guaranteed the right of residence. Should their host state conclude that the individual holds a nationality and is, therefore, not a stateless person? On the other hand, the individual could formally lack the nationality of any state but still be in a position to be granted, through a facilitated procedure, the nationality of a state to which they have personal ties. Should the host state conclude that such an individual is a stateless person? Without deciding the matter at this time, the necessary conclusion is that the formal concept of nationality is not always decisive to whether a specific individual is a stateless person. This is one of the more difficult and at once more interesting problem aspects of statelessness, which will be analysed more extensively in later chapters.

---

a prerequisite for the existence of a set of rights and obligations of the most extensive nature compared to any other status available to an individual within the state.

30 For example J. Jagielski, *Obywatelstwo polskie. Zagadnienia podstawowe*, Warszawa 1998, p. 20.

31 For a more extensive discussion see D. Pudzianowska, *Obywatelstwo...*, pp. 67–85.

32 K. Bianchini, *Protecting...*, p. 72.

Statelessness means the non-existence, also in the external dimension, of any such link between the individual and the state as would have the essence of making the individual a subject of the state. Nationality makes it possible to define the scope of rights and obligations between the individual and the state, as well as the state's rights and obligations *vis-à-vis* the international community in respect of the specific individual. Statelessness means that no state has any rights against or owes any obligations to another state with regard to the individual, as defined by international law (such as diplomatic assistance or the obligation to receive a citizen extradited by a different state).

At present, due to the development of the international law of human rights, a stateless person is not completely bereft of any rights from the perspective of international law. However, it will be expedient to quote L.F. Oppenheim, who, at the beginning of the 20th century, provided this vivid description of the situation in which stateless persons find themselves under international law: 'Since stateless individuals do not own a nationality, the principal link by which they could derive benefits from International Law is missing, and thus they lack protection as far as the law is concerned. Their position may be compared to vessels on the open sea not sailing under the flag of a state, which likewise do not enjoy protection' (emphasis added).[33]

Due to the implication of the absence of any link between the individual and any state in either the domestic or the international dimension, the impact of statelessness on the individual's position is unquestionably negative, as has been discussed above. It also, however, has a negative impact on the position of states and on the international order. This used to be the prevailing outlook on the consequences of statelessness. Statelessness was viewed primarily as a threat to the international order (similarly to dual nationality) and captured states' interest on account of the conflicts it could trigger.[34] The presence in a state of a large number of stateless persons deprived of nationality as a result

33 L.F. Oppenheim, *International Law. A treatise*, London–New York–Bombay 1905, p. 366. In turn, in the oft-cited case of *Dickson Car Wheel Company (U.S.A.) v. Mexico* of 1931, it was noted: 'A State, for example, does not commit an international delinquency in inflicting an injury upon an individual lacking nationality, and consequently, no State is empowered to intervene or complain on his behalf either before or after the injury', US–Mexico General Claims Commission, July 1931, UN Reports of International Arbitral Awards, vol. IV, p. 678. Available at: http://legal.un.org/riaa/cases/vol_IV/669-691.pdf (accessed 2 January 2023).

34 P. Weis, *Nationality and statelessness in international law*, London 1979, p. 162.

of denaturalization, with no options for extraditing them to any other state, was seen as a problem.[35] Statelessness also caused a disturbance in the international order, for it 'created' individuals for whose conduct no state could be held responsible, and that — in theory, at least — opened a gap in the effective application of international law.[36]

The development of the international system of human rights after the Second World War shifted the focus of attention paid to statelessness to its adverse impact on the position of the individual. Even nowadays, however, the perspective of the negative impact of statelessness on the international order has not entirely lost its prominence. In the 1990s, with the fall of Yugoslavia, Czechoslovakia and the USSR, the potential of statelessness to become a source of regional tensions came to surface again.[37] It is noteworthy that the potential of statelessness for triggering tensions resulting in conflicts between communities has provided the basis for the OSCE's mandate in the area.[38]

From the above paragraphs, it can be seen that statelessness is a negative condition meaning the lack of nationality of any state. The circumstance of not holding any nationality results in the negatively defined characteristic of statelessness. However, it must already be noted at this stage that statelessness can also become grounds for the acquisition of a specific status to which specific rights are adjoined, as long as the relevant provisions dealing with the protection of stateless persons have been introduced to the legal system. I will discuss topics relating to the 'status of a stateless person' more extensively in Chapter IV, which deals with the protection of stateless persons.

---

35 C. Seckler-Hudson, *Statelessness. With special reference to the United States*, Washington, D.C. 1934, p. 251.

36 P. Spiro, *Mandated membership, diluted identity. Citizenship, globalization, and international law* [in:] A. Brysk and G. Shafir (eds.), *People out of place. Globalization, human rights, and the citizenship gap*, New York 2004, 92.

37 UNHCR, *Citizenship and prevention of statelessness linked to the disintegration of the Socialist Federal Republic of Yugoslavia*, 3(1) European Series, Geneva, June 1997.

38 OSCE & UNHCR, *Handbook on statelessness in the OSCE Area. International standards and good practices*, 28 February 2017, p. 6.

4. Causes of statelessness

The question of origins of statelessness is an extraordinarily complex one. Statelessness often is the product of the diversity of the regulatory minutiae of the frameworks adopted in domestic or international law. It can arise at birth (original statelessness) or occur later in life (subsequent statelessness). It can be of either individual or collective (mass) nature.[39] It sometimes originates from extralegal circumstances, such as the discrimination of specific racial or ethnic groups by a state's administration. Below, I provide a rundown of the typical causes of statelessness, with detailed historical context for some of them, as well as some examples.

Statelessness can arise from a negative conflict of nationality laws, i.e. lack of synchronization of the various states' provisions of nationality law. Statelessness of this type can arise at birth (original statelessness), such as when the parents' state of nationality follows the *ius soli* and the child is born in the territory of a state adhering to the *ius sanguinis*.[40] A conflict of laws can also produce subsequent statelessness. In the past, it was common for a woman to lose her original nationality upon marriage, although her husband's state of nationality did not always provide for the automatic acquisition of nationality by the wife of a citizen, rendering some of such women stateless. Individual statelessness of this type could also occur as a result of the recognition or adoption of a child, who would

---

39 'Original statelessness' and 'subsequent statelessness' in the sense assigned to them by P. Weis; see P. Weis, *Statelessness as a legal political problem* [in:] British Section of the World Jewish Congress, *The problem of...*, p. 4. Terms 'individual statelessness' and 'mass statelessness', in turn, as defined by A.P. Mutharika, *The regulation of statelessness under international and national law*, New York 1989, p. 2. However, I do not categorize the causes of statelessness in line with those authors' classifications; my use of the terms is merely as aids to explanation.

40 With regard to the legislation governing the acquisition of nationality by birth, states follow one of the two principles — *ius sanguinis* ('right of blood') or *ius soli* ('right of territory') — or at least one of the principles predominates. The *ius sanguinis* principle attaches the acquisition of nationality to the fact of birth from one or both parents holding the nationality of a given state. Under this rule, a child whose one or both parents are nationals acquires the nationality of the relevant state irrespective of the country of birth. Under the *ius soli* principle, a person's nationality is determined by their place of birth. Thus, a child born in a given state acquires its nationality irrespective of the parents' nationality. For a more extensive discussion see D. Pudzianowska, *Obywatelstwo...*, pp. 86–87.

thereupon lose whatever nationality it may previously have held but without automatically acquiring the new parent or parents' nationality.[41]

Statelessness can also be the outcome of loss of nationality as a consequence of the individual's renunciation done before the public authorities of the state. In the majority of European states, the availability of renunciation is conditional, or its effect is contingent, upon holding or being expected in the close future to obtain the nationality of a different state. This, however, does not mean that statelessness cannot originate from renunciation; there are situations in which the renunciation takes effect upon submission of another state's assurance of conferring its nationality on the individual, which that other state does not ultimately do.[42] In certain jurisdictions, the ability to renounce one's citizenship is regarded as a fundamental individual right. For example, in the United States in 1868, Congress adopted The Expatriation Act, which stipulates that the right to renounce citizenship is a person's natural and inherent right.[43]

Statelessness can also result from an involuntary loss of nationality. This can occur *ex lege* or be effected by the decision of a competent authority (deprivation of nationality) when the legally prescribed conditions are met. Statelessness resulting from the involuntary loss of nationality can arise in a variety of factual contexts. Those may involve citizenship fraud, provision of certain services to a foreign state (such as enrolment in foreign armed forces or civil service) or conduct prejudicial to the interests of the state. Some states allow for the loss of nationality resulting in statelessness in connection with a citizen's prolonged sojourn abroad if such a citizen fails to notify the state's consulate of the intention to retain the nationality.[44]

Individual statelessness can also be the consequence of birth from stateless parents. Many modern cases of statelessness are similarly rooted in the past. If a given state does not adopt special provisions to protect children from statelessness in such situations, the consequences of specific events from the past are visited on future generations.

In contradistinction to the above-identified individual causes, mass statelessness is another possibility. Whereas before the First World War the majority

---

41 I address the causes of statelessness of children and women, also in the context of a conflict of laws, more extensively in Chapters V and VI.

42 For more details on this topic see Chapter VIII.

43 'The right of expatriation is a natural and inherent right of all people' — Expatriation Act of July 28, 1868, ch. 249, 15 Stat. 223, R.S. § 1999.

44 I discuss these causes of statelessness in detail in Chapter VII.

of cases of statelessness had been occasioned by individual loss of nationality, during the interwar period some states began to deprive entire groups of population of nationality ('mass denationalization').[45] The process was begun by the USSR and Turkey. By decrees from the first half of the 20s of the 20th century, the government of the USSR withdrew Soviet citizenship from more than a million Russian nationals having left the country as a result of the events relating to the October Revolution of 1917 and the ensuing Civil War (mainly so-called White Russians). As noted by J. Litwin, that was the first case of mass denationalization of punitive nature dictated by political revenge.[46] In 1927, in turn, Turkey stripped its citizenship from hundreds of thousands of Armenians. During the later period, immediately prior to the Second World War and during it, various European states, with Nazi Germany and Fascist Italy chief among them, divested Jews of their nationality.[47] A more modern example of mass denationalization involves the *Ajanib* Kurds of Syria having lost Syrian nationality as a result of failure to meet the registration requirements of the 1962 census. Three hundred thousand Kurds are estimated to have lost nationality in this manner.[48]

Gaps in the legal provisions adopted to regulate the nationality of persons upon state succession can create statelessness on a mass scale. The greatest probability of statelessness exists in connection with the loss of nationality due to the disintegration of the state. Mass statelessness resulting from defective legal frameworks adopted in response to the disintegration of states was a significant problem after the First World War. For example, following the disintegration of the Habsburg Monarchy, the attempt to dispose of the matter of nationality in the peace treaties with Austria and Hungary so as to prevent cases of statelessness from arising proved to be futile. One of the fundamental problems was that the acquisition of the nationality of a successor state was made conditional not

---

45 See P. Abel, *Denationalization*, 6 Modern Law Review 1942–1943, p. 58; L. Preuss, *International law and deprivation of nationality*, 23 Georgetown Law Journal 1934–1935, p. 258; J. Litwin, *Pozbawienie...*, 9 Palestra 1934, p. 573.

46 J. Litwin, *Pozbawienie...*, 9 Palestra 1934, p. 573. A different author writes: 'no denationalization on any such scale as this has hitherto been known in history' — J.F. Williams, *Denationalization*, 8 British Year Book of International Law 1927, pp. 45–46.

47 For a more extensive discussion of mass denationalizations in the period following the First World War see J. Perry, C. Carey, *Some aspects of statelessness since World War I*, 1 The American Political Science Review 1946/40, pp. 114–115.

48 Z. Albarazi, *The Stateless Syrians*, 11 Tilburg Law School Research Paper 2013, May 24, pp. 15–16. The situation of the *Ajanib* Kurds is discussed more extensively in Chapter VIII, section 2.2.

upon the criterion of habitual residence in a given territory but upon proof of having the so-called *Heimatrecht* or *pertinenza* ('right of citizenship'), i.e. affiliation with or 'belonging to' a commune situated in the territory of one of the newly emerging states.[49] Failure to prove such became the cause of the statelessness of hundreds of thousands of individuals.[50]

At present, the question of territorial changes continues to pose a significant problem. Following the disintegration of the USSR, Czechoslovakia and Yugoslavia, the new states decided upon their own criteria for the acquisition and attestation of nationality. In many cases, persons not meeting such criteria would become stateless. Particularly large numbers of stateless persons were created in Estonia and Latvia (approximately 30% of the residents), as the two states, upon winning back their independence, went on to rebuild their statehoods on the foundation of their pre-1940 citizenship bases, denying the automatic acquisition of nationality to thousands of persons having immigrated during Soviet rule (mainly Ethnic Russians and Russian-speaking minorities).[51] The UNHCR estimates that the greatest numbers of stateless persons in Europe are found in these two countries (252,195 in Latvia and 85,301 in Estonia).[52] Persons whose

---

49 Article. 64 of the peace treaty with Austria signed in 1919 in Saint-Germain-en-Laye; Article 56 of the Treaty of Trianon of 1920. The *Heimatrecht* or *pertinenza* (the Polish term was *prawo swojszczyzny*) was a public-law relationship representing the affiliation between the individual and a specific commune and not merely factual residence (W. Ramus, *Instytucje prawa o obywatelstwie polskim*, Warszawa 1980, pp. 65–66). Not all individuals had such a relationship, and some lacked the papers necessary to demonstrate it; in many cases disputes ensued among communes as to where an individual's *Heimatrecht* was placed (P. Weis, *Statelessness...* [in:] British Section of the World Jewish Congress, *The problem of...*, p. 33). As a result, there were numerous cases of statelessness resulting from the inability to prove the *Heimatrecht*. It has also been noted that the aforementioned treaty provisions in themselves were not the cause of the problem, as the provisions of treaties dealing with the protection of ethnic minorities and the interpretation of the treaties by the successor states aspiring to create as ethnically homogeneous states as possible also played a role.

50 M. Stiller, *Statelessness in international law. A historic overview*, 3 Deutsch-Amerikanische Juristen-Vereinigung Newsletter 2012, p. 97.

51 J.-M. Henckaerts, *Mass expulsion in modern international law and practice*, Hague 1995, pp. 92–93.

52 UNHCR, *Global Trends. Forced Displacement in 2015*, Annex 2, 20 June 2016. Both states have awarded this particular category of stateless persons a special status entailing an extensive list of rights. For a broader discussion of the status of so-called non-citizens in Estonia and Latvia, see K. Kruma, *EU Citizenship, nationality and migration*

statelessness takes its source from those events can also be found in states whose existence predates the fall of the USSR. For example, in Poland, the problem of statelessness somewhat often affects individuals having entered the country before 1991 on USSR passports, which subsequently ceased to be valid.[53] One of the largest groups of stateless persons currently in the world are Palestinians. As noted by A. Shiblak, following the termination of the British Mandate in 1948, more than a half of the Palestinian population of eight million have never acquired the nationality of any other state.[54]

Statelessness can also arise from the adoption of domestic frameworks preventing certain groups of people from the acquisition of the nationality of a given state. This is usually due to the introduction of discriminatory laws or practices (on racial or ethnic grounds). For example, the beginning of the 90s of the 20th century in Croatia saw the development of an administrative practice blocking the naturalization of ethnic Serbs, even though they may have been resident in the territory since before independence and satisfied all the conditions.[55] It has been observed that the statelessness of mainly the Romani people in the Western Balkans and Ukraine is the result of the systematic discrimination of their group by administrative authorities.[56]

Certain new and potential sources of statelessness can also be identified. Modern reproductive technologies (e.g. surrogacy) present challenges concerning the nationality of the children. Entering into cross-border surrogacy contracts can result in the statelessness of the child where the law of the contracting parents' state of nationality prohibits such contracts and stipulates that the affected child cannot obtain nationality, while the surrogate mother's state of nationality does not enable the acquisition of its nationality by the child, due

---

status. An ongoing challenge, Leiden–Boston 2014, pp. 361–365; V. Poleshchuk (ed.), *Chance to survive. Minority rights in Estonia and Latvia*, Tallinn 2010.

53 K. Przybysławska, UNHCR and The Halina Nieć Legal Aid Center (eds.), *Mapping statelessness in Poland*, Kraków 2019, 17.

54 A. Shiblak, *Stateless Palestinians*, 26 Forced Migration Review 2006, p. 8.

55 W. Sievers, *A call to Kinship* [in:] R. Bauböck, B. Perching and W. Sievers (eds.), *Citizenship policies in the New Europe*, Amsterdam 2009, p. 443; B. Blitz, *Statelessness, protection and equality*, Forced Migration Policy Briefing 3, Refugee Studies Centre, Oxford University, September 2009, p. 10.

56 *Roma Belong — Statelessness, discrimination and marginalisation of Roma in the Western Balkans and Ukraine*, European Network on Statelessness, European Roma Rights Centre, The Institute on Statelessness and Inclusion, Budapest, October 2017, pp. 20ff.

to recognizing the validity of the surrogacy contract.[57] As for potential causes of statelessness in the future, it has been noted that, in connection with climate changes, the nationals of sinking-island states could become stateless through the physical disappearance of their states of nationality[58] (e.g. the Maldives).

The number of stateless persons worldwide is estimated at more than 10 million. The plurality — as many as 40% — live in the Asia-Pacific Region. Europe's stateless population hovers around 600 thousand. Its members have for the most part been stateless since the respective collapses of the Soviet Union and Yugoslavia in the 1990s. The vast majority of stateless persons living in Europe (80%) is concentrated in four countries (Latvia, Russia, Ukraine and Estonia).[59]

However, it must be stressed that the above-given number of stateless persons does not paint the full picture of the scale of the problem. There are no data being collected as to how many cases of statelessness have been successfully avoided by the application of preventive mechanisms. For example, there is no count of cases in which the states have conferred nationality on otherwise stateless children or refused to allow the renunciation of nationality by a citizen on the grounds of their not holding the nationality of any other state.

Having outlined the typical causes of statelessness and the scale of the problem, it now becomes necessary to emphasize that those individuals who do hold a nationality but are not regarded as a citizen by any state 'under the operation of its law' fall under the definition of a stateless person in Article 1(1) of the 1954 Convention. This means that individuals whose statelessness has the above-understood cause and formal character are not the only ones who can be stateless persons. This topic is discussed more extensively in Chapter II.

5. The regulation of statelessness in international law

Matters relating to statelessness are regulated on two basic levels: firstly, the norms of the international law of human rights (section 5.1); secondly, the

57 S. Rajan, *International surrogacy arrangements and statelessness* [in:] *The World's 2017. Stateless and children*, Institute on Statelessness and Inclusion, January 2017, p. 377.

58 UNHCR, *Expert Meeting – The Concept of Stateless Persons under International Law ('Prato Conclusions')*, May 2010, p. 5, hereinafter the 'Prato Conclusions'.

59 *The World's 2017. Stateless and children...*, pp. 57, 73–75. The exact numbers as stated by the UNHCR are: Latvia: 252,195; Russia: 101,813; Estonia: 85,301; Ukraine: 35,228; Sweden: 31,062; Germany: 12,569; Poland: 10,852; UNHCR, *Global Trends: Forced Displacement in 2015...*.

development of specific instruments intended to regulate statelessness, which entailed the separate regulation of matters relating to refugees (section 5.2).

5.1. Statelessness as a human-rights issue

The development of the international protection of human rights in relation to stateless can be analysed in two fundamental aspects. On the one hand, the development of human rights involves their universalization, i.e. recognition of their existence in 'everyone' rather than in citizens alone. On the other hand, the international law of human rights has witnessed the emergence of a right to nationality.

Firstly, the adoption of the UDHR in 1948 was the first step taken towards the establishment of a new system of protection of individual rights, founded not upon the status of a citizen but upon the inherent dignity of the human person. However, the enjoyment of human rights theoretically available to everyone is often rendered difficult if not outright impossible in the case of apatrides. The main reason is that a stateless person usually has no identity papers or other documents with which to confirm identity. And without proof of identity, one cannot effectively exercise human rights. Such a person's right to be recognized as a subject of law within the meaning of Article 6 UDHR is effectively curtailed,[60] imposing significant difficulties on their enjoyment of other human rights.[61] Stateless persons usually encounter difficulties exercising the right of access to court, the right to a private and family life (marrying, registering child births), and freedom of movement. There is also a risk of unwarranted loss of personal freedom due to arbitrary detention,[62] even when voluntarily approaching the

60 The idea of linking the right to nationality formulated in Article 15 UDHR with Article 6 UDHR is something for which I owe gratitude to the pertinent question asked by Michał Kowalski in a conference held by Polish Academy of Arts and Sciences on 12 October 2018 in Cracow.

61 This could be illustrated by the case of a stateless man originally from Georgia who wanted to marry while incarcerated in a Polish prison. As a result of his lacking identity papers, the administrative authorities denied him the right. His case had to go all the way up to the Supreme Administrative Court, whose judgment was the first to call attention to the connection existing between the legal duty for a stateless person to hold an identity document and the ability to enjoy one's fundamental rights (Polish Supreme Administrative Court (NSA), *II OSK 1251/14*, judgment of 26 January 2016).

62 The ECtHR highlighted the unique vulnerability of stateless persons in this context in *Kim v. Russia* (appl. no. 44260/13), 17 July 2014.

public authorities with the intention of regularizing the situation.[63] A stateless person has limited options for the legalization of their stay and often avoids entering into any contact with the institutions, thus becoming vulnerable to all sorts of discrimination or abuse, even human trafficking.

Secondly, by the present date, international documents in the area of human rights have formulated a certain specific human right — a right to nationality. It made its first appearance in Article 15 UDHR, which provides that everyone has a right to nationality (section 1) and that no one may be arbitrarily deprived of nationality or of the right to change it (section 2). The subsequent development of human rights has been to protect only some of the aspects of this right, of which the extensive formulation in the UDHR had been made possible, among other contributing factors, by the Declaration's non-binding character. No universal convention espouses such a broad formula of the right to nationality as does the UDHR[64]. In particular, the right to nationality is not explicitly affirmed by the ECHR.[65] In the development of international law following the Second World War, the right to nationality has been reflected primarily in the aspect concerned with the prevention, elimination or reduction of statelessness in

63 K. Przybysławska, A. Pilaszek, *Ochrona bezpaństwowców przed arbitralną detencją w Polsce*, report by The Halina Nieć Legal Aid Center and the European Network on Statelessness, Kraków 2015.

64 A similar provision is only contained in the American Convention on Human Rights adopted on 22 November 1969 in San José (entered into force on 18 July 1978) — a regional instrument. Article 20: '1. Every person has the right to a nationality. 2. Every person has the right to the nationality of the state in whose territory he was born if he does not have the right to any other nationality. 3. No one shall be arbitrarily deprived of his nationality or of the right to change it.' The obligation of a state to grant its nationality to a person born in its territory is a reflection of the preference of Latin American states, as historically immigrant communities, for the *ius soli*. This convention takes things further than the UDHR does, affirming the explicit obligation to confer nationality on a stateless person who is born in the territory of a given state.

65 There had been plans for an additional protocol to the Convention to deal with the right to nationality, but the idea fell through due to the determined objection of the states to subjecting the relevant matters to the jurisdiction of the ECtHR. See J.M.M. Chan, *The right to a nationality as a human right. The current trend towards recognition*, 12 (1–2) Human Rights Law Journal, p. 7. Although the ECHR does not contain a provision protecting the right to nationality, the ECtHR extends the subject scope of certain Convention rights (e.g. Article 8) to include citizenship, even though they do not have it as their direct formal object, J.-F. Renucci, *Droit européen des droits de l'Homme*, Paris 2002, p. 312.

children. In other words, the states have reached the consensus that everyone should acquire some nationality or other at birth.[66] Similar consensus is lacking, however, with regard to other cases of statelessness. Importantly, international law still tolerates denationalization in situations leading to statelessness. For example, the penalty for serious crimes such as high treason, espionage or terrorist acts may include deprivation of nationality resulting in statelessness.[67]

One cannot but notice a certain contradiction (or at least tension) written into the international system of human rights with regard to statelessness. The purpose of guaranteeing rights to every individual, irrespective of citizenship status, is not perfectly consistent with the placement of emphasis on nationality or with the making of a special right of it. At the same time, no explicit obligation to prevent statelessness from arising has been formulated in the international human-rights system. Interestingly, the drafters of the UDHR (Drafting Committee on an International Bill of Human Rights) had debated on a different version of Article 15 UDHR, which ultimately was not adopted. The eminent French scholar and promoter of human rights, R. Cassin, not only proposed a provision creating a right to nationality but even asserted: 'It is the duty of the United Nations and Member States to prevent statelessness as being inconsistent with human rights and the interests of the human community.'[68] Moreover, stateless persons are not guaranteed the ability to obtain identity papers, which is a necessary precondition for the enjoyment of their human rights.

5.2. Statelessness and the protection of refugees

The establishment of a specific legal framework dealing with statelessness consisted in the adoption of two conventions: the Convention Relating to the Status of Stateless Persons (1954) and the Convention on the Reduction of Statelessness (1961). Before that could happen, however, topics relating to the protection of refugees were split off to be regulated separately in the UN forum.

Before the Second World War and during the beginning of the works on the Convention Relating to the Status of Stateless Persons at the end of the 40s of the 20th century, the protection of refugees and the protection of stateless persons

66 The category of 'children' in the context of statelessness is discussed more extensively in Chapter VI.

67 I treat more extensively on this problem in Chapter VII, section 1.

68 See Report of the Drafting Committee, E/CN.4/21, 1 July 1947, p. 21, cited after G.S. Goodwin-Gill, *Convention relating to the status of stateless persons*, United Nations Audiovisual Library of International Law, United Nations 2010, p. 1.

were discussed conjointly. At that time, the goal was to regulate the situation of whatever groups were in need of protection, with stateless persons among them. According to G.S. Goodwin-Gill, no distinction had historically been made between refugees and stateless persons, both having 'once walked hand in hand'. After the Second World War, the two terms were regarded as synonyms. The concept of being left without the protection of one's state of origin or any other state (such as could be obtained through the acquisition of a new nationality) was referred to both groups. Nonetheless, '[l]ater their paths diverged, with refugees being identified principally by reference to the reasons for flight, and their statelessness, if it existed, being seen as incidental to the primary cause.'[69]

This 'diverging of paths' between refugee and stateless topics during the drafting works at the UN is a process worth taking a closer look at. As early as 1947, the UN Commission on Human Rights adopted a resolution expecting the UN to consider the legal status of those persons who were left without the protection of any state.[70] In line with that resolution, in March 1948, the ECOSOC adopted its own resolution on stateless persons,[71] asking the UN Secretary General, among other requests, to commence analysis of the existing situation with regard to stateless persons. In 1949, the Secretary General published a voluminous Study of Statelessness.[72] Following the tradition of the pre-war period, the document deals with the topics of refugees and stateless persons conjointly, but it introduces the distinction between *de iure* and *de facto* stateless persons, with a lasting impact on the conceptualization of a stateless person.[73] The Study emphasizes the inability to benefit from the protection of a state of nationality as a characteristic *de iure* and *de facto* stateless persons have in common. In the case of those who are *de iure* stateless, this inability is the consequence of not holding any nationality whatsoever, and in the case of those *de facto* stateless, it derives from not being in a position to claim the protection of their state of nationality

69 G.S. Goodwin-Gill, *The rights of refugees and stateless persons* [in:] K.P. Saksena (ed.), *Human rights perspective & challenges: in 1990 and beyond*, New Delhi 1994, pp. 389 (quotation), 379.

70 Report of the Commission on Human Rights on the Second Session (E/600); Report of the Working Party on an International Convention on Human Rights (E/CN.4/56, 11 December 1947), cited after G.S. Goodwin-Gill, *Convention...*, p. 1.

71 Resolution 116 (VI) D on Stateless Persons, Economic and Social Council, March 1948.

72 United Nations, *A Study of Statelessness*, Lake Success–New York, August 1949, E/1112; E/1112/Add.1, hereinafter the 'Study'.

73 This topic is discussed more extensively in Chapter II.

while formally remaining its citizen.[74] In the Study, the Secretary General made a recommendation to the ECOSOC concerning the necessity of creating a legal framework for the protection of stateless persons. In that same year, having considered the Study, the ECOSOC adopted a resolution[75] appointing an *ad hoc* committee to consider the need for a convention for the protection of refugees and stateless persons and, in the event of an affirmative conclusion, to draft the appropriate text. The committee was also tasked with examining matters pertaining to the elimination of the problem of statelessness. Simultaneously, the Secretary General submitted to the *ad hoc* committee a preliminary working draft of the relevant convention for discussion. Article 2 of the draft stipulated the applicability of the instrument to those refugees who might be *de iure* or *de facto* stateless, as well as to *de iure* stateless persons not being refugees.[76] However, in its report for the ECOSOC, the committee recommended that only a convention addressing the status of refugees be drafted. Agreeing with that position, the Council presented the working draft of a convention dealing solely with the protection of refugees. Simultaneously, it suggested the preparation of an additional protocol concerning stateless persons at a later time.

The ECOSOC's draft focused on the subcategory of individuals defined by the Study. First and foremost, by introducing the criterion that the individual be outside of the territory of their country of origin and unable to claim protection due to a well-founded fear of persecution, the draft offered protection only to a certain part of the individuals termed either *de iure* or *de facto* stateless persons by the Study. Those stateless persons who did not satisfy the condition of being outside of their country of origin and having a well-founded fear of persecution were not accorded protection.

In December 1950, the UN General Assembly decided to hold a conference of plenipotentiaries of states in order to finalize the works on a convention relating to the status of refugees along with a protocol relating to stateless persons. Ultimately, however, the discussion on the protocol was deferred in time, with the document itself returned to the relevant UN bodies for further analysis. In 1951, the Geneva Convention was adopted, and not even four years later, on 26 April 1954, the ECOSOC resolved[77] to hold another conference of plenipotentiaries of

74 United Nations, *A Study of Statelessness…*, p. 6.
75 Economic and Social Council, Resolution 248 (IX) B, August 1949.
76 H. Massey, *UNHCR and De Facto Statelessness*, UNHCR Geneva, LPPR/2010/01, April 2010, p. 9.
77 Resolution 526 A (XVII) of Economic and Social Council, 26 April 1954.

states with a view to regulating and improving the status of stateless persons by means of an international treaty.[78] Thus, the Convention Relating to the Status of Stateless Persons became a separate treaty in its own right rather than a protocol to the 1951 Geneva Convention, and the matters of refugees and stateless persons were regulated by separate instruments of international law.

5.3. United Nations conventions on statelessness

5.3.1. The 1954 Convention relating to the Status of Stateless Persons

The significance of the 1954 Convention [79] consists primarily in that its Article (1)(1) provides the definition of a stateless person nowadays regarded as customary law[80] and enumerates a series of personal, political, economic, social and cultural rights for stateless persons.[81] However, what rights specifically are available to stateless persons is a complex matter, because their rights are distinguished on two levels. On the first level, the situation of stateless persons differs depending on whether the individual is merely physically present in the territory of a given state[82] or is so in compliance with its laws and regulations (i.e. lawfully). As discussed more extensively in Chapter IV, analysis of the provisions of the 1954 Convention permits categories of stateless persons to be distinguished, with a gradual scale of rights accorded to them, depending on the nature and length of their stay in the territory. The second level on which the Convention rights are distinguished refers to the difference in the treatment of stateless persons depending on the type of standard of treatment foreseen for a given right. The Convention sets a minimum standard of treatment of stateless persons — they are to be treated on par with foreigners unless the Convention prescribes more favourable treatment.

78 A. Edwards, L. van Waas, *Statelessness* [in:] G. Loescher, K. Long, N. Sigona and E. Fiddian-Qasmiyeh (eds.), *The Oxford Handbook of Refugee and Forced Migration Studies*, Oxford 2014, 291.

79 The Convention came into force on 6 June 1960.

80 Matters relating to the definition of a stateless person are analysed in Chapter II.

81 For a more extensive discussion of this topic see Chapter IV on the protection of stateless persons.

82 An individual is a stateless person if they meet the definitional criteria under Article 1(1) of the 1954 Convention, whereas the nature of a determination of statelessness in a special procedure is declaratory; UNHCR, *Handbook on Protection of Stateless Persons*, Geneva 2014; hereinafter the 'UNHCR Handbook', paragraph 16.

The rights specifically recognized by the 1954 Convention are very similar to those covered by the 1951 Geneva Convention. However, the level of protection accorded to stateless persons in the 1954 Convention is inferior compared to the earlier Convention. In particular, there is no provision for *non-refoulement* (prohibition against extraditing or reconducting the individual to a territory where their life or freedoms would be in danger) and no ban on imposing penalties for unlawfully entering or being in the territory (Articles 33(1) and 31(1) of the 1951 Geneva Convention, respectively). The omission of these rights can probably be explained by the fact that a stateless person whose status is regulated by the 1954 Convention is not necessarily outside of the territory of their country of origin.[83] Another difference compared to the 1951 Geneva Convention is that the 1954 Convention contains no supervisory mechanism for its implementation (whereas in Article 35 of the 1951 Geneva Convention the states party agree to work with the UNHCR).

Many of the rights guaranteed by the 1954 Convention are currently covered by the general instruments of protection of human rights, and in this sense they supplement the protection system established by the 1954 Convention. Accordingly, in states not having acceded to the 1954 Convention, stateless persons fall within the purview of the international law of human rights, which envisages some additional rights that are of importance in the case of stateless persons and are not included in the 1954 Convention, such as protection from arbitrary detention (Article 9(1) ICCPR) or the right to enter one's 'own country' (Article 12(4) ICCPR), which is understood more broadly than the 'state of nationality'.[84] It needs to be emphasized, however, that the 1954 Convention provides stateless persons with rights not stipulated in any other treaty. Those are the right to be issued identity papers and the right to be issued a travel document. Such is, at present, the main significance of the 1954 Convention.

5.3.2. The 1961 Convention on the Reduction of Statelessness

Having regulated the protection status of stateless persons by the 1954 Convention, the international community diverted its attention to a different purpose: ensuring that no new cases of statelessness would arise in the future. That was by no means a novel goal. Rather, the idea was to reforge the aspirational nature of Article 15 UDHR into some concrete standards to be implemented by

---

83 A. Edwards, L. van Waas, *Statelessness* [in:] G. Loescher, K. Long, N. Sigona and E. Fiddian-Qasmiyeh (eds.), *The Oxford…*, p. 292.

84 UNHCR Handbook, paragraphs 141–142.

the states in their domestic legislations and to devise more complex solutions than those foreseen by the 1930 Hague Convention.

The adoption of the 1961 Convention was preceded by the works of the International Law Commission, which adopted two provisional drafts dealing with statelessness: the Draft Convention on the Elimination of Future Statelessness and the Draft Convention on the Reduction of Future Statelessness. The former was more rigorous and contained stipulations that, if actually adopted by the states, would have had the effect of abolishing the statelessness arising from the causes addressed by the instrument. The latter dealt with similar topics but left the states with the option of subjecting the availability of the safeguards stipulated by it to certain conditions. In the discussions taking place in the course of the Commission's works, the sentiment was leaning in favour of the less stringent convention, so as to make the states more amenable to its ratification.[85] In the aftermath of what proved to be difficult negotiations,[86] the text of the Convention on the Reduction of Statelessness was adopted in 1961.

The purpose of the 1961 Convention[87] is to counteract (prevent and reduce) statelessness in three basic contexts: acquisition of nationality upon birth (Articles 1–4); loss, deprivation or renunciation at a later point in life (Article 5–9); and succession of States (Article 10).

In each case the provisions of the Convention specify which state is responsible for providing an individual who would otherwise be a stateless person with the option to acquire or retain nationality.[88] This is one of the most significant aspects of the Convention, which imposes on the states a positive obligation to confer nationality in certain circumstances, contrasting with the negative obligations of the 1930 Hague Convention.[89] Moreover, as opposed to its predecessor, the 1961 Convention contains provisions devised to counteract that type of statelessness which arises in connection with the loss of nationality. However, the decision to focus on reducing the number of stateless persons rather than eliminating statelessness altogether has the result that the provisions of the 1961 Convention allow for an individual to lose their nationality with the effect of

---

85 H. Suchocka, *Prawo do posiadania obywatelstwa* [in:] R. Wieruszewski (ed.), *Prawa człowieka. Model prawny*, Wrocław 1991, 274.

86 The conference of plenipotentiaries called in 1959 was deferred due to the lack of a consensus on the provision dealing with the deprivation of nationality and was reconvened in 1961.

87 The Convention came into force on 13 December 1975.

88 The legal framework of the 1961 Convention is analysed in more detail in Chapter III.

89 G.S. Goodwin-Gill, *The Rights of Refugees...*, p. 383.

becoming a stateless person (e.g. as a sanction for citizenship fraud — Article 8(2)(b) of the 1961 Convention) or to remain a stateless person when already being one (e.g. the principle of Article 1 of the 1961 Convention concerning the acquisition of nationality *iure soli* by a child who would otherwise be stateless is not unconditional).

Similarly to the 1954 Convention, the 1961 Convention lacks provisions guaranteeing the existence of an effective enforcement mechanism. The proposal of an international court with jurisdiction over disputes arising from the application of the Convention in individual cases was not adopted. Instead, a weaker supervisory mechanism was chosen — an agency empowered to assist individuals desirous to take advantage of the Convention's provisions with referring their cases to the competent authorities (Article 11) — a role filled since the very beginning by the UNHCR.

5.4. The regulation of statelessness in Europe

For many years, the 1954 Convention and the subsequent 1961 Convention had only achieved a scarce number of ratifications, remaining in the side-lines of the international law on refugees. However, in the 90s of the 20th century, awareness of the problem of statelessness began to increase in connection with new waves of stateless persons emerging from the disintegration of the USSR, Czechoslovakia and Yugoslavia. The renewed interest in statelessness in the 90s of the 20th century resulted in the adoption of regional instruments with a view to preventing and reducing statelessness. This particularly includes the ECN of 1997, as well the Council of Europe Convention on the Avoidance of Statelessness in Relation to State Succession of 19 May 2006.[90] The year 1999 saw Recommendation no. R (99) 18 of the Committee of Ministers to member States on the avoidance and reduction of statelessness.[91] In 2009, the Committee issued its Recommendation CM/Rec(2009)13 and explanatory memorandum of the Committee of Ministers to member states on the nationality of children.[92] It should also be noted that the

90 Council of Europe Convention on the Avoidance of Statelessness in relation to State Succession, Strasbourg, 19 May 2006, Council of Europe Treaty Series — No. 200.

91 Recommendation no. R (99) 18 of the Committee of Ministers to member States on the avoidance and reduction of statelessness, 15 September 1999.

92 Recommendation CM/Rec(2009)13 and explanatory memorandum of the Committee of Ministers to member states on the nationality of children, Council of Europe: Committee of Ministers, 9 December 2009, hereinafter the 'Council of Europe Committee of Ministers recommendation of 2009 on the nationality of children'.

ECtHR has made a number of important judgments in the context of statelessness (e.g. *Genovese v. Malta*,[93] *Mennesson v. France*[94] and *Labassée v. France*[95]).

As far as the European Union is concerned, one can only identify certain initiatives undertaken in the field of statelessness that are not binding on the member states. For example, as part of the implementation of the Council of the EU's conclusions on statelessness, the European Commission has ordered the preparation of a document titled *Statelessness in the EU*.[96] Although the EU lacks the power to regulate the conditions for granting or revoking the EU citizenship, the CJEU's judgment of 2 March 2010 in *C-135/08*,[97] for example, is of significant importance to the evaluation of the EU member states' approach to the prevention of statelessness due to the enunciation of the principle that the permissibility of the withdrawal of nationality resulting in statelessness is conditional on having positively verified the merits and proportionality of taking such a measure.

6. Basic legal mechanisms for regulating statelessness

As demonstrated by the preceding paragraphs, there are two basic mechanisms for the regulation of statelessness in international law. On the one hand, there are instruments intended to counteract statelessness, such as the 1961 Convention, and — on the regional level — the ECN. In a gist, the goal is to prevent new cases of statelessness from arising and to reduce statelessness by conferring nationality on stateless persons.[98] On the other hand, there are instruments for the protection of stateless persons, which is the topic of the brunt of the provisions of the 1954 Convention. This system is supplemented by abundant regulation in the field of the international law of human rights.[99]

93 ECtHR, *Genovese v. Malta*, appl. no. 53124/09, judgment of 11 October 2011.

94 ECtHR, *Mennesson v. France*, appl. no. 65192/11, judgment of 26 June 2014.

95 ECtHR, *Labassée v. France*, appl. no. 65941/11, judgement of 26 June 2014.

96 *Statelessness in the EU*, European Migration Network, 11 November 2016. Another example of the European Union's engagement can be found in the EU's pledge of September 2012 that all EU Member States would accede to the 1954 Convention and would consider acceding to the 1961 Convention.

97 Judgment of the Court (Grand Chamber) in *Janko Rottmann v. Freistaat Bayern*, EU:C:2010:104. For a more extensive discussion of this particular case see Chapter VII, section 1.1.1.

98 I discuss these topics in detail in Chapter III.

99 I discuss these topics in detail in Chapter IV.

Although the two mechanisms for the regulation of statelessness (counteraction and protection) are presented in UN documents as mutually complementary, there is a visible tendency to assign priority to instruments of prevention and reduction before instruments of protection.[100] The international community's primary goal is to eliminate statelessness. This approach is already visible in the Study: 'The two problems – the improvement of the status of stateless persons and the elimination of statelessness – though quite distinct, are complementary. However necessary and urgent, the improvement of the status of the stateless person is only a temporary solution designed to attenuate the evils resulting from statelessness. The elimination of statelessness, on the contrary, would have the advantage of abolishing the evil itself, and is therefore the final goal.'[101] As can be seen, during that time statelessness had been viewed as an 'evil' needing to be stopped, whereas protection instruments were presented as transitional solutions for until such time as the individual concerned may be granted the nationality of one state or another.

The position giving priority to mechanisms for the prevention and reduction of statelessness is manifest in modern UN documents dealing with statelessness. With regard to the 1954 Convention, the UNHCR Handbook[102] notes: 'The drafters intended to improve the position of stateless persons by regulating their status. That said, as a general rule, possession of a nationality is preferable to recognition and protection as a stateless person.'[103] A different UNHCR document states that the protection of stateless persons cannot serve as a substitute for nationality and that the 1954 Convention requires the states to facilitate the naturalization of stateless persons.[104] Since 2014, the UNHCR has conducted an extensive campaign titled #IBelong Campaign to End Statelessness with the goal of eliminating statelessness by 2024.[105]

Despite the attempts undertaken on the international level since the 30s of the 20th century to eliminate statelessness, the objective has not been achieved. W.E. Conklin goes as far as calling this problem an 'enigma'.[106] In my view, complete

100 For a more extensive discussion of this topic see K. Swider, *A rights-based approach to statelessness*, doctoral thesis defended at the University of Amsterdam, pp. 137ff, courtesy of the author, with my thanks.

101 United Nations, *A Study of Statelessness…*, p. 10.

102 For more information about this particular document see footnote 246.

103 UNHCR Handbook, paragraph 14.

104 UNHCR, *Introductory Note by the Office of the UNHCR to the 1954 Convention*, Geneva 2014.

105 https://www.unhcr.org/ibelong/ (accessed 2 January 2023).

106 W.E. Conklin, *Statelessness. The Enigma…*

eradication of statelessness is an impossible goal. The aspiration to eliminate all the cases of statelessness from arising focuses primarily on the source of the problem and follows the logic that when the source is eliminated, the problem will be solved. This obfuscates an important aspect of the problem, which is that the term 'statelessness' refers to an extensive and diverse pool of individuals. The perspective in which the elimination of statelessness is the goal ignores the fact that not all of those individuals, not always desire to become the nationals of a specific state or of any state whatsoever. It ignores also the fact that the international community and the individual states do not always have the political will to treat each and every category of stateless persons with the same consistency of purpose with regard to the prevention and reduction of statelessness; this will be discussed in the later chapters of this work.

7. Conclusions

Statelessness as a term refers to the potential or actual occurrence of the 'negative condition' consisting in the lack of the nationality of any state whatsoever. The legal nature of statelessness consists in the absence of the relationship created by nationality both in the domestic and in the external dimension. In principle, statelessness has an adverse impact on the individual's situation and on the international legal order.

To this date, statelessness continues to be an important legal category. At present, the legal framework governing statelessness includes instruments of counteraction of statelessness and instruments for the protection of stateless persons. It could have seemed that the creation of mechanisms to counteract statelessness would have the effect of diminishing its significance; however, that is not the case because, among other reasons, international law permits new cases of statelessness to arise. Furthermore, despite the development of human rights, there continues to exist a need for special protection to be given to how stateless persons' enjoyment of their human rights is met with difficulties or made outright impossible due to the lack of identity documents.

The importance of statelessness as a legal category manifests itself also in how the scope of this problem area includes on the one hand legal provisions dealing with stateless persons as a group of actually existing individuals affected by statelessness (reduction and protection) and on the other hand complex frameworks designed to prevent statelessness from arising. From this perspective, the importance of the problem area that is statelessness cannot be judged solely in the lens of the number of stateless persons in a given country or in the world as a whole; this must also take into account the number of individuals who are prevented from becoming stateless persons thanks to the application of the prevention mechanisms.

'Statelessness' and 'stateless person' are not coterminous; this is the thesis providing direction to the later chapters of this book. The topic of the discussion in Chapter II will be the definition of the term 'stateless person' from the perspective of the different approaches taken to the problem in the various regulatory instruments of domestic jurisdictions.

Chapter II Defining the Stateless Person

The subject-matter of this chapter are definitional issues relating to the concept of a stateless person through the perspective of the terms used and their interpretations. The discussion of the definition of a stateless person adopted in the 1954 Convention and its modern interpretation (section 2) will first make it necessary to expound on the broader meaning of the term 'stateless person' in the international documents originating from the discussions on the adoption of a protection regime for stateless persons (section 1). Towards the end, I will discuss several definitional problems arising in the domestic legal systems of several European states taken as examples (section 3).

1. The meaning of the term 'stateless person'

To answer the question of what the definitional characteristics of a stateless person should be is not a simple task. The precise meaning of the term 'stateless person' has been the topic of debate among scholars in international law essentially since the end of the Second World War. The adoption of a definition of a stateless person in the 1954 Convention has not changed this.

After the Second World War, a division into two analytically separate categories was introduced: the *de iure* and the *de facto* stateless persons. This was done with a view to designing a regulatory framework to protect a variety of persons who were unable to avail themselves of the protection of their state of origin and who were referred to with the umbrella term 'stateless persons' at the time.[107] Whereas the term '*de iure* stateless person' is consistently used in reference to persons formally lacking the nationality of any state whatsoever, the term '*de facto* stateless person' has been used in different meanings evolving over time.

Under the traditional concept of *de facto* statelessness followed in the 40s of the 20th century, the term referred to those individuals who, while holding the nationality of a certain state, were finding themselves outside of its borders and not in a position to avail themselves of its protection and assistance. The understanding of the last-mentioned element varied. It could mean either the state's having denied such persons its diplomatic assistance[108] or, in a broader

107 See Chapter I, section 5.2.

108 Intergovernmental Committee on Refugees, *Statelessness and some of its causes: an outline*, London, March 1946, pp. 3–4.

perspective, the individuals' own refusal to accept the protection offered to them by their state of nationality.[109]

Since the 90s of the 20th century, with the disintegration of the USSR, Czechoslovakia and Yugoslavia, the topic of *de facto* statelessness has begun to be discussed in a new way, from somewhat of a different perspective.[110] The concept of *de facto* statelessness refers to persons who, while remaining outside of the territory of their state of nationality, lack specific rights linked to nationality, such as the right of entry and residence (thus, this is no longer merely about diplomatic assistance).[111] It is also applied to persons who are outside of the borders of the state and unable to prove (confirm) their citizenship status.[112] It is also beginning to be applied to persons being within the territory of their state of nationality but unable to avail themselves of the rights associated with it.[113] In this way, the concept of *de facto* statelessness has become associated with the broadly understood principle of effective nationality.[114] Moreover, the concept of *de facto* statelessness has also been applied to persons having been assigned, as a result of state succession, the nationality of not the state in which they had been born and had had their habitual residence but of one with which they lacked ties, thus forfeiting their existing rights in the state of residence (such as the right to work, own property or access health-care or education).[115]

---

109 United Nations, *A Study of Statelessness…*, p. 7.

110 For a more detailed discussion of the evolution of the term '*de facto* statelessness' see H. Massey, *UNHCR and De Facto...*, p. 27.

111 C.A. Batchelor, *Statelessness and the problem of resolving nationality status*, 10(1/2) International Journal of Refugee Law 1998, p. 173.

112 C.A. Batchelor, *Statelessness...*, p. 173; J.A. Goldston, *Holes in the rights framework. Racial discrimination, citizenship, and the rights of noncitizens*, 20(3) Ethics and International Affairs 2006, pp. 339–340. For example, upon the disintegration of Yugoslavia, this mainly involved the inability to offer proof of previous nationality of one of the constituent republics due to the destruction or loss of registers in war-affected territories (especially Bosnia and Herzegovina and Croatia). UNHCR, *Citizenship and prevention..., Foreword.*

113 D. Weissbrodt, C. Collins, *The human rights of stateless persons*, 28 Human Rights Quarterly 2006, pp. 251–252.

114 For a discussion of the principle of effective nationality see D. Pudzianowska, *Obywatelstwo...*, pp. 59–62.

115 This is the category of individuals identified by C.A. Batchelor, *Statelessness…*, p. 173. The context for distinguishing this category can be found in the situation arising from the succession of nationality after the collapse of the Socialist Federal Republic of Yugoslavia. The principle was adopted that the internal nationality of each of the former republics would become the nationality of the corresponding successor state.

As can already be seen from the above (non-exhaustive) list of meanings of the term '*de facto* stateless person', it is a polysemous and capacious term. It is important to highlight its semantic diversity because the axis of the ever-current dispute is the matter whether stateless persons within the meaning of the definition adopted in international law are only those who are *de iure* stateless (i.e. formally lacking the nationality of any state whatsoever) or also those who are so *de facto*. Due to the fact that the still-ongoing debate surrounding the international law definition of a stateless person invokes the semantic dichotomy between the '*de iure* stateless person' and the '*de facto* stateless person', in the interest of clarity I enclose below a schematic illustration of the meanings of the two terms (Fig. 1).

The '***de iure* stateless (1)**' lack the nationality of any state whatsoever.	The '***de facto* stateless (1)**' are a capacious category including among others those who have a nationality but: - do not enjoy the protection of their state of nationality (whether within its territory or without); - cannot prove or attest the nationality they have; - cannot exercise rights linked to nationality, e.g. right of entry and residence.

Fig. 1. Meanings of terms '*de iure* stateless person' and '*de facto* stateless person' in the historical distinction prevailing until the publication of the Prato Conclusions in 2010.

2. Definition of a stateless person in international law

2.1. General problems

The definition of a stateless person is provided in Article 1(1) of the 1954 Convention:

'For the purpose of this Convention, the term "stateless person" means a person who is not considered as a national by any State under the operation of its law.'

Article 1(2) of the 1954 Convention enumerates the categories of individuals excluded from the protection offered by the treaty and is not an element of the definition. This means either those who, although they fulfil the definition of

---

Although this is noted to have avoided the problem of *de iure* statelessness, many permanent inhabitants of republics other than the one of which they hold the nationality became stateless *de facto*; UNHCR, *Citizenship and prevention…*, *Foreword.*

Article 1(1), do not need protection (due to being given alternative protection on the basis of different provisions),[116] or those who, on account of their own conduct, are undeserving of protection.[117]

The meaning of the term 'state' used in this definition refers to its understanding in international law. The Montevideo Convention on the Rights and Duties of States of 1933 will be of particular importance here.[118] In line with this convention, a state as a subject of international law should have the following qualities: permanent population, sovereign authority, defined territory separated by a border, and the capacity to enter into relations with other states. If the only entity with which the individual has ties is not a state, then the individual is a stateless person.[119]

It should be noted that the definition does not concern itself with the manner in which the individual has become a stateless person. This can include being made stateless by operation of the law (*ex lege*) or by the action (or omission) of the organs of the state.[120] It is irrelevant to this definition whether the statelessness is voluntary or not.[121] In this sense, the definition affirms the objective concept of statelessness, for it refers to the simple circumstance that the individual lacks the nationality of any state whatsoever, without addressing the reasons (causes) of the statelessness; the latter would be the manifestation of a more subjective concept.[122]

The definition refers to stateless persons in a migration context and *in situ*.[123] In other words, it is irrelevant whether the individual is a migrant or has never crossed the border of the state of origin. As regards statelessness linked

---

116 Articles 1(2)(i) and 1(2)(ii) of the 1954 Convention.

117 Article 1(2)(iii) of the 1954 Convention. For a more extensive discussion of the so-called exclusion clauses see Chapter IV, section 1 and Chapter VII, section 2.

118 Montevideo Convention on the Rights and Duties of States, Montevideo, 26 December 1933.

119 UNHCR Handbook, paragraph 17.

120 UNHCR Handbook, paragraphs 25–26.

121 UNHCR Handbook, paragraph 51.

122 Ch. Chiurulli, *La protection des apatrides. État des lieux*, Wavre 2014, p. 21. Already in this place it must be emphasized that although the provisions of the 1954 Convention do not foresee a distinction in treatment between voluntarily and involuntarily (forcibly) stateless persons, instruments of soft law (such as the UNHCR Handbook) provide for the possibility of offering weaker protection to the voluntarily stateless. I will be examining this distinction more closely in Chapter VIII.

123 UNHCR Handbook, paragraph 15.

to migration, it must be noted that the definitions of a stateless person and of a refugee are not mutually exclusive. A stateless person can simultaneously be a refugee (or, more broadly speaking, an individual entitled to international protection).[124]

Returning now to the definition of a stateless person in Article 1(1) of the 1954 Convention, it must be noted that the use of the phrase 'for the purpose of this Convention' implies that the definition is a regulatory one designed for the needs of the specific legal instrument in which it is contained. It is thus not a reporting definition[125] intended to reflect the accepted meaning of the defined term 'stateless person'. This formulation clearly shows that the drafters had considered the existence of a broader meaning (denotation) of the term 'stateless person'; in particular, as I noted above, during their time it had extended to individuals formally holding the nationality of a state but not having the benefit of its protection. At present, however, this definition, although originally designed for the purposes of a specific legal instrument, is regarded as part of customary international law.[126] Accordingly, it has been relied upon to define the term for the purposes of other treaties, such as the 1961 Convention. Furthermore, since it has acquired the status of customary law, it should nowadays be regarded as binding not only on the parties to the 1954 Convention but also on any states not having ratified the Convention but employing the term 'stateless person' for a variety of purposes.[127]

The tersely worded negative definition of a stateless person in Article 1(1) of the 1954 Convention is currently the topic of debate as to its exact meaning. The Convention itself does not contain any provisions dealing with how the definition should be applied in practice. As a result of the relative length of the period

---

124 UNHCR Handbook, paragraphs 15, 128. A stateless person who is simultaneously a refugee should be accorded the higher standard of protection, as established by the 1951 Geneva Convention, among other reasons due to the prohibition of *refoulement*; for a more extensive discussion of this topic see Chapter I, section 5.3.1.

125 Concerning the term 'regulatory definition' (roughly: statutory definition) and 'reporting definition' (roughly: descriptive definition) see Z. Ziembiński, *Logika praktyczna*, Warszawa 2000, pp. 45–46.

126 In 2006, the UN International Law Commission voiced the opinion that this definition 'can no doubt be considered as having acquired a customary nature' — International Law Commission, *Draft Articles on Diplomatic Protection with commentaries*, United Nations 2006, p. 49.

127 L. van Waas, *The UN Statelessness Conventions* [in:] A. Edwords and L. van Waas (eds.), *Nationality and statelessness...*, 72.

during which the Convention had not been the object of great interest on the part of the states, the analysis of the terms used in the definition and of the various aspects of its practical application has begun only somewhat recently and is still in progress.

2.2. Semantic challenges

Two basic interpretations of this definition can be distinguished. The first one can be viewed as a narrow interpretation, corresponding to historical construction, extending only to *de iure* stateless persons in line with the meaning discussed above (section 2.2.1). However, it is also necessary to take note of the various proposals of a broad interpretation, extending the definition not only to *de iure* stateless persons but also to some persons previously regarded as *de facto* stateless (section 2.2.2).

2.2.1. Narrow interpretation of the definition of a stateless person in the 1954 Convention

The question of whether only *de iure* or also *de facto* stateless persons should be seen to fall within the ambit of the definition of a stateless person was the single hottest-debated topic during the works on the 1954 Convention.[128] Eventually, the decision turned to be in favour of applicability only to *de iure* stateless persons, which means that only those formally lacking the nationality of any state whatsoever are stateless persons in the light of the definition.

The goal of this approach was clarity and lack of ambiguity — especially the avoidance of any doubt as to who is a stateless person versus who is a refugee.[129] For the assumption at the time of drafting was that all *de facto* stateless persons (and some of the *de iure* ones, too) would be covered by the 1951 Geneva Convention.[130]

In the 90s of the 20th century, the definition from the 1954 Convention began to be criticized for having left *de facto* stateless persons outside of the system of international protection. By that time, it had become clear that not all stateless

128 N. Robinson, *Convention relating to the status of stateless persons. Its history and interpretation*, New York 1955, reprinted by the Division of International Protection of the UNHCR 1997; Commentary on Article 1 of the 1954 Convention, p. 7 (section 3).

129 D. Weissbrodt, C. Collins, *The Human…*, p. 252.

130 C.A. Batchelor, *Statelessness…*, p. 172; M. Achiron, *Nationality and Statelessness. A Handbook for Parliamentarians*, UNHCR and the Inter-Parliamentary Union, Geneva 2005, p. 12.

persons satisfied the requirements for the protection of the 1951 Geneva Convention. Not all were migrants, and even if those who were, were still not all affected by a well-founded fear of persecution. The narrow approach to statelessness, limited to the optic of *de iure* statelessness, began to be seen as problematic due to its failure to take into account the similarity of the problems facing *de iure* and *de facto* stateless persons, namely the lack of protection and assistance offered by a state of nationality. From this perspective, the distinction between *de iure* and *de facto* stateless persons came to be regarded as arbitrary, denying protection to those who technically held a nationality but who were not in a position to obtain or avail themselves of the rights or protection annexed to it.[131]

Two approaches to the problem of the exceedingly narrow nature of the definition are possible. Firstly, one can take the position that the scope is limited to *de iure* stateless persons and, accepting the utility of the use of the term '*de facto* statelessness', seek avenues to extend protection to such persons. That could be achieved, for example, by introducing domestic provisions to the effect that *de facto* stateless persons are to be offered the same treatment as *de iure* stateless persons for certain purposes (the principle of similar treatment). Secondly, one could give the conventional definition a different (broader) interpretation, so as to expand its applicability to include *de facto* stateless persons as well.

With regard to the first proposal, one must note that although the 1954 Convention itself does not employ the '*de iure*/*de facto* stateless person' terminology, the recommendation of the annexed final act makes a direct reference to the concept of *de facto* statelessness. The recommendation is that 'each Contracting State, when it recognizes as valid the reasons for which a person has renounced the protection of the State of which he is a national, consider sympathetically the possibility of according to the person the treatment which the Convention accords to stateless persons […]'.[132] Similar language can be found in the final act annexed to the 1961 Convention, where the recommendation is that those who are *de facto stateless persons* 'should as far as possible be treated as stateless *de jure* to enable them to acquire an effective nationality.'[133] Additionally, *de facto* statelessness is mentioned in the Recommendation of the Committee of Ministers of the Council of Europe of 2009 concerning the nationality of children: 'with a

131 D. Weissbrodt, C. Collins, *The Human…*, p. 251.

132 Cited after H. Massey, *UNHCR and De Facto...*, p. 19.

133 This was added at Belgium's request with the UNHCR's support so as to ensure that the children of refugees can acquire the nationality of the state of residence; see H. Massey, *UNHCR and De Facto...* p. 23 (also for the quotation).

view to reducing statelessness of children and ensuring their right to a nationality, states should (…) treat children who are factually (*de facto*) stateless, as far as possible, as legally stateless (*de jure*) with respect to the acquisition of nationality'.[134] From these documents, it follows that the states are recommended either to expand the availability of the protection to *de facto* stateless persons or to apply statelessness-reduction mechanisms to *de facto* stateless persons (facilitated naturalization).

States can offer protection to *de facto* stateless persons by according to them similar treatment under domestic provisions as is given to *de iure* stateless persons, at least to a certain extent. One of the examples of such a regulatory approach to statelessness taking into account the situation of *de facto* stateless persons are the Draft Articles on the Protection of Stateless Persons,[135] which contain the proposal of a provision extending the rights of stateless persons to a selected category of *de facto* stateless persons. The recommended provision is worded as follows: 'The rights of stateless persons as recognised under this law shall be extended to those individuals who have a nationality but to whom the authorities of their country do not allow them [sic] to return to it. [...] The migration authority will authorise the temporary residence of said individual for humanitarian reasons, as long as it does not conflict with the criteria of migration regulations on the prohibition of the stay of foreigners. The competent authority may issue that individual a special travel document for foreigners who cannot obtain a passport from the authorities of the country of their nationality.'[136] Clearly, this refers to those who are formally the nationals of some state but are prevented from returning to it.

---

134 Principle 7. The explanatory memorandum specifies that *de facto* stateless persons are those who lack an effective nationality, i.e. cannot exercise rights annexed to nationality — Explanatory memorandum of the Committee of Ministers to member states on the nationality of children, 9 May 2009, CM/Rec(2009)13, commentary on Principle 7.

135 UNHCR, *Draft Articles…* As explained in the foreword, the document was drafted '[…] in consultation with various Latin American countries, which are developing regulations for the protection and naturalisation of stateless persons, with human rights organisations and with civil society organisations. Its purpose is to offer legal counsel to these countries and to respond to the requests for technical assistance received by UNHCR', UNHCR, *Draft Articles…*, p. 3.

136 Article: 'Individuals in a similar situation to stateless persons', UNHCR, *Draft Articles…*, p. 12.

2.2.2. Broad interpretation of the definition of a stateless person in the 1954 Convention

The aforementioned criticism of the conventional definition of a stateless person has led to calls for a broader interpretation of the definition itself. The essence of that interpretation is not to apply the Convention *per analogiam* to *de facto* stateless persons but to encompass a broader range of individuals under the definition (including persons regarded as being *de facto* stateless under the approach discussed in section 2.2.1).

This is the position currently taken by the UNHCR, advocating for departure from the historical dichotomy between *de iure* and *de facto* stateless persons in favour of a uniform definition of a stateless person coextensive with a suitably broad interpretation of the definition contained in the 1954 Convention. According to the Prato Conclusions, the interpretation of the phrase 'under the operation of its law' employed in the definition can include those who are regarded as *de facto* stateless persons. And thus: 'some categories of persons hitherto regarded as *de facto* stateless are actually *de jure* stateless, and therefore particular care should be taken before concluding that a person is *de facto* stateless rather than *de jure* stateless.'[137] The document emphasizes that an important reason for the avoidance of classification of persons as *de facto* stateless is the absence of any treaty framework to protect *de facto* stateless persons and that the recognition of an individual as being a *de facto* stateless person does not entail any rights. As M. Manly observes, the Prato Conclusions marked a breakthrough in attracting attention to the fact that the definition of statelessness had previously (i.e. until 2010) been interpreted too narrowly.[138]

Under the above-described approach, specific individuals can be *de iure* (and not *de facto*) stateless persons due to the fact that specific practices engaged in by states are taken as evidence of not regarding such individuals as their nationals. The phrase 'under the operation of its law' permits a different (broader) interpretation than the historical dichotomy of two categories of statelessness. The UNHCR Handbook points out the necessity of a detailed examination not only of the wording of the domestic provisions but also of the practice of application of nationality legislation in individual cases by the authorities of the state. Thus, the reference to the 'law' in this definition includes situations in which the 'law

137 Prato Conclusions, p. 5.

138 M. Manly, *UNHCR's mandate and activities to address statelessness* [in:] A. Edwards and L. van Waas (eds.), *Nationality and statelessness…*, p. 96.

in books' is significantly modified in the process of its practical application.[139] Moreover, as the UNHCR Handbook goes on to expound: 'Where the competent authorities treat an individual as a non-national even though he or she would appear to meet the criteria for automatic acquisition of nationality under the operation of a country's laws, it is their position rather than the letter of the law that is determinative in concluding that a State does not consider such an individual as a national' (emphasis added).[140] Hence, certain actions of a state may be regarded by other states as *prima facie* evidence of not regarding specific persons as nationals.

It cannot escape notice that in the Prato Conclusions' recommendation for the interpretation of the definition, the term '*de iure* statelessness' is used in a different meaning than it has in the historical dichotomy of *de iure* and *de facto* stateless persons. This simply means the use of the term '*de iure* stateless person' in the sense in which it is normally used in legal sciences, i.e. in reference to all individuals falling within the ambit of the legal definition.[141] In other words, it is a call for the retirement of the dichotomy between *de facto* statelessness and *de iure* stateless in the original understanding (which had involved a narrow interpretation of the conventional definition) in favour of uniform use of the term 'stateless person' only with regard to individuals covered by the legal definition (a new meaning the term '*de iure* stateless person'), provided that the definition should be interpreted broadly.

'*De iure* stateless persons (2)' are persons who fall within the ambit of the definition in the 1954 Convention. This category includes *de iure* stateless persons and part of the *de facto* stateless according to the historical dichotomy (see Fig. 1).	**'*De facto* stateless persons (2)'** are persons who are not covered by the definition in the 1954 Convention and are reckoned as *de facto* stateless persons according to the historical dichotomy (see Fig. 1).

Fig. 2. Meaning of the term '*de iure* stateless person' in a broad interpretation of the definition from Article 1(1) of the 1954 Convention.

139 UNHCR Handbook, paragraph 23.
140 UNHCR Handbook, paragraph 37.
141 Concerning the term 'legal definition' see A. Malinowski, *Polski język prawny. Wybrane zagadnienia*, Warszawa 2006, pp. 155–159.

The use of the broad interpretation of the conventional definition limits the scope of the term '*de facto* stateless persons' (Fig. 3). This term becomes somewhat irrelevant. In the views of some authors, it should never be used at all because the individuals remaining within the category are going to be those in respect of whom specific violations of human rights may be taking place, which, however, does not justify referring to them as 'stateless persons'.[142] Whether this category is useful or not will depend on the specific interpretation of the definition in individual cases in domestic jurisdictions. The broader the interpretation of the conventional definition, the less relevant (up to completely irrelevant) the category of *de facto* stateless persons becomes.

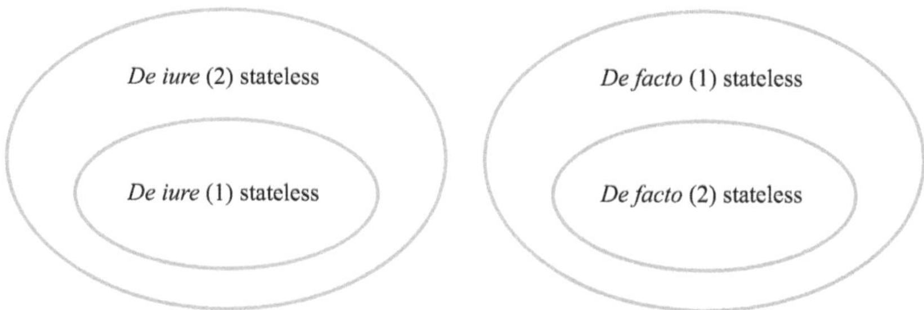

Fig. 3. Relationship between the scopes of terms '*de iure* (1) stateless person' (in the historical dichotomy between *de iure* and *de facto*) and '*de iure* (2) stateless person' (in the broad interpretation of the conventional definition)

The key problem is what individuals can be regarded as stateless persons within the meaning of the conventional definition. The UNHCR Handbook notes that domestic authorities have a certain leeway to determine that an individual is not the national of any state 'under the operation of its law'. What appears to be important in this context is for suitable procedures to be developed within domestic legal systems for the determination of statelessness within the meaning of Article 1(1) of the 1954 Convention.[143] States choosing to follow a broad interpretation of the definition may need to develop suitable evidentiary standards for the determination of which cases of statelessness fall within the scope of the definition of a stateless person in international law.

---

142 L. van Waas, *Nationality Matters. Statelessness under International Law*, 29 School of Human Rights Research Series 2008, p. 27.

143 I discuss the procedures for determining statelessness in more detail in Chapter IV.

In the broader interpretation of the definition, individuals who formally have a nationality but are not in a position to exercise their rights associated with it may be regarded as stateless persons. The fact that an individual is denied certain rights by their state of origin may be taken as evidence that the state does not deem them to be a national 'under the operation of its law'. To what extent the refusal of rights associated with nationality or rather the refusal of which rights is relevant to the determination that the individual is a stateless person will depend on the evidentiary standard adopted in such cases in specific domestic jurisdictions. With the broad interpretation of the conventional definition, it becomes important to address the question of which rights constitute the essence of nationality, with the consequence that the deprivation of an individual of those rights may result in the recognition of such an individual as a stateless person.

Not every bar to enjoyment of such rights as may be associated with nationality can be classified as a case of statelessness. That depends on the facts of the individual case. However, the existence of a special, constitutive relationship between certain rights and nationality is emphasized. For example, the state's duty to allow a national to enter the territory is regarded as being such an essential consequence of nationality as to be almost coterminous with it.[144] There is an opinion that the right to diplomatic assistance also is constitutive to nationality.[145] Denial of these rights may be taken as evidence that the state does not regard the individual as a national 'under the operation of its law'.[146]

It is also noted that those individuals who, due to the discriminatory practices of states, cannot obtain documents confirming their nationality (and thus have no proof of it and cannot obtain any such proof) should be regarded as stateless persons under the conventional definition. A finding that such a situation is taking place should lead to the recognition of the affected individual as a stateless person within the meaning of the 1954 Convention.[147] Other situations potentially classifiable as warranting a broader personal scope of the conventional definition are cases in which a state denies that the individual is its national and those when the individual is unable to identify or prove their nationality.

144 H.F. van Panhuys, *The role of nationality in international law. An outline*, Leyden 1959, p. 56.
145 See Chapter 1, section 3.
146 For a similar view see K. Bianchini, *Protecting...*, p. 72.
147 L. Bingham, J. Harrington Reddy, S. Kohn, *De jure statelessness in the real world. Applying the Prato summary conclusions*, New York 2011, pp. 5–6.

In the above-discussed proposal of a broad definition the problem of interpretation is regarded as a practical one (a question of suitable procedures for determining statelessness). Another possible approach to the interpretation of this provision so as to extend its personal scope to include certain categories of stateless persons who have historically been viewed as belonging to the *de facto* group is to turn attention to the very meaning of the term 'nationality' used in the definition. Some of the cases of statelessness previously viewed as *de facto* can be included in the scope of the definition in Article 1(1) of the 1954 Convention if the interpretation of the term 'national' is to use not the formal definition (as is done under the narrow interpretation) but a definition presupposing nationality to have some specific minimal content (and thus necessarily to entail a certain minimum of rights). This is an interpretation that goes beyond the understanding of nationality as solely a formal relationship. Thus, domestic jurisdictions, the emphasis would be placed not on issues relating to the classification of individuals as stateless persons in the relevant procedures but on the very definition of a stateless person, which could be narrowed down so as to mean that e.g. individuals denied entry into and residence in their state of origin are not considered its nationals.

3. Problems with the definition of a stateless person in selected jurisdictions

Among the states having ratified the 1954 Convention one can find those whose domestic definitions of a stateless person are co-extensive with the conventional definition. Such is the case with, for example, France,[148] Moldova[149] or Germany[150]. However, one can also identify states that, although party to the 1954 Convention, do not have a definition of a stateless person in their domestic law (e.g. in Czech law such persons count as foreigners).[151] In turn, some states,

148 I relied on data gathered for the period until the end of 2018 under the Statelessness Index Survey project completed by the European Network on Statelessness (see footnote 12). Until that time information pertaining to twelve European states had been prepared according to model detailed surveys in the project. Hereinafter information about states based on the data from the project is cited as Statelessness Index Survey (SIS) with reference to the state and survey question, e.g. 'SIS, France, IDP.3.a'.

149 SIS, Moldova, IDP.3.a.

150 SIS, Germany, IDP.12.a.

151 H. Hofmannová, *Legal Status of Stateless Persons in the Czech Republic*, 3(1) The Lawyer Quarterly 2013, pp. 55, 67.

while using the definition formulated in international law, interpret it narrowly in practice (France, Switzerland).[152]

In some states, the definition of a stateless person has been modified so that the 'under the operation of its law' element of Article 1(1) of the 1954 Convention uses a different wording. For example, according to the definition adopted in the Netherlands, Spain and Hungary, a stateless person is an individual nor regarded as a national by any state 'under its law'.[153] Similarly, Ukrainian legislation deems a stateless person to be one who is not the national of any state 'in accordance with its law'. [154] In Slovenia, in turn, this is 'in accordance with the legal acts of the individual states'. The wordings used in the aforementioned European states, referring only to the law (legal instruments, legislation) but not to the practice of its application (which, as demonstrated above, falls under the 'operation of its law'), have the potential to restrict the personal scope of the definition. That is because the element of how the law is applied in practice eludes attention; moreover; any such definition is already difficult to interpret in the light of the above-discussed broad construction. These may, however, be merely problems occasioned by the difficulty of the task of translating the English phrase 'under the operation of its law'.[155] Nor can it be excluded that the practical application of the definitions takes into account the practice of the administrative authorities in cases involving nationality.[156]

The definitions used in some states distinguish multiple categories of stateless persons. The Finnish statute on nationality distinguishes voluntarily stateless persons from those who are stateless against their will. A voluntarily stateless person means an individual who does not hold the nationality of any state and remains stateless voluntarily or due to the decision of a parent or guardian.[157] Attention is

152 For a discussion of the interpretation of the definition of a stateless person in France and Switzerland see Chapter VIII.

153 K. Bianchini, *Protecting...*, p. 209.

154 The incorrectness of the Ukrainian and Russian translations of this provision has been suggested; UNHCR, *The problem of statelessness in Ukraine and the ways of addressing it*, Kyiv 2014, p. 10.

155 In the Polish translation of the 1954 Convention prepared by the UNCHR the definition was mistranslated, with 'under the operation of its law' rendered as *w zakresie obowiązywania tego prawa* (roughly: 'to the extent such law applies'); see translation of the Handbook on Protection of Stateless Persons published by the UNHCR (Polish office) as *Podręcznik dotyczący ochrony bezpaństwowców*.

156 For example, such is the case in Hungary; K. Bianchini, *Protecting…*, p. 209.

157 Article 2(1)(4) of Finnish Nationality Act, 359/2003 (consolidated version incorporating amendments up to and including Act 974/2007 — English translation).

drawn to how a child who is stateless due to the decision of its parent or guardian is regarded as a voluntarily stateless person.[158] An involuntarily stateless person is deemed to be an individual who does not hold the nationality of any state and remains stateless against their will or that of their parent or guardian.[159] Such a distinction on the definitional level entails different treatment of the relevant categories of stateless persons with regard to the rights accorded to them.[160]

Some states insert additional elements in the legal definition of a stateless person, so that the categories of individuals excluded from protection by virtue of so-called exclusion clauses (Article 1(2) of the 1954 Convention) are not regarded as stateless persons Such is the case of the United Kingdom, where the exclusions from Article 1(2) of the 1954 Convention form part of the very definition of a stateless person. According to § 401(c) Immigration Rules,[161] a stateless person is deemed to be one who: satisfies the conditions of Article 1(1) of the 1954 as an individual who is not regarded as a national by any state under the operation of its law; is within the United Kingdom; is not excluded from eligibility for recognition as a stateless person in the light of § 402 (§ 402 copies the exclusion clauses).

In some states, individuals who have become stateless voluntarily are not recognized as stateless persons. As noted above, in the light of the 1954 Convention, it is irrelevant why the individual is a stateless person. However, in states such as Switzerland or France, the lack of any nationality whatsoever is not sufficient for the characterization of an individual as a stateless person. In those countries, voluntarily stateless persons are excluded from recognition as stateless persons by the consistent decision-making history of not recognizing them as stateless within the meaning of the 1954 Convention, except in special circumstances. Said decision-making history has developed certain criteria for assessing whether a set of facts corresponds to the definition of voluntary statelessness. Also in other countries — such as Belgium and Luxembourg — one can find court decisions to the effect that those who are voluntarily stateless cannot be recognized as stateless persons.[162]

---

158 UNHCR, *Mapping Statelessness in Finland*, November 2014, p. 42.

159 Article 2(1)(3) of Finnish Nationality Act.

160 I discuss this topic in more detail in Chapter VIII.

161 Immigration Rules (HC 1039, 6 April 2013) (as amended). These are supplemented by internal guidelines — Home Office, United Kingdom Visas and Immigration, *Asylum Policy Instruction: Statelessness and Applications for Leave to Remain* (18 February 2016), version 2.0, hereinafter the 'British immigration rules'.

162 Concerning this topic, see Chapter VIII and the cases and literature cited therein.

In states not having ratified the 1954 Convention, the situation varies greatly. For example, Polish legislation lacks any separate definition of a stateless person whatsoever. According to the definition contained in the core statute dealing with foreign nationals, i.e. the Act on Foreigners,[163] a foreigner is anyone who does not have Polish nationality (Article 3(2)). This had already been the case under previous legislation.[164] At present, the sole example of a statutory definition of a foreigner that does not cover a stateless person is Article 7 of the Act of 7 May 1989 on Guarantees of Freedom of Conscience and Belief.[165] As a marginal note, Polish provisions have not always consistently included stateless persons in the same category with other foreigners. For example, Article 88 of the Constitution of the Polish People's Republic enacted by the Legislative Sejm on 22 July 1952,[166] with amendments introduced in 1991,[167] distinguished between foreign nationals and stateless persons: 'Foreign nationals and stateless persons may avail themselves of the right of asylum on terms defined by separate statute.'[168]

From the perspective of the definition of a stateless person, counting stateless persons among foreign nationals is not correct. They can, of course, be regarded as foreigners, but only in the sense of lacking the nationality of the state concerned. As argued by M. Vichniac, stateless persons must not be confused with foreign nationals to the effect of losing sight of their not holding the nationality of any state whatsoever.[169] To explain the linguistic angle involving the Polish word *cudzoziemiec* (Latin: *alienigena*) — literally, someone from a foreign land — stateless persons are not 'from a foreign land' (*ex terra aliena*); on the

163 Dz.U.2018.2294, as amended.

164 Article 1 of the Regulation of the President of the Republic of Poland of 13 August 1926 on Foreigners (Dz.U.83.465, as amended); Article 1 of the Act of 29 March 1963 on Foreigners (Dz.U.1992.7.30, as rectified and amended); Article 2 of the Act of 25 June 1997 on Foreigners (Dz.U.2001.127.1400, as amended).

165 Dz.U.2017.1153. 'Article 7 (1) Foreigners being in the territory of the Republic of Poland shall enjoy the freedom of conscience and belief on par with Polish citizens. (2) The provision of section 1 shall apply *mutatis mutandis* to stateless persons.'

166 Dz.U.1976.7.36, as amended.

167 Article 1 of the Act of 18 October 1991 amending the Constitution of the Republic of Poland (Dz.U.119.514).

168 D. Pudzianowska, *„Opatrzność" czy „nieopatrzność" ustawodawcy? O ochronie bezpaństwowców w prawie polskim* [in:] J. Jagielski, M. Wierzbowski (eds.), *Prawo administracyjne dziś i jutro*, Warszawa 2018, p. 687.

169 M. Vichniac, *Le statut international des apatrides*, Recueil des Cours 1933-I, de la Collection 1933/43, p. 136.

contrary, they have no land to call their own (*sine terra propria*). Additionally, failure to distinguish stateless persons as a separate category of non-nationals on the definitional level afflicts them with a sort of invisibility, allowing their highly specific problems to pass unnoticed. In certain ways, the position of a stateless person is similar to that of a foreign national (national of a foreign state). However, it also differs from it in a significant way. In normal circumstances, a foreign national who is not satisfied with the conditions in the host country can return to their country of origin. A stateless person, in principle, has no such option. As argued by A.P. Mutharika: 'To the extent that the stateless person suffers such special disabilities, his situation calls for special attention.'[170]

4. The various categories of stateless persons

The above paragraphs show that the term 'stateless person' does not necessarily denote a homogeneous category of individuals. Firstly, opting for a broad interpretation of the definition of a stateless person in line with the UNHCR's guidelines has the result that the personal scope of the definition is going to encompass a diverse range of individuals. They will include both those who are not formally the nationals of any state but also those who do formally hold the nationality of some state but cannot exercise certain rights attached to it or cannot prove their nationality. The diversity of stateless persons in this perspective could be termed 'diversity according to definitional characteristics'. The assumption that stateless persons constitute a diverse range of individuals enables — in the light of the definition itself — the provisions on statelessness to be extended to a wide circle of individuals while allowing for some diversification in what rights are going to be given to them. Without resorting to a broad definition according a specified minimum of rights to persons historically termed '*de facto* stateless', that particular group of individuals continues to be left without any protection (not even a minimal degree).

Secondly, when it comes to definitional issues in domestic jurisdictions, we can see the exclusion of certain individuals from protection through denial of recognition as stateless persons in the light of the definitional criteria. Such is, for example, the purpose of the distinction made for voluntarily stateless persons in certain legal systems or of the non-recognition of stateless status in those who are excluded by virtue of Article 1(2) of the 1954 Convention. From the perspective of the definition of a stateless person in international law, there are no grounds for any such denial of recognition. However, the concept of differentiating the rights accorded to the

170 A.P. Mutharika, *The regulation…*, p. 20.

different categories of stateless persons is not in itself improper. Specific practical problems induce states to distinguish the various categories of stateless persons due to a preference for different scopes of rights to be accorded to them. That could be termed 'instrumental differentiation'.

5. Conclusions

Although the term 'stateless person' had already been defined in the 1954 Convention, that definition is at present the topic of debate as to its meaning and the possible directions in which its interpretation could be taken. Originally, the definition was conceived by the drafters of the 1954 Convention so as to extend only to individuals holding no nationality of any state whatsoever in the formal sense. However, that interpretation incurred criticism in the face of specific problems arising in the aftermath of the disintegration of the USSR, Yugoslavia and Czechoslovakia in the 90s. Accordingly, the UNHCR embarked on a search for concrete proposals dealing with the application of the conventional definition in domestic administrative law. At present, the need to extend the scope to at least part of those historically termed '*de facto* stateless persons' has been appreciated. When introducing provisions to regulate statelessness, however, the domestic legislator should not copy the conventional definition but rather aspire to resolve — through domestic legislation and appropriate drafting — the problems presented by its ambiguity. It is largely up to the individual states to decide what individuals formally holding the nationality of a state may be recognized as stateless persons in the light of the conventional definition; for that purpose the states should rely on statelessness-identification procedures, which will be discussed more extensively in Chapter IV.

Analysis of the problems relating to the definition of a stateless person shows that the term does not denote a single, homogeneous category of individuals. This already suggests the possible utility of a categorial approach. Moreover, such an approach is also used in international law and in a number of domestic jurisdictions. The differentiation of the various categories of stateless persons is, firstly, the result of the broad interpretation of the conventional definition (distinctions on the basis of definitional criteria). Secondly, it can be the result of a search for legal frameworks adapted to the situation of the various groups of stateless persons (instrumental differentiation). The following chapters discuss topics relating to the counteraction of statelessness (Chapter III) and protection of stateless persons (Chapter IV), with note being taken of the problem of differentiating the legal situation of the various categories of stateless persons (categorization).

Chapter III Counteracting Statelessness

The subject-matter of this chapter are topics relating to the legal mechanisms for the counteraction of statelessness.[171] My chosen method of analysis is to identify international law regulations dealing with the prevention and reduction of statelessness and examples of provisions adopted in European domestic jurisdictions.[172] When discussing international law, I use it as a specific benchmark in the context of which to discuss the domestic regulation. This comes with the caveat that I analyse solutions both from states having ratified the relevant conventions and from those not having done so.

1. Preventing statelessness

1.1. Introductory remarks

Among statelessness-counteraction frameworks I include prevention frameworks, i.e. solutions adopted in the system of international law and in domestic legal systems for the purpose of not allowing statelessness to arise. This includes situations when individuals hold a nationality and the legal provisions contain safeguards against its loss in the event statelessness would be the result. Two types of legal mechanisms can be distinguished here.

The first type provides safeguards against statelessness arising from conflicts of laws ('discordance', in older parlance). This includes loss of nationality due to a change in marital status (e.g. marriage or divorce) and loss of nationality during the marriage due to a change in the spouse's nationality. In the past, the loss of nationality as a consequence of change in marital status or change in the spouse's nationality affected mostly women. These modes of loss of nationality no longer exist in the legal systems of European states. However, in the past, the denationalization of a woman upon marriage to a non-national was the most important cause of individual statelessness.[173] The statelessness of women inspired

171 Concerning the mechanism for the counteraction of statelessness, see Chapter I, section 6.

172 While making the comparison, I relied on the GLOBALCIT (2017) — Global Database on Modes of Loss of Citizenship, version 1.0. San Domenico di Fiesole: Global Citizenship Observatory, Robert Schuman Centre for Advanced Studies, European University Institute, see also footnote 11.

173 See Chapter I.

reflection upon possible instruments of counteracting statelessness and led to the adoption, in domestic jurisdictions and in international law, of the first rules devised to counteract statelessness. I discuss this topic in more detail in Chapter V, which deals with the mechanisms used for the regulation of the statelessness of women.

The second to note are safeguards against statelessness provided by the domestic legal system of a given state in the event of loss of nationality. These will be discussed further in the present chapter. The extent to which international law and domestic legal systems counteract statelessness arising in connection with the loss of nationality will be analysed. Accordingly, the subject-matter is not the general modes of loss of nationality in the various states but those states' safeguards against statelessness arising in connection with the provisions governing denationalization.

The modes of loss of nationality envisaged by domestic jurisdictions can be divided into two basic groups. The first group involves losing one's nationality in consequence of a suitable declaration of intention to do so made before the public authorities (renunciation of nationality). The second group involves the loss of nationality in circumstances not requiring the individual's consent — either *ex lege* or as a result of the decision of a competent authority (deprivation of nationality) upon meeting the legally prescribed conditions.[174] Below, through the perspective of this dichotomy, I discuss safeguards against statelessness arising through the loss of nationality by renunciation (section 1.2) or involuntary loss of nationality (section 1.3).

1.2. Prevention of statelessness upon renunciation of nationality

In principle, international law does not allow renunciation of nationality with the effect of rendering the affected individual stateless. The 1961 Convention provides that if the state's law permits the renunciation of nationality, the latter must not take effect unless the individual in question already holds or is in the process of acquiring the nationality of another state.[175] This prohibition against creating new cases of statelessness through renunciation is limited in situations when its application would collide with Articles 13 and 14 UDHR[176], i.e. the right to claim asylum or the right to leave the territory of the state. From Article 7(3) ECN it also follows that the domestic legislation of a state must not enable

174 For a more extensive discussion see D. Pudzianowska, *Obywatelstwo...*, pp. 92ff.
175 Article 7(1)(a) of the 1961 Convention.
176 Article 7(1)(b) i of the 1961 Convention.

the loss of nationality by renunciation if the individual concerned were to be rendered stateless by proceeding with it. Unlike the 1961 Convention, the ECN does not admit of any exceptions.

The above-identified provisions of international law do not, however, provide for the renunciation to cease to be valid upon failure to acquire the nationality of another state within a set time-frame. In practice, the above sometimes leads to statelessness. From this perspective, the Hague Convention of 1930 offered more effective protection. It contained the institution of an 'expatriation permit', which, to the extent relevant for our needs, corresponded to the modern institution of renunciation of nationality.[177] The 'expatriation permit', entailing release from and consequent loss of the nationality of the state granting it, contained a safeguard against statelessness — either the recipient had to hold another nationality, or the loss of the existing nationality would only become effective upon the acquisition of a new one. The higher standard — as compared to the ECN and the 1961 Convention — was owing to the second paragraph of Article 7 of the Hague Convention: 'An expatriation permit shall lapse if the holder does not acquire a new nationality within the period fixed by the State which has issued the permit.'

As regards domestic frameworks, out of all European states permitting this mode of loss of nationality, most stipulate that renunciation must not result in statelessness. The sole exception is the provision in the Greek Citizenship Code[178] that an adult residing abroad may be released from nationality upon declaring the lack of any ties to Greece.[179] This provision does not contain a safeguard to prevent statelessness.

Some of the states stipulating that the renunciation of nationality must not result in statelessness have adopted the principle that the renunciation will not take effect if another nationality is not obtained within a set time-frame. Provisions to such an effect have been introduced in twelve European states.[180] For example, a

177 O. Vonk, M.P. Vink, G.-R. de Groot, *Protection against statelessness. Trends and regulations in Europe*, 1 EUDO Citizenship Observatory 2013, p. 66.

178 Article 18 of Greek Citizenship Code, Law 3284/2004, 10 November 2004.

179 In comparative studies, the term 'release from nationality' refers to one of the modes of loss of nationality. This involves the surrender of citizenship by the individual concerned, although subject to the approval of the competent domestic authorities. By contrast, surrender of citizenship as a matter of right without requiring the state's leave is termed 'renunciation by declaration'. See Glossary on Citizenship and Nationality at https://globalcit.eu/glossary/ (accessed 3 January 2023).

180 O. Vonk, M.P. Vink, G.-R. de Groot, *Protection…*, p. 67.

German citizen may be released from nationality upon request if applying for a foreign nationality, where the competent foreign authority has given assurances of conferring it.[181] However, the renunciation will be regarded as null and void if the individual concerned does not acquire the promised foreign nationality within one year of the certification of the release.[182] This means that German law contains an express guarantee of retention of German nationality by the renouncing citizen in the event of failure to obtain the nationality of another state. A similar solution featuring a one-year time-limit for the acquisition of foreign nationality can be found in North Macedonia's nationality statute — where another nationality is not acquired within the time-limit, the release is withdrawn and loss of nationality does not take place.[183] In the United Kingdom, the regulations prescribe a shorter time-limit for the acquisition of foreign nationality (six months), and if the latter is not forthcoming, the individual is deemed never to have ceased to be a British national.[184] In Slovenia[185] and Turkey,[186] the corresponding period is two years. In all of the aforementioned states, the effect of retention of the old nationality is mandatory if the individual concerned fails to acquire a new one. However, it is still possible to find examples of states in which such provisions are only an option at the individual's disposal, in the sense that the loss of nationality will be prevented if the individual submits a request to that effect (and not in every case of non-acquisition of foreign nationality). One such example is the nationality legislation of Montenegro, under which the renunciation of nationality will be invalidated at the request of the individual concerned upon failure to obtain a foreign nationality within one year of renouncing Montenegrin nationality. The relevant application to that effect must be filed within three months of the time-limit for the acquisition of a foreign nationality.[187].

181 Article 18 of German Nationality Act of 22 July 1913, Reich Law Gazette I, p. 583 — Federal Law Gazette III 102-1, as last amended by Article 2 of the Act to Implement the EU Directive on Highly Qualified Workers of 1 June 2012, Federal Law Gazette I, p. 1224.

182 Article 24 of German Nationality Act.

183 Article. 18 of the Law on the Citizenship of the Republic of Macedonia 67/92, published in the Official Gazette on 3 November 1992.

184 Article 12(3) of British Nationality Act 1981.

185 Article 19 of the Act on the Citizenship of the Republic of Slovenia as amended by an Amending Act, Official Gazette No. 127/2006 of 7 December 2006.

186 Article 26(2) of Law no. 5901/2009 — Turkish Citizenship Law.

187 Article 23 of Montenegrin Citizenship Act of 14 February 2008, Official Gazette of Montenegro, No. 13/08 of 26 February 2008.

Not in all states the safeguards against statelessness manifest themselves in such a clear manner. In the Polish example, neither the Constitution nor the provisions of the Act on Polish Citizenship contain any explicit guarantee that renunciation of nationality cannot take effect if the individual concerned is to become stateless as a result. However, the fact that renunciation of Polish nationality is by application to the President of the Republic of Poland with a document confirming foreign nationality or assurances of its conferral prescribed as a mandatory attachment,[188] on pain of disregarding the application (upon futile notice to cure the defects),[189] indicates that foreign nationality is a circumstance taken into advisement in the renunciation procedure. An application lacking the required attachments relating to the possession or assurance of foreign nationality will not proceed. This means that the President's approval cannot be granted in those cases in which the application does not contain the relevant documents.[190] Nonetheless, it must be noted that this provision does not offer complete protection from statelessness, because an individual who submits a foreign authority's assurances of conferral of nationality but does not subsequently obtain it will become a stateless person. There are no such provisions in the above-discussed Polish framework as to withdraw the presidential approval if the foreign nationality is not acquired. This problem is illustrated by the intersection of Polish law and the German and Austrian regulations providing for an assurance of conferral of nationality, which will be discussed below.

The risk of statelessness can also arise in connection with the requirement of renunciation of one's original nationality as a condition of naturalization. Renunciation of the old nationality is usually required for naturalization in e.g. Austria,[191] Germany[192] or Ukraine.[193] In Austria, upon successful verification that the individual meets the requirements, they will be given the competent

188 Article 48(4)(3) of the Act on Polish Citizenship.
189 Article 49(2) of the Act on Polish Citizenship.
190 Similarly J. Jagielski: 'Yet, the *ratio* of the discussed norm cannot be ignored. (…). Its message is clear: a Polish national renouncing Polish nationality cannot become a stateless person with the approval of the public authority' — J. Jagielski, *Obywatelstwo polskie. Komentarz do ustawy*, LEX 2016, Commentary on Article 48 (of the Act on Polish Citizenship).
191 Article 10(3) of Federal Law on Austrian Nationality 1985, consolidated version as amended by BGBl. I Nr. 37/2006.
192 Article 10(4) of German Nationality Act.
193 Article 9(2) of the Law N 2235-III (2235-14) on the Citizenship of Ukraine (as amended by Law N 2663-IV (2663-15) of 16 June 2005).

administrative authority's assurances of conferral of Austrian nationality (*Einbürgerungszusicherung*) on condition of submitting proof of surrender of their previous nationality within two years. However, when the individual has already renounced their previous nationality, the authorities still verify that the requirements of naturalization are met. If not, the promise of naturalization may be withdrawn.[194]

It is notable that a risk of statelessness arising for this reason used to exist, for example, in Poland. In the case of a grant of citizenship, the acquisition of Polish nationality could be made conditional on submitting proof of loss of or release from foreign nationality (Article 8(3) of the Act of 15 February 1962 on Polish Citizenship).[195] In practice, where the authorities decided to avail themselves of that option, the foreigner received a promise of naturalization conditional on submitting proof of renunciation of previous nationality within two years. The individual could still become stateless in cases in which the renunciation took effect but the two-year time-limit was exceeded. There are known cases of foreigners being refused Polish citizenship and becoming stateless during that period.[196]

---

194 Article 20 of Austrian Citizenship Act. On 29 September 2011, the Austrian Constitutional Court held that the different grounds of revoking a promise of naturalization ought to be given different treatment. The analysed case involved a woman who had renounced her previous nationality upon receipt of a promise of naturalization and thereafter lost her employment through no fault of her own prior to acquiring Austrian nationality, for which reason she had ceased to meet the income requirement. The Constitutional Court found it to be problematic that the loss of employment after the renunciation of original nationality required before the acquisition of Austrian nationality can render the individual unable to seek lawful employment and for that reason unable to meet one of the requirements of naturalization. As a result of the decision in that case, the Austrian Citizenship Act was amended in 2013. The loss of one's livelihood in the period between the promise of naturalization and the naturalization itself is no longer grounds for revocation. However, the promise may still be withdrawn if any other naturalization requirement fails to be satisfied, H. Chahrokh, *Mapping Statelessness in Austria*, UNHCR, January 2017, pp. 90–91.

195 Dz.U.2000.28.353, as amended.

196 Dorota Gajos-Kaniewska, *Sukces HFPC: bezpaństwowa Viktoriia dostała polskie obywatelstwo*, Rzeczpospolita, 19 July 2017.

1.3. Statelessness prevention in involuntary loss of nationality

Renunciation is not the only mode of loss of nationality having the possible effect of statelessness. Statelessness ensuing from the involuntary loss of nationality in specific situations is permitted in international law and domestic legal systems.

1.3.1. Loss of nationality due to the lack of an effective link to the state

The 1961 Convention provides that in certain situations nationality may be forfeited in connection with residence abroad even if statelessness is going to be result. The conventional principle that nationality must not be lost with the effect of making the individual a stateless person in connection with travelling or residing abroad, failure to comply with mandatory registration or other similar reasons (Article 7(3) of the 1961 Convention) admits of certain exceptions. The first such exception refers to naturalized citizens.[197] They may be denaturalized upon having resided uninterruptedly in a new country for at least seven years (the exact time-limit is determined by domestic legislation) without notifying the competent authority of the intention to retain their nationality (Article 7(4) of the 1961 Convention). In this case, accordingly, international law allows different categories of nationals to be treated differently (i.e. nationals by birth as opposed to naturalized individuals). Another exception applies to those born abroad — domestic provisions may stipulate that the retention of nationality beyond one year of coming of age requires either residence within the territory of the state or registration with the appropriate authorities during the time (Article 7(5) of the 1961 Convention).

A different standard is laid down by the ECN, which provides that the loss of nationality owing to the lack of a genuine link between the state and its national habitually residing abroad is not possible where it would lead to statelessness (Article 7(1)(e) in conjunction with Article 7(3) ECN). Additionally, Article 5(2) ECN established the principle of non-discrimination of nationals, whether

---

197 As for the meaning of the term 'naturalization' in this provision, see Resolution no. 2 adopted during the Conference, which states that for the purposes of Article 7(4) of the 1961 Convention, the term 'naturalized person' should be interpreted as referring to an individual having been conferred nationality through a discretionary naturalization procedure.

they be such by birth or subsequent naturalization.[198] As one can see, the ECN standard for prevention mechanisms is higher.

In the majority of European states, residence abroad cannot lead to loss of nationality with the effect of statelessness. Exceptions exist in countries such as Cyprus, Ireland and Malta.[199] The Cypriot regulations enable the loss of nationality owing to residence abroad, which may result in statelessness, if the individual is a naturalized citizen having resided abroad uninterruptedly for seven years without notifying the consulate every year in the legally prescribed form of their intention to remain a Cypriot national. The loss of nationality does not take place where the individual resides abroad providing services to the state or to an international organization of which Cyprus is a member.[200] Irish and Maltese regulations contain very similar provisions,[201] albeit Ireland makes an exception for a naturalized 'person of Irish descent or associations'.[202]

1.3.2. Loss of nationality due to fraud in naturalization procedures

Article 8(2) of the 1961 Convention provides that an individual may be deprived of nationality, even with the result of rendering them stateless, due to misrepresentation or fraud in the naturalization procedure (Article 8(2)(b)). The ECN, too, provides for this ground of forfeiture of nationality even in situations in which the individual concerned is going to become stateless as a result. This is the only exception from the principle laid down in Article 7(3) ECN. In line with Article 7(1)(b) when read in conjunction with Article 7(3) ECN, a state's domestic legislation may enable the loss of nationality, even with statelessness ensuing as a result, where the nationality was obtained fraudulently or by means of culpable misstatement or concealment.[203]

As understood in comparative studies in denationalization, the term 'fraud' is construed very broadly and extends to different types of conduct specified in the various provisions of the Convention, such as resorting to threats or conferring

198 From this perspective, the provision of Article 7(4) of the Convention 1961 is discriminatory in the light of Article 5(2) ECN.

199 O. Vonk, M.P. Vink, G.-R. de Groot, *Protection…*, table, pp. 71–72.

200 Article 113(4) of Law no. 141(I)/2002: The Civil Registry Law 2002.

201 Article 14(2)(d)of Maltese Citizenship Act, as amended by Act XV of 2013.

202 Article 19(1)(c) of Irish Nationality and Citizenship Acts 1956–2004, as amended by Act no. 38 of 2004.

203 *Verbatim*: 'by means of fraudulent conduct, false information or concealment of any relevant fact attributable to the applicant.'

an economic benefit in the naturalization procedure. I would be reluctant to deprive myself of the utility of this term when used in such a broad meaning. However, this calls for the caveat that in both of the Conventions — ECN and the 1961 Convention — the term 'fraud' is given a narrower meaning. In turn, the wider construction of fraud encompasses two types of situations. One type is misleading the naturalization authority, and the other is exerting undue influence on the decision-making process.

While there are states not recognizing any mode of loss of nationality other than renunciation (such is the case e.g. in Polish[204] and North Macedonian law[205]), that is a rarity. Numerous states provide for various modes of involuntary loss of nationality even in cases in which statelessness is the end result. I discuss this in detail in Chapter VII.

1.3.3. Loss of nationality due to disloyal conduct

International law permits statelessness to arise in a variety of situations involving broadly understood disloyalty to the state of nationality. The standards differ between the 1961 Convention and the ECN. The 1961 Convention stipulates a few cases in which states may deprive individuals of nationality, even if statelessness is going to be the result of that act, for disloyal conduct. Firstly, this involves the situation of one who — in violation of the duty of loyalty to their state of nationality and in disregard of a clear prohibition issued by that state — has entered the service of another state or has not ceased to provide services or has received emoluments from a foreign state (Article 8(3)(a)(i) of the 1961 Convention). Secondly, one who — in violation of the duty of loyalty to one's state of nationality — has engaged in conduct seriously prejudicial to the state's vital interests (Article 8(3)(a)(ii) of the 1961 Convention). And, thirdly, one who — in violation of the duty of loyalty to the state of nationality — has sworn an oath or made a formal declaration or in some other way given proof of loyalty to another state (Article 8(3)(b) of the 1961 Convention).[206] By contrast, the ECN standard in

204 Article 34(2) of Polish Constitution.

205 Article 4 of the Constitution of North Macedonia of 17 November 1991; M. Smilevska, *Ending childhood statelessness. A study on Macedonia*, 2 European Network on Statelessness, Working Paper 2015, p. 10.

206 The permissibility of denationalization on such grounds is conditional upon the relevant state's having reserved, when signing, ratifying or acceding to the Convention, a right to do so already existing in its domestic legal system at the time of accession (the first sentence of Article 8(3) of the 1961 Convention).

this regard is higher when it comes to the prevention of stateless, as it does not allow the loss of nationality on the above grounds to occur if the affected individual would be left stateless. While the Convention does provide that states may revoke citizenship on the grounds of service in foreign armed forces or conduct seriously prejudicial to the vital interests of the state, doing so may not result in statelessness. Numerous European states envisage the deprivation of nationality on the disloyalty grounds as specified in the 1961 Convention, even with statelessness ensuing from it. I discuss this in detail in Chapter VII.

1.3.4. Loss of nationality by a child due to parentage redetermination, adoption or parental loss of nationality

Statelessness prevention in the event of changes in findings relating to the child's parentage or in the event of adoption, or loss of nationality as a result of its loss by the child's parent, is explained more extensive in the Chapter discussing the statelessness of children.[207] Here, it must be mentioned that the loss of nationality in connection with changes relating to the determination of the child's parentage (e.g. denial of paternity, annulment of recognition) or adoption must not result in statelessness, in the light of the 1961 Convention and the ECN (Article 5(1) of the 1961 Convention and Articles 7(1)(f) and 7(1)(g) EEN). In the majority of states whose domestic legislations provide for the loss of nationality by the child as a result of denial of origin from a national, statelessness is prevented from arising in such situations by making the effectiveness of the loss of nationality conditional on holding the nationality of another state. Similarly, the majority of countries foreseeing the loss of nationality through adoption have introduced mechanisms to prevent statelessness. In the end, both the 1961 Convention and the ECN make the child's denationalization as a result of loss of nationality by the child's parent conditional on the child's having another nationality (or being in a position to acquire it). The sole exception is stipulated by the ECN and deals with the parent's denaturalization for fraud (Article 7(1)(b) in conjunction with Article 7(3) ECN). In such cases, the provisions of the Convention allow the child to become stateless in the footsteps of the parent.

207 This already calls for the proviso that my use of the term 'child' here is not as the synonym of a minor. It refers to persons in specific family configurations (sons or daughters) regardless of age. For a more extensive discussion see Chapter VI.

2. Reducing statelessness

2.1. Introductory remarks

Among legal instruments intended to counteract statelessness, I also count those devised for the purpose of reducing its scale. In the case of reduction, the solution is to confer nationality on those who do not acquire any other upon birth or are stateless for other reasons. The terminology calls for a brief explanation. I use the term 'reduction', even though sometimes the term 'prevention of statelessness' is used in aspects relating to children. In my view, the term 'prevention' is a better fit for situations of 'potential statelessness' the legal system endeavours to prevent from arising (such as in the cases discussed above). In the case of statelessness occurring at birth, the use of the term 'prevention' presupposes a certain legal fiction, because in reality the child is born stateless, which is fact having to be established before the authorities can confirm the acquisition of nationality either *ex lege* or by option. While the use of the term 'prevention' is justified in the case of frameworks providing for the *ex lege* acquisition of nationality by birth, it is not a good fit for those situations in which the acquisition depends on the making of a request.

2.2. Reduction of statelessness occurring at birth

The topics of reduction of statelessness largely involve children and are discussed extensively in Chapter VI, which deals with the statelessness of children. Here, one should note that the nature of the legal mechanisms devised for the reduction of statelessness in children is somewhat complex. The general international standard in this area is set by the ICCPR and the CRC, which affirm the right of every child to acquire a nationality; this right is currently recognized as belonging to customary international law.[208] Topics of reduction of statelessness at birth refer mainly to the situation of 'foundlings' (children of unknown parents) and the situation of the 'otherwise stateless' children, whose statelessness has a different cause (for example, the parents are known but prevented from transmitting nationality to the child). Although specific legal provisions addressing this problem on the international level are extensive and casuistic, with considerable differences arising in the approaches taken to specific issues from one state to the next, it can be said in general terms that all European states

208 For a discussion of this topic see Chapter VI, section 2.

have some sort of mechanism in place to reduce statelessness in children. I discuss these topics in detail in Chapter VI.

2.3. Reduction of statelessness occurring later in life

The reduction of statelessness can be looked upon from the perspective of the state in which the individual is currently present. Such is the predominant conception of this matter in the various instruments of international law. I will deal with this aspect below. However, it must be noted right away that the various aspects of reduction of statelessness can also be cast in the perspective of solutions designed with a view to securing the individual's return to their country of origin, if there are any prospects of acquiring the nationality of the state of origin.[209]

2.3.1. The international standard

In so far as the international obligations of the individual's state of residence are concerned, in accordance with Article 32 of the 1954 Convention, the parties should facilitate the 'assimilation and naturalization' of stateless persons to the greatest extent possible. In particular, they ought to '(...) make every effort to expedite naturalization proceedings and to reduce as far as possible the charges and costs of such proceedings.' In several documents adopted in 2006–2008, the UNHCR encourages the states to consider facilitating the naturalization of stateless persons lawfully and habitually resident in the territory and to take steps to disseminate information on this topic.[210] According to T. Molnar, we are dealing with a 'gradual strengthening of the norm obliging [s]tates to grant facilitated access to nationality for those lacking it', which has by now become a more developed principle than it had been at the time of the adoption of the 1954 Convention.[211] The introduction in domestic jurisdictions of facilitated naturalization for lawful and habitual residents who are stateless persons is envisaged by Article 6(4)(g) ECN. As can be seen, the various international frameworks do not guarantee to stateless persons a right to obtain the nationality of the state of

---

209 This aspect of the problem of reduction of statelessness is important primarily with regard to the category of 'voluntarily stateless persons' and will be discussed in Chapter VIII.

210 For a more detailed discussion of this topic see T. Molnar, *A fresh examination of facilitated naturalisation as a solution for stateless persons* [in:] L. van Waas and M.J. Khanna (eds.), *Solving statelessness*, Oisterwijk 2017, p. 234.

211 T. Molnar, *A fresh...*, pp. 240, 245.

residence. They merely establish an obligation to facilitate the acquisition of nationality, with precious little guidance as to what principles should be adopted by the states to that end.

Moreover, the ECN standard, in which the various facilitations in the acquisition of nationality are only intended to apply to stateless persons who are 'lawfully and habitually resident' is lower than that of the 1954 Convention, which does not come with any such proviso. The ECN's explanatory report mentions the sufficiency of providing favourable conditions for the naturalization of individuals belonging to this category. Examples could include reducing the requirements concerning the length of stay and proficiency in the language, as well as simplifying the procedure and reducing the fees. The decision whether to confer nationality on such applicants remains in the competence of the states party to the Convention. States in which the conditions for naturalization are already highly favourable (e.g. short length of residence for all applicants) are not required to take any additional measures.[212] It is also noteworthy that according to the explanatory report persons having voluntarily renounced nationality are not entitled to facilitated naturalization.[213]

Additionally, Recommendation no. R (99) 18 of the Committee of Ministers to member States on the avoidance and reduction of statelessness, 15 September 1999,[214] deals with the question of how to regulate the various aspects of naturalization of stateless persons. In line with the Recommendation, every state ought to facilitate the naturalization of stateless persons 'lawfully and habitually resident' in its territory. In this regard, the Recommendation offers guidance on both substantive and procedural aspects of naturalization. Concerning the substantive one, states should: (1) reduce the required length of residence compared to the normally required duration; (2) not require familiarity with more than one official language (where domestic law establishes more than one official language); (3) ensure that in situations in which a criminal record can influence the naturalization decision, this

---

212 ECN explanatory report, § 52.

213 'Persons who have deliberately become stateless, in disregard of the principles of this Convention (for example persons originating from a State with an internal law which, contrary to Article 8 of this Convention, permits the renunciation of nationality without the prior acquisition of another nationality) shall not be entitled to acquire nationality in a facilitated manner' — ECN explanatory report, § 57.

214 Council of Europe: Committee of Ministers, Recommendation no. R (99) 18 of the Committee of Ministers to member States on the avoidance and reduction of statelessness, 15 September 1999, no. R (99) 18.

does not present an unreasonable barrier to stateless persons in their access to nationality. The procedural requirement is one of (4) ensuring that the naturalization procedure is easily accessible, that it can proceed without delays and that concessions from the fees are available.

2.3.2. Regulatory frameworks in selected jurisdictions

The first observation to make with regard to domestic laws and regulations is that not all states enable a facilitated procedure for the acquisition of nationality by stateless persons. Only a minority of European states do not have such solutions in place (Austria, Croatia, Cyprus, Iceland, Lithuania, Luxembourg, Malta, Portugal, Romania, Serbia, Spain and Turkey).[215]

In the majority of states facilitating the naturalization procedures for stateless persons, the facilitation consists in shorter requirements of residence. In some countries the shortening is considerable,[216] for example by half or more in countries such as: Belgium (2 years instead of 5),[217] Slovakia (3 years instead of 8),[218] Greece (3 years instead of 7),[219] or Italy (5 years instead of 10)[220]. In others the shortening is not relatively as large but is still significant; for example Hungary (5 years instead of 8),[221] Bulgaria and the Netherlands (3 years instead of 5),[222] Germany and North Macedonia (6 years instead of 8)[223]. Lastly, there are examples of states in which the mandatory residence

215 O. Vonk, M.P. Vink, G.-R. de Groot, *Protection…*, p. 66.

216 This comparison takes the specific kind (type) of residence requirement into account.

217 Article 19(2) of Belgian Nationality Law of 1984, French consolidated version of 24 July 2017.

218 Article 7(2)(h) of Act no. 40/1993 Coll. on Citizenship of the Slovak Republic (consolidated version as last amended by Act no. 250/2010 Coll. — English translation).

219 Articles 5(1)(d) and 6(3)(d) of Greek Citizenship Code.

220 Article 9(1) of Italian Act no. 91/92 (L. 5 February 1992, n. 91, as amended by Act no. 94/2009).

221 Articles 4(4) and 5a(1)(b) of Act LV of 1993 on Hungarian Nationality, version of 1 January 2009.

222 Article 14 of the Law on Bulgarian Citizenship, consolidated version as amended by Law of 19 February 2013; Article 8(4) of the Kingdom Act on Netherlands Nationality, consolidated version including amendment of 25 November 2013.

223 Article 8 of German Nationality Act; Articles 7 and 7a of the (North) Macedonia Nationality Act.

is insignificantly shorter: Denmark (8 years instead of 9),[224] Sweden (4 years instead of 5),[225] and Poland (2 years instead of 3)[226].

Some states grant additional facilitations beyond the shortening of the residence requirement. For example, Greece not only shortens the required length of residence but also waives the language test and the citizenship test, as well as requirements dealing with specific documents (such as birth certificate). In the United Kingdom, in addition to the abbreviated residence requirement (from five to three years), stateless persons are exempted from the language test and from the so-called citizenship test.[227] One of the examples of a state according such different facilitations without an abbreviated residence requirement is Montenegro — the required residence is not shortened (ten years), but the requirements of housing, sufficient income source and language proficiency are not applied.[228]

In some countries facilitated naturalization is applicable only to selected groups of stateless persons. For example, in Estonia, facilitations extend only to stateless children younger than fifteen years of age who are habitually resident in Estonian territory.[229] In Switzerland, too, only minors may benefit from the facilitations (five years' residence instead of twelve). Until 2013, Latvian law accorded facilitations only to adopted stateless persons younger than sixteen years of age (where the adoptive parents are spouses of whom one is a Latvian national and the other a foreigner permanently residing in Latvia).[230] It must be noted that in the cases of Estonia and Switzerland the naturalization facilitations offered to minors are prompted by the lack of acquisition of nationality *ex lege* at birth by

224 Article 6 of Act no. 113 of 20 February 2003 on Danish Nationality; as amended by Act no. 311 of 5 May 2004).

225 Article 11(4)(b) of Swedish Nationality Act (Law 2001:82: Swedish Citizenship Act, consolidated version as last amended by Law 2006:222 — English translation).

226 Article 30(1)(2)(b) of the Act on Polish Citizenship. The facilitation applies only to cases when the residence has been authorized by a permanent residence permit, long-term EU residence permit or right of permanent residence.

227 O. Vonk, M.P. Vink, G.-R. de Groot, *Protection...*, table, pp. 64–65.

228 Articles 8 and 14 of Montenegrin Nationality Act.

229 V. Poleshchuk, *Naturalisation procedures for immigrants. Estonia*, EUDO Citizenship Observatory, SCAS/EUDO-CIT-NP 2013/8, p. 8.

230 Article 15(3) of the Latvian Law on Citizenship 1994, as amended by Law of 9 May 2013.

the subsidiary application of the *ius soli*, which, on the contrary, is the case in many other European countries.[231]

A unique solution from the perspective of distinguishing the treatment of a specific group of stateless persons is in place in France, where facilitated naturalization is available to those above the age of seventy who have been lawful and habitual residents for fifteen years. Since 2003, such persons have been exempted from the language requirement.[232] A similar provision can be found in Estonian law. Persons born before 1 January 1930 are exempted from the written examination in the naturalization procedure.[233]

Moreover, some states distinguish the treatment of voluntarily and involuntary statelessness. For example, Finland accords facilitated treatment in naturalization only to involuntarily stateless persons.[234] This is a solution reflective of the approach taken in the ECN explanatory report (discussed above), which holds that voluntarily stateless persons are not entitled to the facilitated procedure prescribed by the ECN.

3. Conclusions

From the perspective of the adoption of instruments regulating statelessness in domestic jurisdictions, it is important to emphasize that the problem area of statelessness is not limited to the protection of stateless persons. Statelessness law also includes instruments of counteraction (prevention and reduction) of statelessness, which are traditionally regarded as part of the discipline of nationality law. It is important for the drafting works on domestic legislation dealing with statelessness to address aspects of both counteraction and protection, of which the latter will be discussed in the next chapter.

---

231 'It should be noted that stateless minors under the age of 15 are entitled to a simplified naturalisation procedure. In other words, they are not recognised as Estonian citizens solely due to the fact that they were born in Estonian territory' – A. Semjonov, J. Karzetskaja and E. Ezhova in: L. van Waas (ed.), *Ending Childhood Statelessness: a Study on Estonia*, 4 European Network on Statelessness, Working Paper 2015.

232 Article 21-24-1 of French Civil Code, Book I, Title I bis on French Nationality, as amended by Act no. 2006-399 of 4 April 2006.

233 Estonian Government Easing Citizenship Laws For Children and Elderly, 2 October 2014, ERR news https://news.err.ee/113784/estonian-government-easing-citizenship-laws-for-children-and-elderly (accessed 2 January 2023).

234 Article 20 of Finnish Nationality Act.

There exist gaps in prevention of statelessness in international law and in the domestic legislation of European states, which means that new cases of statelessness can still arise and that not always, not all stateless persons are in a position to take advantage of the various mechanisms of reduction of statelessness. The above can be the outcome either of poor drafting or of an intentional design. Aspirations to create a comprehensive regulatory framework for the counteraction of statelessness in the domestic legal system should thus not lose sight of how the international standard and foreign domestic legislation do not always supply a fitting point of reference, as they allow new cases of statelessness to arise and existing cases to be maintained in some situations.

The way in which statelessness is regulated shows signs of a categorial approach. The efforts of the international community and the individual states' willingness to counteract statelessness with regard to different categories of individuals are not on the same levels. This diversification of the regulatory landscape is linked to the treatment of specific cases of statelessness from the perspective of assessing the situation of specific categories of individuals. For example, individuals committing naturalization fraud are excluded from prevention mechanisms, whereas mechanisms preventing the statelessness of women in the event of change in marital status have been universally adopted. In a different aspect, the reduction of statelessness in children is a priority compared to cases of statelessness arising in circumstances unrelated to birth.

Chapter IV Protection of Stateless Persons; Statelessness-Determination Procedures

1. Preliminary issues

The significance of the 1954 Convention consists primarily in that its Article (1) (1) provides the definition of a stateless person nowadays regarded as customary law,[235] as well as a considerable number of rights for stateless persons. The rights include freedom of religious practice (Article 4), ability to acquire movable and immovable property (Article 13), protection of artistic rights and industrial property (Article 14), the right of association (Article 15), access to courts (Article 16), right to engage in gainful employment, including self-employment and liberal professions (Articles 17–19), access to products that are in short supply 'where a rationing system exists' (Article 20), access to public housing services (Article 21), access to public education (Article 22), access to public relief and social security and right to appropriate labour standards (Articles 23–24), right to administrative assistance (Article 25), freedom of movement (Article 26), right to be issued identity papers (Article 27) and travel documents (Article 28), prohibition of fiscal charges other or higher than levied on nationals (Article 29), protection from expulsion for reasons other than national security and public order (Article 31), and access to facilitated naturalization (Article 32). The 1954 Convention also guarantees the non-discriminatory treatment of stateless persons in respect of to the rights stipulated in the Convention without regard to race, religion and country of origin (Article 3).

However, what rights specifically are available to stateless persons is a complex matter, because their rights under the 1954 Convention are distinguished on two levels. On the first level, the situation of stateless persons is modified depending on whether a given stateless person is merely physically present in the territory of a given state or is so in compliance with the state's laws and regulations ('lawfully in'; *résidant régulièrement*). Within the latter category, a broader range of rights is available to the 'lawfully staying' and the broadest one to those who are also 'habitually resident'. The first group includes persons whose stay is relatively longer, such as those holding a timed permit for a duration exceeding

235 See Chapter II, section 2.1.

several months. The second group covers those to whom permanent residence has been permitted but also those having settled down in the state and remained lawfully in it for many years without such a permit.[236]

The second level on which the rights under the 1954 Convention are distinguished refers to the difference in the treatment of stateless persons depending on the type of standard of treatment foreseen in respect of a given right. The 1954 Convention defines a minimum standard of treatment of stateless persons — they are to be treated as foreigners unless the Convention prescribes a more favourable treatment. The majority of rights are available on a most-favourable-treatment basis (meaning an obligation to treat stateless persons on par with foreign nationals in the same circumstances),[237] and in exceptional cases national treatment is envisaged (treatment of stateless persons on par with own nationals).[238]

Analysis of the provisions of the 1954 Convention permits categories of stateless persons to be distinguished with a gradual scale of rights conditioned by the nature and length of their stay in the territory. The closer the stateless person's ties to the state, the more rights the stateless person has. In consequence, only some of the rights must be guaranteed to all categories of stateless persons, while the majority are prescribed for those stateless persons who are 'lawfully in'.[239] The minimum of rights that are mandatory to guarantee under the 1954 Convention are the right to be issued identity papers (Article 27), access to courts (Article 16), access to public education (Article 22), ability to acquire property

---

236 UNHCR Handbook, paragraphs 132, 137 and 139.

237 As observed by C. Mik, the most-favoured standard is in reference to the treatment of third-state nationals, because for the national treatment the reference point is 'not only the treatment of Polish citizens but also, in principle, of the citizens of EU member states' — see C. Mik, *Analiza…*, p. 86.

238 National treatment is stipulated only for the freedom of religious practice (Article 4 of the 1954 Convention); protection of artistic rights and industrial property (Article 14 of the 1954 Convention); access to courts (Article 16(2) of the 1954 Convention); right of access to goods in short supply (where a rationing system is in place) (Article 20 of the 1954 Convention); and access to elementary education (Article 22(1) of the 1954 Convention).

239 For example, any stateless person has a right to be issued identity papers, but only a stateless person who is lawfully staying in the territory has a right to receive travel documents. Lastly, some rights are reserved to habitual residents. These are the right of access on national terms to the court system and legal assistance, with exemption from the *cautio iudicatum solvi* (Article 16(2) of the 1954 Convention) and the protection of artistic and industrial property (Article 14 of the 1954 Convention).

(Article 13), and access to products in short supply (Article 20). The prohibition of fiscal charges other or higher than levied upon own nationals also applies to all stateless persons (Article 29).[240]

The core issue from the perspective of giving to stateless persons the rights prescribed by the 1954 Convention is to whom the rights are attributed. Fundamental significance belongs to the question of who is a stateless person in the light of Article 1(1) of the 1954 Convention (so-called inclusion clause). Nonetheless, at the stage of decision-making about protection, it is also important what individuals are excluded from it in the light of Article 1(2) of the 1954 Convention (so-called exclusion clause). Article 1(2) of the 1954 Convention identifies the categories of individuals excluded from the protection offered by the provisions of the treaty. It refers to those who either meet the definition of a stateless person according to Article 1(1) of the 1954 but do not need protection (because they enjoy alternative protection granted under separate provisions)[241] or are excluded from protection because of e.g. important reasons to believe that they are guilty of criminal offences or of conduct incompatible with the goals and principles of the United Nations.[242]

2. Procedures for the determination of statelessness

2.1. Preliminary issues

The standard of treatment of stateless persons prescribed by the 1954 Convention can only be effective when it is known who is entitled to protection. Procedures for the determination (identification) of statelessness are, therefore, of key importance. The 1954 Convention does not require states party to introduce any procedures of this type.[243] The matter is addressed by the UNHCR Handbook dealing with the protection of stateless persons, as I discuss below.

---

240 Regardless of the nature of the sojourn, stateless persons must also be guaranteed access to facilitated naturalization (Article 32 of the 1954 Convention), which I discuss as a mechanism for the reduction of statelessness (see Chapter III).

241 See Articles 1(2)(i) and 1(2)(ii) of the 1954 Convention. These exclude persons who are in receipt of assistance provided by a different UN agency, as is the case of those receiving assistance and protection from the United Nations Relief and Works Agency for Palestine Refugees in the Near East (UNRWA). For a more extensive discussion of this exclusion ground see K. Bianchini, *Protecting…*, pp. 86–96.

242 See Article 1(2)(iii) of the 1954 Convention. Topics relating to persons excluded from protection on the basis of this provision are discussed in Chapter VII, section 2.

243 It should be noted that a similar situation exists with regard to the Geneva Convention of 1951 and the New York Protocol of 1967, neither of which contains any provisions

According to the position taken by the UNHCR, the introduction of mechanisms for the identification of stateless persons is in the interest of the persons whose rights are concerned. Although the necessity of the introduction of such procedures is not stated explicitly in the 1954 Convention, it nonetheless constitutes an assumption written into it, considering that the determination of who is a stateless person is a necessary precondition of the ability to guarantee appropriate treatment. Furthermore, the introduction of statelessness-determination procedures has a positive impact on respect for stateless persons' human rights, providing an important mechanism to mitigate the risk that prolonged or unlawful administrative detention will occur. The introduction of such procedures is, moreover, in the best interests of the states themselves, as it has a positive effect on compliance with the obligations of the 1954 Convention. Firstly, in those states in which statelessness is mainly a problem specific to migrant populations, statelessness-determination procedures assists governments to evaluate the size and structure of the stateless population in their territories. Secondly, identification of stateless persons can also be instrumental to counteracting statelessness by revealing its sources and any novel trends in the area.[244]

An interest in matters relating to the determination of statelessness is also visible in the EU, although no regulations requiring the member states to introduce statelessness-determination procedures have been adopted until the present date. According to the European Commission's document titled *Statelessness in the EU*, identification mechanisms are a practical prerequisite of the ability to

---

dealing with the identification of refugees. However, the assumption followed in subsequently enacted instruments of soft law has been that the protection of refugees begins with identifying those to whom the protection should be given. Conclusions of the UNHCR's Executive Committee contain recommendations in this regard. Those address not only the relevance of the procedures themselves but also the standards they must meet: Conclusion no. 8 (XXVIII) Determination of Refugee Status (1977), paragraphs a and e; Conclusion no. 11 (XXIX) General (1978), paragraphs h and i; Conclusion No. 14 (XXX) General (1979), paragraph f; Conclusion No. 16 (XXXI) General (1980), paragraph h [in:] Conclusions Adopted by the Executive Committee on the International Protection of Refugees 1975–2009 (Conclusion No. 1–109), UNHCR December 2009. With time, regulations adopted within the European Union have developed a procedural standard binding upon the member states (although it has been observed not to conform fully to the provisions of the Geneva Convention of 1951; see e.g. A. Potyrała, *Ochrona uchodźców w ustawodawstwie państw członkowskich Unii Europejskiej z Europy środkowej i wschodniej*, 1 Środkowoeuropejskie Studia Polityczne 2012, p. 234).

244 UNHCR Handbook, paragraph 10.

guarantee the protection of stateless persons, and although the 1954 Convention does not specify any methods by which to determine statelessness, the states must determine who is eligible for the state's protection pursuant to Article 1 of the 1954 Convention for the purpose of extending to such an individual the standard protection prescribed by the treaty.[245] The Council of Europe, by contrast, does not preoccupy itself with such procedures.

Below, I discuss the UNHCR's guidance on procedures for the determination of statelessness (section 2.2) and solutions in place having regulated stateless status and introduced procedures for the identification of stateless persons (section 2.3). For clarity of presentation with regard to UNHCR guidelines on procedures, I will use the term 'statelessness-determination procedures' (SDP). By contrast, with regard to procedures adopted in domestic jurisdictions, I will use the term 'statelessness-identification procedures' (SIP).

2.2. UNHCR guidance on the introduction of statelessness-determination procedures in domestic jurisdictions

2.2.1. Preliminary issues

As has been noted, the matter of statelessness-determination procedures is addressed by the UNHCR Handbook on Protection of Stateless Persons (2014), currently the only document formulating comprehensive guidelines on SDP. The Handbook is an official UNHCR document arising from several years of that entity's collaboration with external experts in a series of meetings on the 50th anniversary of the adoption of the 1961 Convention.[246] While the status of

245 *Statelessness in the EU*, p. 5.

246 It will be worth saying a couple of words on the drafting process of the UNHCR Handbook of Protection of Stateless Persons. In 2006, the UNHCR Executive Committee resolved for the UNHCR to develop technical guidelines for the states concerning the adoption and implementation of mechanisms of counteraction of statelessness and implementation of the 1954 Convention due to the degree of complexity of the topics of the 1954 and 1961 Conventions (see *Conclusion on Identification, Prevention and Reduction of Statelessness and Protection of Stateless Persons*, no. 106 (LVII) — 2006, paragraph s). In response, the UNHCR's Division of International Protection designed guidelines concerning the key issues of the Conventions, by a process begun by consultations with external experts (e.g. representatives of the government administration of the various states, judges, representatives of non-government organizations, practising lawyers, and scholars) and UNHCR representatives. As a result, the year 2012 saw the publication of, among others, *Guidelines on Statelessness no. 1: The definition of "Stateless Person" in Article 1(1) of the 1954 Convention relating to the Status of Stateless*

the guidelines on SDP contained in the UNHCR Handbook is not imperatively binding, they should be taken into account by the states party to the 1954 Convention. Simultaneously, to states not party to the 1954 Convention but planning the introduction of such procedures, the guidelines serve as an important source of information on the international standard in this area. For this reason, the UNHCR recommendations provided by the UNHCR Handbook will be the object of more in-depth analysis in this book.

Two introductory remarks must precede the analysis of the guidelines contained in the UNHCR Handbook. Firstly, the standard defined by the UNHCR is applicable only to those procedures of which either the sole purpose or one of several purposes is the determination of statelessness. Accordingly, it does not apply to all procedures in which matters relating to an individual's nationality or statelessness are being determined. In particular, the UNHCR Handbook explicitly states that the standard is not applicable to procedures conducted for the purpose of applying such laws and regulations dealing with the prevention and reduction of statelessness as are prescribed by the 1961 Convention.[247] Secondly, the application of SDP will sometimes not be warranted in a *mutatis mutandis* manner with regard to certain stateless populations. Statelessness can occur either with regard to persons who are in a migration situation or to those who are not immigrants but are living in their 'own country'.[248] To the last-mentioned category of stateless persons (who are also referred to as the *in-situ* stateless), SDP should not be held to be applicable because those are individuals having a permanent link to the state in whose territory they reside (often having been born in it), while lacking any such ties to any other country. Depending on the specific situation, the recommendation is for the states to organize campaigns encouraging such populations of stateless persons to acquire nationality and take

Persons, HCR/GS/12/01, 2012; *Guidelines on Statelessness no. 2: Procedures for Determining whether an Individual is a Stateless Person*, HCR/GS/12/02, 5 April 2012; and *Guidelines on Statelessness no. 3: The Status of Stateless Persons at the National Level*, HRC/GS/12/03, 17 July 2012. The aforesaid guidelines were subsequently consolidated and, with small edits, published as the UNHCR Handbook; see M. Manly, *UNHCR's mandate…*, pp. 95–97; UNHCR Handbook, Foreword, pp. 1–2.

247 Among others, these will include procedures enabling nationality to be acquired through facilitated-naturalization procedures or procedures for the confirmation of acquisition of nationality *iure soli* by an otherwise stateless child born in the territory of the relevant state.

248 Within the meaning of Article 12(4) ICCPR. Concerning stateless persons residing in their 'own country' see also paragraph 164 of the UNHCR Handbook.

advantage of existing procedures for the confirmation (verification) of nationality.[249] The purpose of the last-mentioned type of procedures is to assist individuals residing in the territory of a state in which they experience difficulties acquiring proof of nationality.[250]

The UNHCR Handbook notes that the states have broad leeway with regard to the establishment and implementation of SDP, given as the 1954 Convention does not address them directly. The procedures should, however, be regulated by legislation,[251] and thus they should not be a mere reflection of specific administrative or judicial practice. The concrete shape of such procedures should depend on local circumstances such as the number and structure of the stateless population and the complexity of legal and evidentiary issues. Regardless of any specific procedural outcomes, the primary purpose of the procedure (although not necessarily its sole purpose) should be the determination of statelessness.[252]

2.2.2. The administrative framework

According to the UNHCR Handbook, states are free to designate a central determination authority or empower local authorities to serve as the decision-makers in statelessness-determination procedures. A centralized administrative structure, however, is preferred because it makes the development, with time, of suitable expertise among the officials responsible for statelessness determinations a more likely prospect.[253] The UNHCR notes that applications in statelessness-determination procedures should be examined by appropriately trained civil servants specialized in the handling of cases involving statelessness, due to the significant complexity of matters relating to the determination of statelessness.[254]

Nonetheless, if a centralized model is selected, applicants' access to SDP can be fraught with difficulties. In this connection, the UNHCR stresses the necessity

---

249 UNHCR Handbook, paragraph 58.

250 UNHCR Handbook, paragraph 60. As noted by another UNHCR document, in those cases in which the direct purpose of the procedure is the acquisition, re-acquisition or confirmation of nationality of the state of residence by the members of a given population, resources should not be expended on formal determinations of statelessness; UNHCR, *Action to address statelessness. A strategy note*, March 2010, paragraph 50.

251 UNHCR Handbook, paragraph 71.

252 UNHCR Handbook, paragraph 62.

253 UNHCR Handbook, paragraph 63.

254 UNHCR, *Establishing statelessness determination procedures to protect stateless persons*, Good Practices Paper, Action 6, 11 July 2016, p. 4.

of making sure that such a centralized procedure is easily accessible to applicants located in different parts of the country. That can be achieved, for example, by permitting applications to be filed with local administrative bodies and subsequently forwarded by them to the competent central determination authority.[255] In essence, therefore, this guideline means that where a centralized administrative model is selected for the decision-making in statelessness-determination cases, states should strive to achieve deconcentration by enabling technical aspects such as receiving applications to be handled by administrative bodies on the local level.

2.2.3. The accessibility of the procedure

The UN High Commissioner for Refugees recommends that wide accessibility of the procedures be guaranteed. This particular angle has already been discussed above with regard to various aspects of administrative organization. Further guidelines concern the recommendation to enable the procedures to be initiated not only by the application of the interested party but also *ex officio*. Moreover, any individual within the territory of the state should be able to submit such an application. The 1954 Convention admits of no grounds on which to restrict the ability to file applications only to those individuals who are 'lawfully in'. As the Handbook observes, a requirement of such kind would be particularly harmful to stateless persons, as their lack of nationality is what often impedes their ability to obtain precisely the documents that are required for lawful entry or residence anywhere. Additionally, no time limits should be imposed on the filing of the applications. Any such limits can have the effect of groundlessly depriving an individual of the protection of the 1954 Convention.[256] It is noted that information about SDP and procedural rights relating to statelessness determination should be circulated by the states broadly in different languages, so as to ensure the wide accessibility of such procedures.

2.2.4. Procedural safeguards

The UNHCR Handbook provides a number of recommendations for procedural guarantees in statelessness-determination procedures. Firstly, it is important for the states to design appropriate frameworks to ensure that applicants may receive assistance at the stage of preparing their applications and throughout the entire

---

255 UNHCR Handbook, paragraph 63.
256 UNHCR Handbook, paragraphs 68–70.

proceedings. Applicants should have the opportunity to obtain the necessary information about SDP in a language they can understand. Legal assistance, the assistance of an interpreter and an opportunity to contact the UNHCR should be guaranteed in the proceedings. In states having a system of unpaid legal assistance, such assistance should be extended to stateless persons lacking the financial means.[257]

Secondly, SDP should guarantee the applicant's opportunity to be heard. The right to be heard — with the simultaneous assurance of the necessary assistance of an interpreter — is necessary in order to make sure that applicants have the opportunity to present their case in a holistic manner and to explain everything that may be relevant to the outcome of the case.[258] The above also creates an important avenue for the decision-making authority to clarify any doubts concerning the evidence presented to it.[259]

2.2.5. Burden and standard of proof

The Handbook addresses the matter of the distribution of the burden of proof and specifies the evidentiary standard for SDP. The UN High Commissioner for Refugees recommends having a shared burden of proof, so that it rests on both the applicant and the authorities. It is noted that the evidence gathering and fact finding requires a collaborative effort between the applicant and the authority. Applicants have a duty to communicate truthfully and present their personal situation with as much accuracy as possible, as well as to submit all such evidence as may be available to them. The case-handling authority, in turn, has a duty to gather and adduce all such evidence as it may be reasonably expected to gather, so as to be in a position to make an objective assessment of the applicant's status. It is regarded as a sufficient evidentiary threshold if the circumstances relating to the individual's statelessness are proved to a reasonable degree.[260] Thus, with regard to evidentiary matters, the procedure should assume the applicant's duty to establish the circumstances relating to statelessness as plausible.

It is rightly pointed out that the burden of proof should be shared between the applicant and the determination authority, and that the evidentiary standard must not be unreasonably elevated in such type of proceedings. It is necessary

---

257 UNHCR Handbook, paragraph 71.
258 UNHCR Handbook, paragraph 73.
259 UNHCR Handbook, paragraph 100.
260 UNHCR Handbook, paragraph 89.

to 'take into consideration the difficulties inherent in proving statelessness'.[261] In other words, statelessness-determination procedures involve specific evidentiary problems — the formal object of the evidence is a negative fact (i.e. the fact of not holding the nationality of any state), which in practice is difficult for applicants to prove. It must be emphasized that, for reasons relating to the very nature of statelessness, individuals often cannot support their claims with documentary evidence. Many are not in a position to do so or do not know that they need to carry out their own analysis of the nationality legislation of the states with which they are connected by birth in the territory or of parents being nationals, or by marriage or habitual residence. Another aspect of fundamental importance to the outcome of the determination of the individual's statelessness status is contacting the authorities of other states for information about the individual's case or about the nationality laws and regulations of the requested state and the practice of their application. In many cases, the authorities of other states will only respond to such enquiries when presented by officials representing the authorities of other states rather than by private individuals.[262]

The UN High Commissioner for Refugees also emphasizes that if the determination of statelessness is handled by a court of law, the process should be 'inquisitorial rather than adversarial'.[263] The meaning of this particular guideline is not perfectly clear. In essence, it appears to touch on the question of the degree of active intervention on the part of the judge required in order to ensure the due process of the law. Here, the judge should assume an active role in the identification of problems to address and in the gathering of evidence and should remain actively in control of the proceedings.[264]

The process of determination of statelessness is closely linked to the interpretation of the definition of a stateless person from Article 1(1) of the 1954 Convention. As mentioned in Chapter II, the UNHCR is of the position that the definition should be interpreted broadly. The UNHCR Handbook notes that the determination of statelessness requires the holistic evaluation of factual circumstances and points of other states' law. This means that such cases cannot

---

261 UNHCR Handbook, paragraph 91.

262 UNHCR, *Establishing statelessness…*, pp. 5–6.

263 UNHCR Handbook, paragraph 71.

264 R. Thomas, *From 'Adversarial v. Inquisitorial' to 'Active, Enabling, and Investigative': Developments in UK Administrative Tribunals* [in:] L. Jacobs, S. Baglay (eds.), *The nature of inquisitorial processes in administrative regimes. Global perspectives*, London–New York 2016, pp. 51–52.

be resolved solely by analysing the nationality laws and regulations of the state with which the individual has a connection. According to the UNHCR Handbook, the definition of a stateless person in Article 1(1) of the 1954 Convention requires the 'evaluation of the application of [such] laws in practice'.[265] Notably, '[a]pplying this approach of examining an individual's position in practice may lead to a different conclusion than one derived from a purely formalistic analysis of the application of nationality laws of a country to an individual's case. A State may not in practice follow the letter of the law, even going so far as to ignore its substance.'[266]

As has already been mentioned,[267] the states may need to develop appropriate standards to be followed in the evidentiary process so as to specify what cases of statelessness fall within the definition of a stateless person under international law. Legal provisions may explicitly state that specific conduct of a state (administrative practice) may be regarded as *prima facie* evidence that such a state does not regard the individuals concerned as its nationals. For example, individuals who are nationals from a formal legal standpoint but cannot exercise the right of entry and residence in their state of nationality or cannot obtain proof of nationality may be regarded as stateless persons.

Types of evidence potentially relevant to such proceedings can be divided into two categories — evidence of personal circumstances and evidence of laws and regulations and of the practice of their application in the state concerned. The former group of evidence serves to determine what states and what nationality laws need to be considered when determining the applicant's nationality status. Such evidence includes the applicant's own testimony (e.g. written application or interview), responses from foreign states to queries concerning the individual's citizenship status, identity papers, travel documents, documents relating to citizenship applications or proof of citizenship, proof of renunciation, school certificates, marriage certificates and residence cards. The latter group of evidence comprises foreign nationality laws and regulations, their implementations and administrative practices in specific states, as well as the general legal state of affairs in such countries with regard to the administrative authorities' compliance with court judgments. Such evidence may be obtained from government and non-government sources. In some cases, the complexity of the matter covered by provisions relating to nationality justifies sourcing expert opinions.[268]

265 UNHCR Handbook, paragraph 83.
266 UNHCR Handbook, paragraph 24.
267 See Chapter II, section 2.2.2.
268 UNHCR Handbook, paragraphs 83–85.

According to the UNHCR Handbook, the proceedings should be completed as expeditiously as possible. In cases in which the evidence submitted with the application is clear and claims of the individual's statelessness are well-substantiated, the proceedings should not take longer than a couple of months to finish. Solutions from states having a set time-limit in place for the making and communication of the decision, counted from the day the application was filed, are cited as examples of good practice. In principle, the duration should not exceed six months. In exceptional circumstances, this could take up to twelve months when it involves querying foreign authorities for information relevant to the applicant's nationality.[269]

The UN High Commissioner for Refugees notes that the applicant should be accorded protection throughout the proceedings. States ought to refrain from the expulsion of applicants for statelessness status.[270] The UNHCR Handbook also takes up the matter of the administrative detention of stateless persons pending SDP due to the fact that they often lack identity papers or travel documents. Detention is described as a last-resort measure, and routine detention of individuals applying for protection as stateless persons is asserted to be impermissible. Detention can only be applied in a non-discriminatory manner where it is both necessary and proportionate in each individual case.[271]

According to the UNHCR Handbook, decisions concerning the determination of statelessness should be delivered in written form and accompanied by a statement of reasons.[272] The right to appeal a negative decision of the first-instance authority to an independent organ should be guaranteed. Appeals should be permitted not only on points of law but also of fact. It is up to the states to decide whether the appellate body is to be empowered to enter its own decision on the merits or merely to reverse and remand. In other words, either the cassatory or the reformatory model may be chosen for appeals in statelessness-determination cases. At this stage of the proceedings, the UNHCR Handbook explicitly affirms the necessity of guaranteeing access to legal assistance and of providing individuals who are in need of unpaid legal assistance with an opportunity to obtain it in those states in which a system for such assistance exists. Moreover, states may choose to allow judicial review of the administrative decisions issued in statelessness-determination procedures, provided that the procedural aspects of

269 UNHCR Handbook, paragraphs 74–75.
270 UNHCR Handbook, paragraph 72.
271 UNHCR Handbook, paragraphs 112–115.
272 UNHCR Handbook, paragraph 29.

any such review should conform to the procedural model followed in general in a given state.[273]

It will be expedient to pay some attention to the guidelines formulated in soft-law instruments with regard to the need of offering special protection to the most vulnerable persons. It is noted that age, sex and other individual characteristics may require additional procedural guarantees e.g. to make sure that individuals have access to SDP. Such additional procedural guarantees for children and women are discussed in the dedicated chapters of this book. Here, it will suffice to mention that it is recommended for the specific needs with regard to the protection of persons with disabilities (e.g. intellectual disabilities) who can experience difficulties communicating information about their nationality to be taken into account in the whole course of all relevant procedures. The decision-making officials should also consider the greater risk of persons with disabilities lacking identity papers and other documents as a result of discrimination. Such persons could be given access to procedural and evidentiary facilitations similar to those enabled for minors, such as priority consideration of their applications, availability of suitably trained legal counsel, interviewers and interpreters, as well as a guarantee that the burden of proof rests for the most part on the state.[274]

As can be seen from the above, the purpose of SDP is to determine whether the individual is a stateless person. It must be emphasized, however, that the determination of statelessness through SDP is declaratory in nature.[275] This means that identifying an individual as a stateless person confirms the existing fact that the individual is a stateless person — it does not 'create' statelessness (it is not a constitutive act). Accordingly, the rights stipulated in the 1954 Convention are not restricted to individuals who have been declared stateless through an SDP.[276] As discussed above, the rights specified by the 1954 Convention are linked to the nature of a person's sojourn in the territory of the state (mere presence in the territory, lawful stay, long-term lawful stay, habitual residence). However, it is accepted that persons who are in the process of undergoing a statelessness-determination procedure must be regarded as being 'lawfully in' the state, and

273 UNHCR Handbook, paragraphs 76–77.

274 UNHCR Handbook, paragraph 118. Similarly the guidelines developed jointly by the OSCE and the UNHCR in 2017 — OSCE and UNHCR, *Handbook on statelessness in the OSCE Area. International Standards and Good Practices*, 28 February 2017; UNHCR, *Establishing Statelessness…*, p. 7.

275 UNHCR Handbook, paragraph 16.

276 UNHCR Handbook, paragraph 126.

that the determination of statelessness through the relevant procedure may lead to the acquisition of a specific status in domestic jurisdictions.

3. Regulatory frameworks in selected jurisdictions

3.1. Preliminary issues

On the basis of available data gathered by comparative study, one can distinguish three basic types of approach taken by European states to the shaping of the situation of stateless persons.[277] The first category includes states regulating the status of a stateless person and having adopted a special statelessness-identification procedure (SIP). These are, among others: Spain, Hungary, United Kingdom, Moldova, Switzerland, France, Italy, Latvia and Luxembourg (all have ratified the 1954 Convention). The second category includes states in which the status of a stateless person is regulated but no special statelessness-identification procedure (SIP) is in place. These include Ukraine and Serbia (both are states party to the 1954 Convention). At last, the third category includes states not regulating the status of a stateless person and not having adopted any specific model of identification of statelessness. Among others, these are Germany, Greece, Sweden, Czech Republic, the Netherlands, Poland, Slovenia and North Macedonia. In those states, the matter of statelessness comes to surface in procedures relating to international protection, residence status or travel documents or return procedures. This group includes states not having ratified the 1954 Convention, as well as those having ratified it. The later part of this chapter will focus on examples of solutions from states having implemented the Convention standard in the fullest degree, which could serve as points of reference for the process of designing the appropriate solutions (the first category).

Of all states having adopted special procedures for the determination of statelessness in their legal orders, only two have gathered them in separate legal instruments. These are Spain, where the matter is regulated by Royal Decree of 20 July 2001 no. 865/2001 on the Recognition of the Status of a Stateless Person (hereinafter the 'Spanish Decree on Stateless Persons')[278], and Latvia, with

277 Data gathered under the Statelessness Index Survey project of the European Network on Statelessness (see footnote 148). I also include regulatory examples from countries not covered by the study (Luxembourg, Italy, Latvia, Spain), identifying the source of the information at each time.

278 BOE no. 174, of 21 July 2001, pp. 26603–26606.

its Act on Stateless Persons of 2004 (hereinafter the 'Latvian Act on Stateless Persons').[279]

In other states envisaging SIP, the procedures can be regulated in two ways. Firstly, provisions dealing with SIP can be part of a statute governing foreigners. This is, for example, the case in Hungary (Act on the Admission and Rights of Residence of Third-Country Nationals, Chapter VIII, Articles 76–86, hereinafter the 'Hungarian Act on Foreigners'),[280] in the United Kingdom (British Immigration Rules, part 14)[281], in Moldova (Foreigners Act, Chapter X^1, hereinafter the 'Moldovan Foreigners Act')[282] and France (Code on Entry and Residence of Foreigners and Right of Asylum, chapter titled 'Status of a Stateless Person', Article L. 812-1–812-8, hereinafter the 'French Foreigners Code').[283] Notably, the French procedure for the determination of statelessness has the longest history in Europe, going back to the 50s of the 20th century (having been introduced by the Act on the Right of Asylum of 1952).[284] Secondly, the determination of statelessness can be handled under the general provisions regulating administrative procedures. Such is, for example, the case in Switzerland, where the determination of statelessness takes place in an administrative procedure, subject to additional administrative regulations enacted by the National Secretariat of State for Migrations (*Secrétariat d'Etat aux migrations*; hereinafter the 'SEM'), titled 'Instructions on Asylum and Returns'. Similarly, in Luxembourg, the determination of

279 English translation available as Latvia: Law of 2004 on Stateless Persons [Latvia] at http://www.refworld.org/docid/41387c6c4.html (accessed 10 December 2018). Latvia also regulates the status of a 'non-citizen of Latvia', without, however, regarded such individuals as stateless persons. Accordingly, the Act applies only to those stateless persons who are not such non-citizens. The legal status of the latter is regulated by Latvian Act of 25 April 1995 on the Status of Former USSR Citizens Who Do Not Have the Citizenship of Latvia or That of Any Other State. At the same time, an individual having lost the status of a non-citizen of Latvia will be regarded as a stateless person if not having the nationality or assurance of conferral of nationality of any other state (Article 3(2) of Latvian Act on Stateless Persons). K. Kruma, *EU Citizenship…*, pp. 361–365.

280 Act II of 2007 on the Admission and Rights of Residence of Third-Country Nationals.

281 See footnote 161.

282 Law no. 200 of 16 July 2010 on Foreigners.

283 Code de l'entrée et du séjour des étrangers et du droit d'asile.

284 *Loi relative au droit d'asile n°52-893 du 25 juillet 1952.*

statelessness is handled directly on the basis of the provisions of administrative procedure (hereinafter 'Luxembourgian Administrative Provisions').[285]

The Italian provisions on SIP stand out in a particular way. Italy has two parallel mechanisms for the determination of statelessness: an administrative path and a judicial path.[286] The basis for the administrative procedure for the determination of statelessness is supplied by Article 17 of Presidential Decree no. 572/93 of 12 October 1993 (hereinafter the 'Italian Decree').[287] Statelessness determination through a judicial procedure takes place on the basis of the provisions of the Civil Code (Section 2697 of Italian Civil Code; hereinafter the 'Italian Civil Code').[288]

3.2. The administrative framework

The vast majority of states have adopted an administrative model in which the submissions of SIP applications are received by one central determination authority also making the case decisions. Different bodies are responsible for the examination of the cases and for the making of the decisions in different states. In Spain, that is the Office for Asylum and Refuge (*Oficina de Asilo y Refugio* — OAR),[289] which conducts the evidentiary proceedings and forwards its recommendation for the decision of the case to the Minister for the Interior (through the Directorate General for Foreigners and Immigration), who makes the decision.[290] In the United Kingdom, statelessness determination is the province of the Home Office.[291] In Moldova, applications are considered by the Statelessness Section of the Department for Migration and Asylum (*Biroul migrație și azil*) of the Ministry of the Interior.[292] In Switzerland, the matter is handled by the SEM, which is the central administrative body for matters of migration on the federal level.[293] In France, the competent body is the OFPRA — French Office for

285 French text available at http://www.guichet.public.lu/citoyens/fr/immigration/cas-specifiques/apatride/demande-statut-apatride/index.html (accessed 15 November 2018).

286 In the majority of cases the applicant may choose the procedure to use, but in complicated cases the court will be the competent authority; C.A. Batchelor, *The 1954 Convention relating to the status of stateless persons. Implementation within the European Union member states and recommendation for harmonization*, 22(2) Refuge 2005, p. 39.

287 Presidential Decree no. 572 of 12 October 1993.

288 Royal Decree no. 262 of 16 March 1942.

289 Article 2 of Spanish Decree on Stateless Persons.

290 Articles 10 and 11 of Spanish Decree on Stateless Persons.

291 SIS, United Kingdom, question IDP.2.a, p. 14.

292 SIS, Moldova, question IDP.2.a, p. 13.

293 SIS, Switzerland, question IDP.2.a, p. 17.

the Protection of Refugees and Stateless Persons (*Office français de protection de réfugiés et apatrides*).[294] In Luxembourg, granting the status of a stateless person belongs to the responsibilities of the minister competent for immigration, and statelessness determination is the responsibility of the Directorate for Immigration at the Ministry of Foreign and European Affairs.[295]

In the majority of states having adopted the centralized model, the application must be submitted directly to the central determination authority (in person or by post). Spanish regulations are exceptional in providing that the application must be addressed to the OAR but may be filed either through specified bodies (police units, migration authorities) or directly with the OAR.[296] Spain thus follows the deconcentrated model recommended by the UNHCR. The Spanish solution, in which applications may be filed throughout the country but are decided by a single specialized central authority, is cited as an example of good practice.[297] The deconcentrated model has also been adopted by Hungary. Decisions on the applications are made by the Citizenship and Immigration Authority (*Bevándorlási és Állampolgársági Hivatal*), which has seven regional offices throughout the country. Each such regional office may receive applications and each of them makes the decisions relating to statelessness. The downside of this solution, however, is that different regional offices reach different case outcomes.[298]

Only in some countries do the case-handling officials specialize in matters relating to statelessness. This is the case e.g. in Hungary (although, as noted above, the nature of the officials' specialization is not harmonized throughout the entire administrative structure)[299] and the United Kingdom (Home Office has a specialized unit in Liverpool for statelessness)[300].

3.3. The accessibility of the procedure

Methods of initiating the procedure are no exception from the diversity of the regulatory landscape of SIP. In the overwhelming majority of states, the

---

294 SIS, France, question IDP.2.a, p. 17.

295 Luxembourgian Administrative Provisions, p. 2.

296 Article 2(3) of Spanish Decree on Stateless Persons.

297 UNHCR, *Establishing statelessness...*, p. 4.

298 G. Gyulai, *Statelessness in Hungary. The protection of stateless persons and the prevention and reduction of statelessness*, Hungarian Helsinki Committee 2010, p. 21.

299 G. Gyulai, *Statelessness...*, p. 21.

300 SIS, United Kingdom, question IDP.2.j, p. 15.

procedure can only be initiated by a written application. Only Moldova[301] and Hungary[302] accept applications made orally on the record.

Some states require the application to be on a special form. This is the solution under French,[303] British[304] and Luxembourgian[305] regulations. By contrast, Moldova allows the initial written application to be in any form, with the receiving official's task being to complete the relevant forms during the interview.[306]

In the majority of states, applications have to be made in the state's official language. For example, in Switzerland, the application may be submitted in one of the country's official languages (German, French or Italian). By way of exception, the authorities may accept submissions in different languages.[307] In the administrative procedure used in Italy, the application must be in Italian.[308] Only Hungary[309] and Moldova[310] permit the use of any language of the applicant's choice.

Only in exceptional situations do the discussed provisions allow SIP to be initiated *ex officio*. In Spain, that is the case when the OAR becomes aware of facts, data or information suggesting the existence of circumstances compelling the determination of statelessness. The *Oficina de Asilo y Refugio* notifies the individual concerned, so as to give them the opportunity to present a case.[311] This is similar in Moldova, where the proceedings can be brought *ex officio*, but the statute provides no precise indication of when that is expected to happen.[312] It is also worth mentioning the Hungarian provisions under which the procedure cannot be initiated *ex officio*, but the authorities have a duty to advise of its ability any potentially stateless person within any migration procedure.[313]

---

301 Article 87^1(2) of Moldovan Foreigners Act.
302 Section 76 of Hungarian Foreigners Act.
303 SIS, France, question IDP.2.b, p. 14.
304 SIS, United Kingdom, question IDP.2.b, p. 14.
305 *Demande en obtention du statut d'apatride au sens de la Convention de New York du 28 septembre 1954 relative au statut des apatrides.* Form available at https://guichet.public.lu/citoyens/catalogue-formulaires/immigration/apatride/demande-statut-apatride/formulaire-demande-FR.pdf (accessed 12 November 2018).
306 SIS, Moldova, question IDP.2.b, p. 13.
307 SIS, Switzerland, question IDP.2.b, pp. 15– 16.
308 *Ad-Hoc Query on Recognition of Stateless Persons*, European Commission and European Migration Network, 4 May 2015, p. 19.
309 Section 77(2) of Hungarian Foreigners Act.
310 SIS, Moldova, question IDP.2.b, p. 13.
311 Articles 2(1) and 2(2) of Spanish Decree on Stateless Persons.
312 Article 87^{i} (1) of Moldovan Foreigners Act.
313 Section 22(2) of Hungarian Foreigners Act.

Against the background of the diversity of regulatory approaches taken to SIP, it can be seen that only a minority of states (Spain and Moldova) have heeded the UNHCR recommendation to enable the procedures to be initiated *ex officio*. When evaluating the regulations in the various states, the UNHCR recognized the opportunity to apply in any language as an example of good practice (Hungary and Moldova).[314]

Although most do not, some states prescribe time limits for applying. Spanish regulations allow applications no later than one month of entering the territory. An exception applies when the individual has been in Spain lawfully for a long time, in which case the application must be filed before the end of the lawful stay. If the applicant has been unlawfully in Spain for at least a month and has submitted the application while already ordered to leave, the application will be regarded as manifestly ill-founded.[315] In the United Kingdom, by contrast, there is no time-limit for applying.[316] However, it is noted that, in practice, failure to disclose all facts and claims during prior contacts with the authorities will be taken into advisement by the decision-making authority when making the decision.[317]

The regulations in some states impose the requirement of being lawfully in their territory at the time of filing, which is incompatible with the UNHCR's recommendations. Such a requirement features in the Italian administrative procedure (but not on the judicial path).[318] A similar limitation at the stage of filing used to apply in Hungary. Until February 2015, an application for stateless status could only be made by an applicant lawfully in Hungary. The Hungarian Constitutional Court found that requirement to be in violation of the 1954 Convention.[319]

---

314 UNHCR, *Establishing statelessness…*, Action 6, p. 5.

315 Article 4(2) of Spanish Decree on Stateless Persons.

316 SIS, United Kingdom, question IDP.2.i, p. 17.

317 K. Bianchini, *A comparative analysis of statelessness determination procedures in 10 EU states*, 29(1) International Journal of Refugee Law 2017, p. 53.

318 *Ad-hoc Query…*, p. 19.

319 Hungarian Constitutional Court, 6/2015, judgment, 25 February 2015; text available at http://www.refworld.org/cases,HUN_CC,5542301a4.html (accessed 20 November 2018). Moreover, Hungarian regulations exclude from the scope of SIP those stateless persons who have deliberately renounced their previous nationality with the intention of obtaining the status of a stateless person (section 78 of Hungarian Foreigners Act). For a more extensive discussion of that category of stateless persons, whom I term the 'voluntarily stateless', see Chapter VII.

3.4. Procedural safeguards

As regards the opportunity to present one's case in person during the status interview, in most countries holding an interview is not mandatory. In Italy, that is not done.[320] In France, it may be done, but the authorities do not have an obligation to do so.[321] In Switzerland, the procedure is written, and an interview may be held only on an exceptional basis.[322] In Luxembourg, an interview may be held according to need.[323] In the United Kingdom, the authorities may refuse to hold an interview in specific situations, such as when 'there is already sufficient evidence that an individual is stateless, is not admissible to any other country and is eligible for leave to remain on this basis.'[324] Only Moldova[325] and Hungary[326] legally guarantee a right to be heard through an interview.

None of the countries charge a fee for applying. However, costs may arise if there is a need to present the required documents in a legally specified form. For example, in Italy, the costs of the procedure are affected by the requirement of authentication of copies before submission.[327] A cost-reducing facilitation available in the Hungarian SIP consists in the option to submit the documents without an accompanying translation or apostille (the standard requirement in any administrative procedure).[328]

Access to unpaid legal assistance in SIP presents a highly diversified landscape. It is guaranteed at every stage of the proceedings in Hungary[329] and Moldova,[330] for example. In some states, such as Spain or the United Kingdom, the availability of legal assistance is restricted to the appellate

320 K. Bianchini, *A comparative…*, p. 61.
321 SIS, France, question IDP.5.b, p. 22.
322 SIS, Switzerland, question IDP.5.b, p. 22.
323 Luxembourgian Administrative Provisions, p. 2.
324 Asylum Policy Instruction…, p. 10, paragraph 3.4.
325 SIS, Moldova, question IDP.5.b, p. 19.
326 Section 77(1) of Hungarian Foreigners Act.
327 K. Bianchini, *A comparative…*, p. 61.
328 K. Bianchini, *A comparative…*, p. 53.
329 SIS, Hungary, question IDP.4.a, p. 21.
330 With regard to Moldova, it is noted that although legal assistance is formally guaranteed by the provisions regulating administrative procedures, in practice the assistance is provided by an NGO while state-provided assistance is only available at the court stage (SIS, Moldova, question IDP.5.a, p. 19).

stage.[331] In Switzerland, in principle, unpaid assistance is guaranteed both at the first instance and on appeal. In practice, however, unpaid assistance is never granted in first-instance proceedings.[332] In France, unpaid assistance may be granted on an exceptional basis. An application for legal assistance is allowed to be made at the appellate stage. In practice, in such cases, the assistance is usually granted.[333] In Italy, unpaid legal assistance is available only in the judicial procedure. A stateless person is legally eligible for such assistance if lawfully in Italy. Nonetheless, court decisions have expanded the availability of this right also to those not lawfully in Italy.[334]

Only some states impose a limit on the duration of the proceedings. For example, in Spain it should not exceed six months.[335] In Hungary, the decision should be reached within sixty days of the day of filing of the application.[336] In Italy, the administrative proceedings should be completed within 350 days, but this may be extended to 895 days if the Ministry of the Interior has to query embassies or the Foreign Ministry for information for the purpose of determining whether an individual is a national of a given state.[337] In Latvia, the proceedings should be completed within three months of submission of the application along with the required documents. For justified reasons, the duration may be extended by a maximum of one month.[338] In Luxembourg, the time window for the decision is three months of the date of filing. This may be extended in exceptional circumstances relating to the complexity of the case.[339] No time-limit is prescribed in the United Kingdom,[340] Switzerland[341] or France[342].

331 K. Bianchini, *A comparative...*, p. 56.
332 SIS, Switzerland, question IDP.5.a, p. 22.
333 SIS, France, question IDP.5.a, question IDP.7.b; p. 27.
334 K. Bianchini, *A comparative...*, p. 65.
335 Article 11 of Spanish Decree on Stateless Persons.
336 SIS, Hungary, question IDP.5.e, p. 25.
337 *Ad-Hoc Query...*, p. 19. The procedures are protracted, and it is noted that some cases have taken almost a decade; see K. Bianchini, *A comparative...*, p. 64.
338 Article 5 of Latvian Act on Stateless Persons.
339 Luxembourgian Administrative Provisions, p. 2.
340 SIS, United Kingdom, question IDP.6.e, p. 27.
341 SIS, Switzerland, question IDP.6.e, p. 25.
342 In practice, contacting diplomatic missions for the purpose of verification of details relating to nationality takes a long time (in several cases it has taken 2–3 years; SIS, France, question IDP.6.e, p. 26.

As regards the situation of stateless persons undergoing SIP during the procedure, only some states give such individuals a permit. Such guarantees exist, for example, in Moldova[343] and Hungary[344]. In Hungary, moreover, the applicant is protected from expulsion pending the outcome of the proceedings.[345] By contrast, for example, in the United Kingdom,[346] Switzerland,[347] France[348] and Luxembourg[349] applicants are not given leave to remain and are not protected from expulsion.

In the majority of countries with statelessness-identification procedures in place, the applicant is issued a reasoned decision in writing in the state's official language. There is usually no administrative appeal. Judicial review most often is available, and, depending on the country, the process can be either reformatory (allowing the modification of the disputed decision) or cassatory (resulting in a reversal and remand if successful).

For example, the reformatory model is followed in proceedings before courts of the first instance in Spain, Hungary and Switzerland. In Spain, the appeals are heard by the *Audiencia Nacional in Madrid* (a criminal and administrative court), and in Hungary by the Regional Court in Budapest (*Fővárosi Törvényszék*), which may enter their own decision on the merits when reversing the administrative ruling, or they can remit the case to the administrative authority for reconsideration. An extraordinary appeal is allowed to the Supreme Court as the court of second instance, though the review is only for the legality of the decision.[350] In Switzerland, the SEM's decision may be reviewed by the Federal Administrative Court (FTA), which decides on the merits of the case, and thereafter to the Federal Supreme Court of Switzerland (TF), which makes decisions on facts only if there is a manifest error (*offensichtlich unrichtige Sachverhaltsfeststellung*).[351]

The cassatory model (reversal and remand) has been adopted, for example, in the United Kingdom and in France. In the United Kingdom, judicial recourse goes to the Administrative Court, which reviews the disputed decision only for legality; if needed, the case may be remanded to the Home Office (for

343 SIS, Moldova, question IDP.6.a, p. 21.
344 SIS, Hungary, question IDP.5.a, p. 23.
345 SIS, Moldova, question IDP.6.b, p. 21.
346 SIS, United Kingdom, question IDP.6.a, p. 25.
347 SIS, Switzerland, question IDP.6.a, p. 23.
348 SIS, France, question IDP.6.a, p. 23.
349 Luxembourgian Administrative Provisions, p. 2.
350 K. Bianchini, *Protecting...*, pp. 153–154.
351 SIS, Switzerland, question IDP.7.a, p. 25.

reconsideration).[352] In France, the applicant may seek review from the administrative tribunal (*tribunal administratif*) of their place of residence and thereafter the Administrative Court of Appeals (*Cour administrative d'appel*) and ultimately the Council of State (*Conseil d'Etat*).[353] French courts only review for legality and do not enter reformatory decisions.[354]

The time-limits for appealing the statelessness decision to the court differ from one state to the next. For example, in Hungary, the window is short: only fifteen days of the day of service of the disputed decision on the recipient.[355] Luxembourg, by contrast, allows three months.[356] As for the costs, not all countries have abolished the appellate fee. Those having abolished it include Hungary[357] and France[358]. In some, such as in the United Kingdom, the fee may be waived upon request.[359]

3.5. Burden and standard of proof

The distribution of the burden of proof and the standard of proof in SIP are usually not defined explicitly in the provisions. Hungary is an exception, with a clearly defined evidentiary standard in place. In principle, the burden of proof is on the applicant. However, at the applicant's motion the deciding authority has a duty to assist with fact-finding through Hungarian diplomatic missions.[360] Moreover, some types of evidence typically considered in the decision-making are mentioned: information provided by specified entities (such the UNHCR, foreign authorities or Hungarian diplomatic missions), nationality law of the state of origin, and such other evidence as may be offered by the applicant.[361]

In other countries, the regulations on this matter do not easily yield to a clear assessment. Nonetheless, comparative studies can supply examples of states taking different approaches to this issue. In some countries, the burden of proof

---

352 An appeal to the Administrative Court requires the permission of the Upper Tribunal; K. Bianchini, *Protecting…*, p. 153.
353 Article L. 812-3 of French Foreigners Code.
354 *Guide de Procedures de l'Ofpra*, p. 42, available at https://ofpra.gouv.fr (accessed 12 November 2018).
355 SIS, Hungary, question IDP.6.a, p. 25.
356 Luxembourgian Administrative Provisions, p. 3.
357 SIS, Hungary, question IDP.6.c, p. 26.
358 SIS, France, question IDP.7.c, p. 27.
359 SIS, United Kingdom, question IDP.7.c, p. 28.
360 Section 79(1) of Hungarian Foreigners Act.
361 SIS, Hungary, question IDP.3.a, p. 18.

is shared between the applicant and the administrative authority, which conforms to the UNHCR's recommendations. For example, this is the case in Moldova.[362] In some countries, in turn, the burden is on the applicant. Such is the case in Switzerland,[363] the United Kingdom[364] and Luxembourg. SEM guidelines, for example, spell it out clearly that statelessness is not presumed but must be proved by the applicant with sufficiently 'precise and serious' evidence. [365] The practice in Latvia is that the burden of proof is on the applicant (e.g. the authority responsible for the determination will not approach the embassies of other states to verify the applicant's nationality).[366]

In the context of the Italian procedure, there is a notable decision of the Court of Cassation that the burden of proof upon the applicant in the judicial statelessness procedure must be reduced. In the Court's view, the judge has a right and at once a duty to seek evidence to fill the gaps in, or supplement, the evidence presented by the applicant. According to the Court, the judge must approach foreign or Italian diplomatic missions for information and documents concerning the applicant's nationality and information about nationality laws and their practical application.[367]

As for the evidentiary standard, it is variously set. Moldovan provisions do not include a precise demarcation, but in practice the standard is seen to be on par with the one applicable to refugee cases (i.e. demonstration of the relevant circumstance to a reasonable degree).[368] In the United Kingdom[369] and in France,[370] the evidentiary standard is higher than in proceedings for international protection. Switzerland, by contrast, has no special rules governing the evidentiary standard in such cases, and — in line with the general principles of administrative procedure — the applicant has to prove their claim of statelessness.[371]

---

362 SIS, Moldova, question IDP.4.a, p. 17.
363 SIS, Switzerland, question IDP.4.a, p. 19.
364 *Asylum Policy Instruction...*, paragraph 4.2, p. 11.
365 Luxembourgian Administrative Provisions, p. 2.
366 *Ad-hoc Query…*, p. 21.
367 Italian Court of Cassation, case no. 4262, judgment of 3 April 2015, cited by K. Bianchini, *A comparative…*, p. 62.
368 SIS, Moldova, question IDP.4.b, p. 18.
369 SIS, United Kingdom, question IDP.3.b, p. 21.
370 SIS, France, question IDP.4.b, p. 20.
371 SIS, Switzerland, question IDP.3.b, p. 20.

As can be seen from the above, the provisions governing the procedures relating to statelessness determinations in different states do not present a uniform model in any degree. On the contrary, they paint a diverse picture containing only certain types or patterns of regulatory frameworks, which are either more widely followed or less.

4. The status of statelessness

4.1. The 1954 Convention relating to the Status of Stateless Persons

The 1954 Convention does not specify the legal status to be conferred on an individual whose statelessness has been established. In particular, it does not specify that such an individual should be given a residence permit. Without that, the matter of the stabilization of residence, which is one of the most crucial issues from the perspective of a stateless person, is not resolved. The individual continues to face a constant threat without having the guarantee of safe residence in any state whatsoever. This is a significant weakness of the 1954 Convention.

The matter of the status that should be given to the stateless person at the end of SDP is addressed by the UNHCR Handbook. The Handbook argues that individuals having successfully completed SDP should be regarded not only as 'lawfully in' the country but also as meeting the qualified requirements of residence opening access to the broadest range of rights contemplated by the 1954 Convention (this means persons who are 'lawfully in' and have 'habitual residence').

The UNHCR recommends that, in principle, persons found to be stateless through SDP be given a residence permit valid for at least two years, with a preference for longer permits (such as five years). The permit should be renewable and should lead to the option of entering a facilitated naturalization procedure in the future (Article 32 of the 1954 Convention).[372]

4.2. Regulatory frameworks in selected domestic jurisdictions

Domestic regulations of different states define the status of a stateless person differently. It is always a special status in the sense that its acquisition opens access to an 'encoded bundle of rights and obligations'.[373] However, in the vast majority

---

372 UNHCR Handbook, paragraphs 147–148.

373 Concerning the special status see J. Jagielski, P. Dąbrowski, *Specjalny status prawny* [in:] R. Hauser, Z. Niewiadomski, A. Wróbel (eds.), *System Prawa Administracyjnego*, vol. 7, *Prawo administracyjne materialne*, Warszawa 2017, p. 521.

of states, the determination of statelessness and the status of a stateless person do not directly entail the acquisition of rights. A very special right to which in many states the access is opened by obtaining the status of a stateless person is the right to be issued a travel document. Such a document is issued automatically in, for example, Hungary,[374] Latvia,[375] Hungary,[376] Moldova[377] or Spain[378]. There are, however, states in which travel documents require a separate application. Such is the case, for example, in France, where the travel document is issued upon request, following verification that the applicant does not present a threat to the security of the state.[379]

By contrast, access to the majority of the rights is usually not direct but indirect. An individual holding the status of a stateless person enters the pool of individuals eligible for a permit, and the latter is what opens the way to specific rights. The rights that should be linked to the determination of the status of a stateless person, according to the UNHCR guidelines, are those reserved to individuals who are 'lawfully staying' or 'habitually resident'. The most important among such rights are the right to work (Article 17 of the 1954 Convention), the right of access to publicly financed housing services (Article 21 of the 1954 Convention), the right of access to social assistance and security (Articles 23–24 of the 1954 Convention) and the right to be issued a travel document (Article 28 of the 1954 Convention).

Examples of states issuing an automatic residence permit to an individual recognized as a stateless person include Spain[380] and Moldova[381]. Moreover, those states' regulations provide that the right of permanent residence is to be granted immediately. In Spain, a stateless person is issued a special document confirming their rights — a stateless person's card (*tarjeta acreditativa del reconocimento de apatrida*).[382]

In those states in which a separate application must be made for a residence permit, the regulations usually specify additional requirements to be met before the permit may be granted. For example, in the United Kingdom, in order to be

---

374 SIS, Hungary, question IDP.7.d, p. 28.
375 *Ad-hoc Query…*, p. 22.
376 *Statelessness in the EU*, p. 9.
377 SIS, Moldova, question IDP.8.d, p. 25.
378 Article 13(2) of Spanish Decree on Stateless Persons.
379 SIS, France, question IDP.8.d, p. 30.
380 Article 13(1) of Spanish Decree on Stateless Persons.
381 SIS, Moldova, question IDP.8.b, p. 24.
382 *Statelessness in the EU*, p. 9.

given leave to remain, an individual holding the status of a stateless person must satisfy regulatory conditions such as not presenting a threat to the national security or to the public order.[383] In France, the prefect[384] may withhold the permit from an individual deemed to present a threat to the public order. In Switzerland, an individual holding the status of a stateless person will not be given a permit (which falls within the purview of the cantonal authorities)[385] if convicted of a criminal offence and sentenced to a long prison term or if presenting a threat to public security, public or internal order or external security. Other circumstances posing a bar to the issuance of a residence permit have also been identified in certain states. For example, in the United Kingdom, the authorities verify that the individual cannot be returned to their previous state of residence or any other state, and in Switzerland a person whose expulsion from Swiss territory has been made impossible due to their own fault will not be issued a permit.

The durations for which residence permits are granted vary greatly, from indefinite (the aforementioned Moldova and Spain) to temporary, initially very short (Switzerland, France) or somewhat longer (Italy: two years[386]; United Kingdom: three months; Hungary: three years[387]; Latvia: five years[388]). In all states envisaging timed permits, there is always the option to renew and eventually apply for permanent residence, though that is usually conditional upon meeting some additional requirements.

The accessibility of the rights linked to the various categories of residence permits presents a varied picture. Access to the labour market is guaranteed, for example, in Spain,[389] the United Kingdom,[390] Italy,[391] Moldova,[392] France,[393] Switzerland[394] and Latvia.[395] Access to all tiers of education is guaranteed in such

383 Articles 403(c) and 404 of British Immigration Rules.
384 The competent authority for permits is not the OFPRA but the territorial representatives of the government administration, i.e. prefects.
385 The competent authority to grant leave to remain is not the SEM but the cantonal authorities.
386 *Ad-hoc Query*..., p. 20.
387 G. Gyulai, *Statelessness*..., p. 31.
388 *Ad-Hoc Query*..., p. 21.
389 Article 13 of Spanish Decree on Stateless Persons.
390 SIS, United Kingdom, question IDP.8.g, p. 32.
391 *Statelessness in the EU*, p. 10.
392 SIS, Moldova, question IDP.8.g, p. 26.
393 SIS, France, question IDP.8.g, p. 31.
394 SIS, Switzerland, question IDP.8.g, p. 29.
395 *Statelessness in the EU*, p. 10.

countries as the United Kingdom,[396] Moldova,[397] France,[398] Hungary[399] and Italy[400]. Health-care and social assistance are available in Moldova, Switzerland, France and Italy.[401] Some states impose certain special restrictions on access to health-care and social assistance. For example, in the United Kingdom, persons with statelessness status can access the majority of social and health-care benefits but not public housing assistance.[402] In Hungary, access to social assistance and health-care is conditional on having employment.[403]

5. Conclusions

The effective protection of stateless persons requires domestic jurisdictions to adopt procedures for the identification of such individuals. States have broad leeway to define the shape to be taken by such procedures. Consequently, the regulatory frameworks differ greatly from one state to the next. According to the UNCHR's guidelines, individuals who are formally the nationals of a state may still be deemed to be stateless persons where specific conduct (actions or omissions) of the administrative authorities of the relevant state can be viewed as constituting evidence of not regarding such an individual as a national of the state (e.g. no right of entry and residence).

The 1954 Convention allows for the use of a gradual scale of rights accorded to stateless persons. Analysis of the provisions of the Convention allows the discernment of specific categories of stateless persons whose rights can be distinguished on a gradual scale depending on the nature and length of their stay in the territory. The closer the stateless person's ties to the state, the more rights the stateless person will have. In consequence, only some of the rights must be guaranteed to all categories of stateless persons, while the majority are prescribed for those stateless persons who are in the state lawfully. Such a flexible approach to the regulation of the status of a stateless person is not found in the regulatory frameworks of states having established statelessness-identification procedures.

---

396 The accessibility of the higher tier of education, however, is limited by the lack of access to student finance. SIS, United Kingdom, questions IDP.8 h, i; p. 33.

397 SIS, Moldova, question IDP.8.h, i; pp. 26– 27.

398 SIS, France, questions IDP.8.h, i; p. 32.

399 SIS, Hungary, questions IDP.7.h and i; p. 30.

400 *Statelessness in the EU*, p. 10.

401 *Statelessness in the EU*, p. 10.

402 SIS, United Kingdom, question IDP.8.j, p. 34.

403 SIS, Hungary, question IDP.7.j, p. 30.

In other words, the states do not take advantage of the option to assign status categories reflecting the internal diversification within the broader group of stateless persons. Moreover, the 1954 Convention enables the exclusion of certain specific categories of stateless persons from protection. An exclusion clause is provided in Article 1(2), whereby e.g. persons undeserving of protection on account of having committed certain criminal offences or being guilty of conduct incompatible with the goals and principles of the United Nations cannot receive protection. As I have demonstrated, the majority of states having established statelessness-identification procedures require applications to be made for residence permits and, at that stage, verify additional conditions to be met by the applicants, such as not presenting a threat to national security.

Part II

Chapter V The Category of 'Women' in the Law of Statelessness

In the past, women were a numerous category of stateless persons, and their statelessness had very specific causes (section 1). The problem of statelessness among women prompted the advent of the first instruments adopted with a view to the prevention of statelessness in international law, translating into concrete regulatory frameworks in domestic jurisdictions (section 2). From this perspective, the identification of women as a distinct category of stateless persons is primarily of historical significance. It is, therefore, a justified question to what extent it makes sense to maintain such a distinction in modern times and whether there exist any specific regulatory problems relating to statelessness reduction and protection of stateless persons with regard to women (section 3).

1. Causes of statelessness in women

1.1. Introductory remarks

Many women were affected by statelessness in the first half of the 20th century. As noted by legal historian L. Kerber, the majority of individual cases of statelessness in the United States of America during the interwar period were women.[404] As she puts it: 'Gender has, in fact, been a key factor in the history of statelessness.'[405]

The reason for statelessness was usually the loss of original nationality upon marriage in connection with conflicts of laws. Until the First World War, the nationality laws of almost all countries of the world viewed a married woman's nationality as being dependent on that of her husband (the principle of dependent nationality).[406] That was consistent with the idea — accepted by the

404 Concerning the distinction between individual and mass statelessness see Chapter I.

405 L.K. Kerber, *Toward a history of statelessness in America*, 57(3) American Quarterly Sept. 2005, p. 729.

406 It will be expedient to note that this practice first occurred when, in 1804, the French Civil Code made the woman's nationality dependent on that of her husband, which provided the model followed by the majority of European and Latin American States; Shanks v. Dupont 28 U.S. 242 (1830) https://supreme.justia.com/cases/federal/us/28/242/case.html (accessed 4 January 2023). Before that time, for example in English and American common law, marriage had no bearing on a woman's nationality. According to W. Samore, citing C. Seckler-Hudson: '(…) the motive for this practice was not the

majority of states at the time — of unity of nationality in a family, according to which all family members should have the same nationality, defined by that of the man. Women's nationality thus 'followed' that of their foreign husbands, and the women themselves were thus excluded from their national communities of origin. In a model view, the principle of 'dependent nationality' presented as follows: (1) a woman marrying a foreigner automatically acquired her husband's nationality and lost her original nationality; (2) if the husband acquired a nationality by naturalization during the marriage, the woman also acquired it; if he lost his nationality during the marriage, the woman also lost that nationality; (3) upon divorce, the woman lost the nationality acquired by marriage and automatically reverted to her original nationality (previously forfeited by marriage to a foreigner).

The majority of states adhered to the concept of 'dependent' nationality of a woman until the day of the Second World War, though infrequent examples of states adopting the principle of 'independence' ('autonomy') of a woman's nationality from her husband's existed already in the interwar period.[407] And precisely the conflict of these two principles — the principle of 'dependent nationality' prevailing in the majority of states versus the rarer principle of 'autonomous nationality' — constituted a frequent cause of statelessness in women. In the 30s of the 20th century, the frequency of conflicts increased due to more and more states joining the independent-nationality camp,[408] leading to the statelessness of a growing number of women.[409]

As noted above, as a result of a conflict of laws a woman could lose her nationality firstly upon marriage (section 1.2), secondly during the marriage (section 1.3), and thirdly due to the termination of the marriage by divorce or death of the spouse (section 1.4).

---

independence of women's citizenship, but the doctrine of indissoluble allegiance', W. Samore, *Statelessness as a consequence of the conflict of nationality laws*, 45(3) American Journal of International Law 1951, p. 483. For a more extensive discussion of the principle of indissoluble allegiance, see D. Pudzianowska, *Obywatelstwo…*, p. 36.

407 Examples of states adopting the principle of independence of a woman's nationality in a family included the USA (1922) and the USSR (1918).

408 B. Studer, K. Sturge, *Citizenship as contingent national belonging. Married women and foreigners in twentieth-century Switzerland*, 13(3) Gender & History 2001, p. 629.

409 K. Knop, Ch. Chinkin, *Final report on women's equality and nationality in international law*, Committee on Feminism and International Law, International Law Association, London Conference 2000, p. 29.

1.2. Women's statelessness upon marriage

Women became stateless when the legislation of their original state of nationality prescribed its loss by marriage to a foreigner and simultaneously the new husband's state did not automatically confer its nationality on the wife of a citizen upon marriage. Cases of statelessness ensued where one of the states followed the principle that marriage should not affect the spouses' respective nationalities and the other state foresaw the automatic loss of nationality upon marriage. At the beginning of the 50s of the 20th century, the majority of states adhered to the principle of unity of nationality in family, resulting in the unconditional loss of nationality by women marrying foreigners. Examples include: Bolivia, Egypt, Germany, Hungary, India, Iran, Iraq, Ireland, New Zealand, Peru, Spain and Switzerland.[410] Examples of states not conferring nationality on a foreign woman marrying a citizen during that period include: Argentina, Australia, Bulgaria, Brazil, Canada, Chile, Czechoslovakia, Guatemala, Mexico, United Kingdom, USA and USSR.[411]

In some cases the acquisition of nationality by the spouse was made conditional on meeting specific requirements. If the woman did not meet such requirements, then — by forfeiting her original nationality upon marriage — she became stateless. For example, in Greece a foreign woman marrying a Greek man acquired her husband's nationality only where the marriage was performed in the Orthodox Church. That was required for the validity of the marriage under Greek law.[412] In Liberia, a foreign wife had to be black in order to acquire the country's nationality by marriage.[413]

Sometimes, the automatic loss of nationality was only applicable to specific situations. For example, with the adoption by the US of so-called Cable Act of 1922, the automatic loss of a woman's citizenship upon marriage to a foreigner was abolished but only where the foreign husband satisfied the criteria for naturalization. Before the passage of the act, the principle of dependent nationality applied to all women. After the amendments introduced by the Cable Act, women no longer lost their nationality by marrying those foreigners who were eligible for naturalization. Thus, only women whose husbands were ineligible for naturalization continued to lose their nationality by marrying a foreigner. Those deemed ineligible for naturalization

410 W. Samore, *Statelessness…*, p. 484.

411 W. Samore, *Statelessness…*, p. 484. Historian B. Studer states that in 1933 there were 22 states not automatically conferring nationality on a foreign woman upon marriage to a national; B. Studer, K. Sturge, *Citizenship…*, p. 629.

412 C. Seckler-Hudson, *Statelessness…*, p. 41.

413 W. Samore, *Statelessness…*, p. 485.

were primarily individuals of specific racial origin (initially Chinese, but more groups were added later, such as South Asians (Indians) in 1923 and Filipinos in 1925) but also men having refused to defend the country.[414]

Statelessness could also result from marrying a man who did not have the nationality of any state. This problem largely applied to foreign women marrying (or having married) German Jews after the promulgation of a Third-Reich law depriving Jews of German nationality. B. Studer describes the case of former Swiss citizen Irma Bornheim, having become a stateless person by marrying a German Jew during the war. In 1942, after the borders of Switzerland were closed, she petitioned the President of Switzerland for the reinstatement of her Swiss nationality. However, because her husband had been declared missing, she was unable to meet the necessary requirement that was the termination of her marriage. After a year of administrative formalities, she was allowed to enter her original country as a refugee.[415]

1.3. Women's statelessness during marriage

Many states' laws extended the effect of a change of the husband's nationality during the marriage onto his wife. States adhering to this rule included Hungary, Iraq, Spain and Switzerland. Poland, too, had such provisions prior to the adoption of the Act of 8 January 1951 on Polish Citizenship.[416] This was consistent with the principle of 'dependent nationality'. The statelessness of women arose in situations when husbands hailing originally from one of such states obtained the nationality of a state that did not automatically confer their nationality on a citizen's wife (e.g. Argentina, Australia, Belgium, Brazil, Bulgaria, Canada, France, Romania and Sweden) or conferred it only if certain additional conditions were met (e.g. in Norway and Finland residence in the state's territory was required).[417]

In many cases, women became stateless as a result of their husbands' loss of nationality without even being aware of the fact.[418] This is illustrated by the case of Mary K., a natural-born US citizen who in 1914 married a US citizen of Indian origin, Taraknath Das. He had been naturalized before the marriage. However, in

414 L. Volpp, *Divesting citizenship. On Asian American history and the loss of citizenship through marriage*, 53(2) UCLA Law Review 2005, p. 433.

415 B. Studer, K. Sturge, *Citizenship...*, p. 623.

416 Dz.U.4.25.

417 W. Samore, *Statelessness...*, pp. 485–486.

418 K. Knop, Ch. Chinkin, *Remembering Chrystal MacMillan: Women's Equality and Nationality in International Law*, 22(4) Michigan Journal of International Law 2001, p. 545.

1923, the Supreme Court declared his naturalization null and void due to South Asians being deemed 'racially ineligible for citizenship' and thus incapable of naturalization.[419] When the woman applied for a US passport, she was informed that she had forfeited her US citizenship due to her husband's loss of it and that she was a stateless person.[420]

An interesting example of the statelessness of women arising from a conflict of laws already during the marriage is provided by a historical conflict of Soviet and Spanish legislation. Decree of the Council of State no. 142/42, of 30 August 1956, specified the modes of loss of Soviet nationality by Spanish nationals residing in the USSR in 1936–1940 who had left its territory to settle down in Spain. Such persons lost their Soviet nationality upon crossing the Soviet border. Spanish law, in turn, held the wife's nationality to be 'dependent' on the husband's. Thus, if a woman of Spanish origin migrated out of the USSR and her Soviet husband renounced Soviet nationality for himself by migrating with her, she too became stateless.[421]

1.4. Women's statelessness resulting from the termination of marriage

A woman who had previously obtained her husband's nationality, forfeiting her own nationality of origin, could become a stateless person by divorce. Those were not frequent cases, because the majority of states adhering to the principle of unity of nationality in a family allowed a woman who had become their national by marriage to retain her nationality upon divorce. Exceptions included Thailand and the Vatican, where the woman automatically lost nationality upon the dissolution of her marriage. In some states, the law prescribed that nationality was to be lost upon divorce on condition that the woman was residing abroad when it occurred.[422]

The statelessness of women could also result from divergent rulings on the validity of her marriage. That happened when, on the one hand, her original

419 United States v. Thind, 261 U.S. 204 (1923).

420 M.K. Das, *A woman without a country*, 123 The Nation 1926, cited after: L. Volpp, *Divesting…*, p. 435. The only way for her to recover her US citizenship was by terminating the marriage, which is what the Department of State advised her to do; C.L. Bredbenner, *A nationality of her own. Women, marriage, and the law of citizenship*, Berkeley 1998, p. 135.

421 G. Ginsburgs, *The Citizenship law of the USSR*, Hague–Boston 1983, p. 169.

422 W. Samore, *Statelessness…*, p. 488.

state of nationality recognized the validity of her marriage with the resulting loss of her original nationality, and on the other hand her husband's state viewed the marriage as a nullity (a sham marriage) and declined to recognize the woman's acquisition of nationality through that marriage.[423]

2. Prevention of statelessness in women

2.1. Prevention of women's statelessness on the international level

As discussed above, the conflict between the principle of the woman's 'dependent nationality' followed by almost all states before the First World War and the rarer principle of 'autonomous' nationality resulted in cases of statelessness. As P. Spiro observes, preventing that result was the main goal of the international efforts undertaken for the codification of nationality in the 20s of the 20th century.[424]

The problem of statelessness of married women was largely regarded as a technical issue created by a conflict of laws. From the very beginning, however, it had also been put in the perspective of the need for the adoption of a new principle in international law — the principle of the 'independent nationality' of women. The argument was made that the universal adoption of such a principle would eliminate the problem of statelessness of married women arising from a conflict of laws and would simultaneously be an expression of the equality of men and women. The conclusions of the 31st Conference of the International Law Commission in Buenos Aires in 1922 asserted: '(...) it would be desirable to fix uniformly by treaty the nationality of married women, reserving to a married women, as far as possible, the right to choose her own nationality.'[425] However, the 33rd Conference saw the adoption of a draft offering protection from statelessness but without the introduction of the principle of 'autonomous nationality'.[426] In 1925, the Committee of Experts for the Progressive Codification of International Law appointed by the League of Nations created a subcommittee to deal with problems of nationality in relation to a conflict of laws.[427] The rapporteur was a Polish jurist, Szymon Rundstein. In order to find a solution to

423 United Nations, *A Study of Statelessness...*, p. 67.
424 P.J. Spiro, *A new international law of citizenship*, 105(4) The American Journal of International Law 2011, pp. 694–746, 712.
425 International Law Association, 31st Conference report (1922), p. 257.
426 International Law Association, 33rd Conference report (1924), p. 24.
427 Sub-Committee to address questions relating to legal conflicts of nationality.

the increasing number of conflicts caused by the 'reforms lately introduced in the area of married women's nationality', the subcommittee proposed a working draft of a convention aimed to solve the problem of the statelessness of a woman having lost her nationality upon marriage and desiring to revert to it upon the dissolution of that marriage.[428] The proposal to adopt such provisions was subsequently the starting point for the discussions on solutions to prevent the statelessness of women held during the codification conference at The Hague in 1930.

The outcome of the Conference was the adoption of the Hague Convention on Certain Questions Relating to the Conflict of Nationality Law (1930) as the first treaty devised to counteract the statelessness of women. Two articles of the Convention (8 and 9) were devised for the purpose of preventing it. Article 8 stipulated: 'If the national law of the wife causes her to lose her nationality on marriage with a foreigner, this consequence shall be conditional on her acquiring the nationality of the husband.' Article 9, in turn: 'If the national law of the wife causes her to lose her nationality upon a change in the nationality of her husband occurring during marriage, this consequence shall be conditional on her acquiring her husband's new nationality.' In both cases — marrying and change of nationality during marriage — the woman's loss of nationality was made conditional on her acquisition of her husband's nationality.

The 1930 Hague Convention addressed the problem of nationality of women as a legal technicality arising from a conflict of nationality laws. The preamble states: 'it is in the general interest of the international community to secure that all its members should recognise that every person should have a nationality.' From the perspective of solutions to statelessness, adherence the principle of 'dependent nationality' was equally as satisfactory as adoption of the principle of 'autonomous nationality', because problems arose only where the rules followed by the states diverged.[429]

The solutions devised to prevent the statelessness of women were thus not necessarily consistent with the principle of equality of women's rights in respect of nationality. Those of the equal-rights camp, therefore, were critical of the provisions, which they decried as an attempt to prevent statelessness 'at the expense

---

428 See League of Nations Archives, R1290, 19/47029, CPD 120, League of Nations, Expert Committee for the Gradual Codification of International Law, sub-committee reports, 12 November 1925 and 10 December 1925, CPD 120 (annex), cited after: L. Guerry, *Married women's nationality in the international context (1918–1935)*, 1(43) Clio. Women, Gender, History 2016, p. 79.

429 K. Knop, Ch. Chinkin, *Remembering...*, p. 31.

(…) of the woman', suggesting the existence of an 'obsession' with the prevention of statelessness.[430] US delegates campaigned for the adoption of the principle of 'autonomous nationality' of a married woman. As a result, the USA did not sign the 1930 Hague Convention, which was deemed to be insufficiently progressive for having failed to accommodate calls for equality.[431] However, as M.O. Hudson observed, the adoption of the principle of 'independent nationality': '(…) would constitute a reform which may be desirable in the national laws of various states. Yet the principle cannot serve as a guide for international legislation the very object of which is to resolve conflicts resulting from differences in national laws. If all national laws were based on a single principle, such legislation would be unnecessary. In this field, it seems impossible to achieve by international action a reform in national legislations for which many peoples are not prepared.'[432]

Another convention important to the prevention of statelessness was the 1957 Convention on the Nationality of Married Women, which did introduce the principle of autonomous (independent) nationality of women. Its Article 1 provides: 'Each Contracting State agrees that neither the celebration nor the dissolution of a marriage between one of its nationals and an alien, nor the change of nationality by the husband during marriage, shall automatically affect the nationality of the wife.' The principal goal was not to prevent statelessness but to bring the equality of men and women with regard to nationality. It was decided that the prevention of statelessness would be, in a way, a side-effect of the states' adoption of the principle of the woman's independent nationality rather than merely a solution to a conflict of laws. Thus, the driving force of the change was the principle of equal treatment, rather than the right to nationality formulated in the UDHR.[433]

---

430 In reference to Article 9 of the 1930 Hague Convention, J.B. Scott wrote: '(…) *obsessed with the idea of obviating statelessness, at the expense, be it said, of the woman, the wife is not to lose her original nationality, unless by the law of the husband's new state she acquires his new nationality at one and the same time*' — J.B. Scott, *Unprogressive Codification of Nationality at The Hague*, 18 Women Lawyers' Journal 1930, p. 39.

431 L. Guerry, *Married...*, p. 83; N.F. Cott, *Marriage and women's citizenship in the United States, 1830–1934*, 103(5) The American Historical Review" 1998, p. 1470.

432 M.O. Hudson, *The Hague Convention of 1930 and the nationality of women*, 27(1) The American Journal of International Law" 1933, p. 121. As a marginal note, Article 10 of the 1930 Hague Convention expresses the concept of independent nationality of a married woman without having the prevention of statelessness as its goal. It provides that the naturalization of the husband during the marriage does not entail the naturalization of the wife, unless by her consent.

433 P.J. Spiro, *A new international…*, p. 714.

It would seem that from this point onward we are dealing with an evolution inscribing the statelessness of married women in the topic range of the equality of the sexes. However, the next Convention specifically addressing statelessness, i.e. the 1961 Convention, does not seem to embrace such a perspective. Its Article 5(1) provides: 'If the law of a Contracting State entails loss of nationality as a consequence of any change in the personal status of a person such as marriage, termination of marriage (emphasis added), legitimation, recognition or adoption, such loss shall be conditional upon possession or acquisition of another nationality.' And Article 6: 'If the law of a Contracting State provides for loss of its nationality by a person's spouse or children as a consequence of that person losing or being deprived of that nationality, such loss shall be conditional upon their possession or acquisition of another nationality.' It is especially noteworthy how these norms prohibit the woman's nationality from 'following' that of her husband not in all cases but only in those involving statelessness.

Ultimately, the year 1979 saw the adoption of CEDAW, which contains a provision dealing specifically with the nationality of women. Article 9(1): 'States Parties shall grant women equal rights with men (emphasis added) to acquire, change or retain their nationality. They shall ensure in particular that neither marriage to an alien nor change of nationality by the husband during marriage shall automatically change the nationality of the wife, render her stateless or force upon her the nationality of the husband.' From the perspective of topic of our discussion, it is important that this provision reiterates the principle of Article 1 of the 1957 Convention. At the same time, it addresses statelessness directly, which the 1957 Convention does not.

At present, the independence of a woman's nationality from that of her husband's is commonly accepted in Europe, although there are still states maintaining reservations against Article 9(1) CEDAW. Interestingly, some states cite the counteraction of statelessness as the reason for doing so. For example, according to Turkey's declaration, Article 9(1) CEDAW is not incompatible with Turkish nationality law because the intention of the provisions regulating the acquisition of nationality by marriage is the prevention of statelessness.[434]

The approach taken to the statelessness of women has thus evolved over time. Eventually, it was decided that the counteraction of the statelessness of women could not be kept separate from the pursuit of the principle of equal rights. In that way, matters relating to the statelessness of women were integrated into the broader area of human rights that is the equality of men and women. At present,

434 K. Knop, Ch. Chinkin, *Remembering…*, p. 31.

one could venture the conclusion there exists an obligation to introduce provisions that are not discriminatory to women and do not lead to their becoming stateless persons.[435] In the 20s and 30s of the 20th century, the adoption of any such solution would have been impossible due to the lack of a consensus among the states on the matter.

Simultaneously, time has shown the low effectiveness of treaties aimed strictly to counteract the statelessness of women. Over many years, both the 1930 Convention and the 1961 Convention had achieved a low number of ratifications, which largely frustrated their effectiveness.[436] Things became different with the 1957 Convention and with CEDAW, which the states were more eager to adopt from the very onset. As I will expound below, these conventions have popularized the independent-nationality standard across domestic jurisdictions, translating into reduction of statelessness by elimination of conflicts of rules through the broader adoption of one of the competing principles.

2.2. Prevention of women's statelessness in domestic jurisdictions

After the Second World War, the vast majority of European states adopted the principle of independent nationality of women. This was connected with the formation of the aforementioned consensus in the international forum as to the necessity of the introduction of such a rule. It will be expedient to note, nonetheless, that some European states had enacted safeguards against the statelessness of women already before the Hague Convention of 1930. For example, in France, Napoleon's Code was amended in 1889 so that a woman only lost her French nationality upon marrying a foreigner whose state of nationality automatically made her a national by that marriage. Switzerland, in turn, developed its own safeguards through court decisions. In 1910, the Federal Court (relying on a precedent from 1798) found that in the situation of potential stateless a woman ought to be able to retain her Swiss nationality.[437] The Act of 20 January 1920 on the Citizenship of the Polish State, too, protected female nationals who

435 R. Govil, A. Edwards, *Women, nationality and statelessness* [in:] A. Edwards and L. van Waas (eds.), *Nationality and Statelessness under International Law*, Cambridge 2014, p. 179.

436 R. Govil, A. Edwards, *Women...*, p. 188.

437 Decisions of the Swiss federal court (BGE) 36, I, pp. 225–227, cited after: B. Studer, K. Sturge, *Citizenship...*, pp. 629–630.

were marrying foreigners from statelessness. Such women did not lose their Polish nationality automatically but only upon the acquisition of a foreign one.[438]

By contrast, some states introduced mechanisms for the prevention of statelessness of women at a much later time — the 70s of the 20th century. For example, in Italy, it had to wait until 1975.[439] Among other reasons, the amendment was a necessary adaptation of the statutory law to the Italian Constitutional Court's judgment no. 87, of 9 April 1975, in which the loss of nationality by a woman upon marriage was held to be a violation of Article 3 of the Constitution of Italy.[440] Another late adopter was Liechtenstein, in 1974. In the words of M.S. D'Elia: 'A first step towards achieving formal equivalence on citizenship for Liechtenstein women was taken in 1974, with the implementation of the «Liechtensteinerin bleiben» proposal («remain a Liechtenstein citizen» (as a woman)) (…). This removed the automatic loss of Liechtenstein citizenship for women marrying a foreigner – who could now remain Liechtenstein citizens.'[441]

At present, comparative studies[442] show that there are no more states in Europe retaining marriage to a foreigner or dissolution of marriage as a cause of loss of nationality. Moreover, no European state's legal provisions continue to extend the loss of nationality onto one's spouse.[443] Bulgaria is an exception, with its

---

438 There was no express language to such effect, but the conclusion could be drawn from how the conditions for the loss of Polish nationality were defined in Article 11 of the Act. As a marginal note, the progressive solution in the Polish statute is owed to the aforementioned S. Rundstein (the author of the idea and one of the drafters of the provisions preventing the statelessness of women in the Hague Convention of 1930), who served as one of the drafters of the Act.

439 G. Zincone, M. Basili, *Country report Italy*, Country Report, RSCAS/EUDO-CIT-CR 2010/35, p. 9.

440 Article 3 (*in principio*) of the Italian Constitution provides: 'All citizens have equal social dignity and are equal before the law, without distinction of sex, race, language, religion, political opinion, personal and social conditions'— see translation at: https://www.constituteproject.org/constitution/Italy_2020?lang=en (accessed 4 January 2023).

441 Amendment by Act of 4 January 1934 on the Acquisition and Loss of Citizenship; reissued in 1960; see M. Sochin D'Elia, *Country report: Lichtenstein*, RSCAS/EUDO-CIT-CR 2013/29, p. 9.

442 Data from GLOBALCIT (2017), *Modes of Loss*.

443 In Poland, the changes were introduced in 1951. The principle was adopted that a change in the nationality of a spouse should not trigger the same change in the other spouse. It was stipulated that marriage to a non-citizen would have no bearing on the spouses' respective nationalities.

nationality law containing a provision for the denaturalization of an individual having acquired nationality on the basis of the same false or concealed information or facts as their spouse.[444]

Nowadays, provisions of similar type are almost nowhere to be found in any other parts of the world, either. In the Americas, for example, the USA and Belize are the sole exceptions. Under Belizean law, a married person forfeits nationality when their spouse does. The same situation also exists in the USA, but the difference is that the effect depends on the grounds on which the spouse's loss of nationality occurs (only naturalization fraud or specific criminal offences).[445] Neither in the USA nor in Belize is there any regulatory safeguard against statelessness resulting from such cases. In this scope, the two countries' regulations are incompatible with CEDAW and — which is of particular interest to our discussion — can be the source of statelessness of women.

3. Current issues relating to the prevention of women's statelessness and protection of stateless women

The primary intention behind designating stateless women as a separate category of stateless persons is to highlight the specific causes of their statelessness, successfully eliminated through the universal adoption of regulations tailored to meet the problem in domestic jurisdictions. It is also worth examining whether there may be other, more contemporary bases for distinguishing stateless women as a category of stateless persons, in a search for solutions providing a more adequate response to their situation.

3.1. Preventing statelessness

At present, the statelessness of women continues to arise for a variety of reasons, usually affecting men in an equal degree (e.g. renunciation or deprivation of nationality) rather than stemming from discriminatory legislation. Some writers observe, however, that certain gaps in regulatory frameworks failing to envisage different solutions for women in pursuance of the principle of equality may have a disproportionate impact on women. A rather spectacular example comes from outside of the European context and will be discussed below in order to provide

444 GLOBALCIT (2017), *Modes of Loss*, Bulgaria, mode L12.

445 O.W. Vonk, *Nationality law in the western hemisphere. A study on grounds for acquisition and loss of citizenship in the Americas and the Caribbean*, Leiden–Boston 2015, p. 398.

illustration for the claim that certain solutions can have a disproportionate effect on the situation of women.

As discussed in Chapter III, statelessness can result from renunciation of nationality even in those states in which the law permits the loss of nationality only if the renouncing individual already has or is going to acquire the nationality of a different state. The problem is that numerous states do not make the loss of their nationality conditional on the successful acquisition of another.[446] Such regulations were at the root of the statelessness of several thousand women of Vietnamese origin having renounced their Vietnamese nationality in order to obtain that of their foreign spouse's state. Between 1995 and 2002, more than 55 thousand Vietnamese women married foreigners, usually older than themselves, mostly impecunious labourers from Taiwan and South Korea (but also Hong Kong and Singapore) who could not find a partner in their country of origin or afford expensive wedding celebrations. In the majority of cases, the women entering such marriages were motivated by economic reasons. Problems relating to the loss of nationality began to occur when they attempted to obtain the nationality of their new spouse's country of origin. In Taiwan, renouncing Vietnamese nationality was a precondition for naturalization. Thus, if the spouses separated or divorced before the naturalization could be obtained but already after the woman's renunciation of her original nationality, she would become a stateless person. According to government data, approximately three thousand women became stateless in this manner.[447] New nationality legislation of 2008[448] introduced a special solution for this category of individuals, permitting their reintegration.[449]

Furthermore, the introduction of mechanisms to prevent the statelessness of women addressed causes relating to the formal loss of nationality. In the context of the problems discussed more extensively in Chapter II, which deals with the definition of a stateless person, it should be noted that where a broad interpretation of the definition is used, SIP may lead to conferring recognition as stateless persons on women having fallen victim of human trafficking and been deprived of their identity documents, leaving them with no way of proving their

446 See Chapter III, section 1.

447 K. McKinsey, *Lose a Husband, Lose a Country*, 147(3) Refugees Magazine 2007, pp. 26–27; R. Govil, A. Edwards, *Women...*, p. 179.

448 Law on Vietnamese Nationality, No. 24/2008/QH-12 (13 November 2008).

449 Report on Citizenship Law: Vietnam, RSCAS/GLOBALCIT-CR 2017/13, September 2017, pp. 15–16; Article 23(f) of the Act on Vietnamese Citizenship.

nationality according to the host state's rules for the identification of stateless persons. In this sense, it is possibly to identify such characteristic causes of statelessness as human trafficking — a criminal enterprise that predominately targets women.[450]

3.2. Reducing statelessness

R. Govil and A. Edwards observe that the use of identical naturalization procedures for men and women can result in the discrimination of the latter.[451] If there are no special provisions such as to enable a facilitated naturalization procedure for women (e.g. by eliminating certain requirements), women can find it especially difficult to acquire nationality. It has been observed that where, in addition to other criteria, interviews are held to test the applicant's command of the host country's language, that can be present a special difficulty for women. The argument is that women often have little chance to learn the language due to their activities being limited to household management, while the men are the breadwinners undertaking various activities outside of the family home, which provides them with more opportunities for language acquisition.[452] For similar reasons, for example, a cultural-knowledge test could also be more difficult to pass. Recommendation 1261 of the Parliamentary Assembly of the Council of Europe reflects this spirit: 'The Assembly is concerned by the situation of immigrant women, a large number of whom live on the margins of society and are confronted by more serious difficulties than those facing immigrant men. When they are married, they are often confined to the home doing housework and isolated from the local community, without real opportunities to learn the language of the host country, thus further aggravating their isolation. When they are employed, they are often doing menial jobs unconducive to greater autonomy or to their integration into the host society.'[453].

3.3. Protection of stateless women

It will be expedient to mention the guidelines formulated in soft-law instruments with regard to the need for special protection of the most vulnerable individuals.

---

450 A.T. Gallagher, *The international law of human trafficking*, Cambridge 2011, p. 159.

451 R. Govil, A. Edwards, *Women...*, pp. 180–181.

452 K. Knop, Ch. Chinkin, *Remembering...*, p. 549.

453 Recommendation 1261 (1995) on the situation of immigrant women in Europe, adopted by the Committee of Ministers on 7 June 1995.

When discussing statelessness-identification procedures, it is necessary to bear in mind that — through discrimination — women can encounter additional barriers to the acquisition of documents needed in order to prove one's nationality, such as birth certificates or identity papers. Furthermore, circumstances relating to the individual's gender may call for additional procedural safeguards in order to guarantee access to SIP, among other things.[454] One of the ways of accommodating special challenges relating to gender within such procedures is to ensure that the interviewers and interpreters are of the same sex as the applicant. Interviewers and interpreters should also be trained for awareness of cultural differences potentially affecting how certain questions or phrasing might be received by interviewees and for the ability to respond to such differences.[455]

4. Conclusions

The approach taken to the problem of statelessness of women has evolved. In time, matters relating to the statelessness of women became part of the broader topic range of human rights. Whereas the Hague Convention of 1930 only won a small number of ratifications, the 1957 Convention boasted many more, and — later together with CEDAW, after that one was adopted — successfully popularized the independent-nationality standard. In a twist, that translated into a reduction of statelessness through the elimination of the previously existing conflict of principles, achieved by making one of the conflicting principles predominate. In the 20s and 30s of the 20th century no such reduction would have been possible. We owe the successful elimination of this specific cause of the statelessness of women not to regulations dealing with the area of statelessness or nationality but to the inclusion of the statelessness of women in the broader human-rights paradigm of equality between the sexes. That way, the states could be 'persuaded' more easily to amend their nationality legislation previously regarded as part and parcel of state sovereignty. The above analysis demonstrates that this could be a good method for the reduction of stateless affecting certain categories of individuals (as I will demonstrate in the following chapter, a similar strategy is already in evidence with regard to children).

454 UNHCR Handbook, paragraph 118. Similarly the guidelines developed jointly by the OSCE and the UNHCR in 2017 — *Handbook on Statelessness...*; UNHCR, *Good Practices Paper...*, p. 7.

455 UNHCR Handbook, paragraphs 118–121.

At present, the continued relevance of stateless women as a category of stateless persons is visible through the practice of application of protection mechanisms. In women's case, the inability to prove their nationality with the effect of being classified as stateless persons can be the outcome of certain specific circumstances such as being victims of human trafficking or the additional obstacles sometimes encountered by women as a result of discrimination, compounding the difficulty of the acquisition of documents needed to prove nationality. One can also point toward the possible existence of certain special needs of stateless women within statelessness-identification procedures, potentially indicating the necessity of taking specific circumstances relating to the individual's gender into account.

Chapter VI The Category of 'Children' in the Law of Statelessness

1. Introductory remarks

Children (minors)[456] constitute approximately a half of the entire stateless population of the world.[457] Their particular vulnerability has come to notice.[458] In a greater degree compared to adult stateless persons, they are exposed to all sorts of violations of their rights, being uniquely dependent on the state. Among other expressions of this particular vulnerability, J. Bhabha place children's reliance on the state for access to basic services relating to key aspects of their lives. That includes access to education and health-care.[459] Stateless children often have neither birth certificates nor identity documents, which poses a considerable barrier to the enjoyment of their rights. In many states in the world, stateless children have no access to health-care, because specific documentation is required of them before admission to treatment. In almost twenty countries of the world, stateless children are not eligible for state-funded vaccines.[460] Stateless children are denied access to education. Even where public education is available to them on the elementary level, they are hindered from taking state examinations and rarely enter above-elementary education. This leaves them more vulnerable to poverty and various forms of exploitation, such as forced labour.

---

456 For the most part, the problems of statelessness of children discussed in this chapter affect minors. However, although the purpose of the regulation in this area is to counteract statelessness among minor children, the provisions can still sometimes find application to adults. With adults, this will always involve a cause arising at birth in connection with specific family circumstances involving their parents.

457 UNHCR estimates, cited after: UNHCR & Plan, *Under the radar and under protected. The urgent need to address stateless children's rights*, June 2012, p. 1.

458 See e.g. O.W. Vonk, C. Dumbrava, M.P. Vink and G.-R. de Groot, *"Benchmarking" legal protection against statelessness* [in:] L. van Waas and M.J. Khanna (eds.), *Solving Statelessness*, Wolf Legal Publishers 2017, p. 168 (*particularly vulnerable*); P.T. Lenard, *The right to family. Protecting stateless children* [in:] T. Bloom, K. Tonkiss and P. Cole (eds.), *Understanding statelessness. Lives in limbo*, New York 2017 (*profound vulnerability*), p. 227.

459 J. Bhabha, *Children without a state. A global human rights challenge*, London 2011, pp. 13–14.

460 M. Lynch, M. Teff, *Childhood Statelessness*, 32 Forced Migration Review 2009, p. 32.

Faced with natural disasters and other safety risks, stateless children encounter greater difficulty finding shelter or food or other assistance needed for survival. If they go missing, it is more difficult to search for them. They are uniquely vulnerable to exploitation and abuse, including human trafficking, forced labour and sexual exploitation, being held in detention together with adults, or deportation.[461] Of course, the situation of stateless children is not uniform throughout the world. In Europe, stateless children often have multiple rights guaranteed to them, albeit practical barriers to the enjoyment of such rights present a problem (e.g. due to lacking identity papers).[462]

2. Causes of children's statelessness

Statelessness in children arises mainly at birth, which is when they fail to acquire the nationality of any state (so-called original statelessness). An important cause of stateless originating at birth is the conflict of nationality laws. The majority of children acquire some nationality at birth either by 'right of the soil' (*iure soli*) or by 'right of the blood' (*iure sanguinis*). In an international system composed of states, regulations governing the acquisition of nationality upon birth often act as a primary classification mechanism, defining the allegiance of every person who is born. However, there are gaps in the system, as a result of which individuals are sometimes born without acquiring the nationality of any state.[463]

The simplest example for the illustration of the above problem is when a child is born in a state adhering to the principle of *ius sanguinis* to foreign parents whose state of nationality follows the principle of *ius soli* for the acquisition of nationality by birth. At present, European states are affected by this problem in a lesser degree then they used to be, because of the establishment of legal frameworks to prevent statelessness (which I will discuss more extensively below). Still, problems of the same kind continue to occur. For example, a child born in Poland to Cuban parents (holding no other nationality) becomes stateless as a result of a conflict of laws. This is because Cuba follows the *ius soli*, whereas Poland

461 UNHCR & Plan, *Under the radar…*, pp. 8–9.

462 For a more detailed discussion of problems affecting stateless children see the selection of texts in J. Bhabha, *Children…*

463 From this perspective, dual nationality likewise constitutes an anomaly. de Groot G.-R., Vink M.P., *Birthright citizenship. Trends and regulations in Europe*, 8 EUDO Citizenship Observatory, 2010, p. 3.

has no safeguards in place against statelessness in a situation of a child's birth in its territory to parents of known identity whose nationality is also known.[464]

Another cause of statelessness arising at birth is the 'inheritance' of the status from stateless parents. Children become stateless through birth to parents having no nationality whatsoever in a state that does not confer its nationality by virtue of birth in its territory. The statelessness of children also affects foundlings.

Yet another cause of statelessness in children arises from various kinds of regulations discriminating against either men or women in the transmission of nationality. Already in the 50s of the 20th century, nationality regulations somewhat universally restricted the transmission of nationality through the mother. Thus, a child could become stateless upon failure to inherit nationality from the father, e.g. due to the father's being a stateless person. At present, the legal systems of a number of European states prevent men from being able to pass their nationality onto their children on the same terms as women can if the child is born out of wedlock and abroad.[465] In the latter case, if the mother is a stateless person or is unable to transmit her nationality to the child, that child will become a stateless person. Statelessness can also result from regulations discriminating against same-sex couples in the transmission of nationality to their children.[466]

Statelessness can also arise after birth, later in the child's life (so-called subsequent statelessness). This can be linked to different circumstances involving the loss of nationality. The loss of a child's nationality can be entailed by the loss of nationality by one or both of its parents. For example, the parents surrender their citizenship and their children forfeit theirs as a consequence, without acquiring the nationality of any other state. The parents could also be stripped of nationality as a penalty, triggering the loss of nationality by their children. Loss of nationality by children can also be the result of situations such as invalidation of acknowledgement of parentage, or transnational adoption.

This preliminary rundown of examples already demonstrates the diversity of causes of statelessness in children, making the matter of statelessness reduction

---

464 For a closer look upon this case, see D. Pudzianowska, M. Szczepanik, *Wokół problemu...*, pp. 87–88.

465 Provisions to such effect were found to be discriminatory by the ECtHR in *Genovese v. Malta*, appl. no. 53124/09, judgment of 11 October 2011. Only Finland has no safeguards against statelessness for children born abroad out of wedlock to a male national; see Article 9(1) of Finnish Nationality Act.

466 See D. Pudzianowska, P. Korzec, *Citizenship 'on paper'. On the risk of statelessness of Polish children raised in same-sex unions abroad*, 16(2) National Taiwan University Law Review, 2021

and prevention in this category of stateless persons a very complex one on account of the need to adapt the provisions to an extensive range of dissimilar factual configurations.

3. General principles in international law

In international law, the statelessness of children receives priority treatment. Although the right to nationality has been formulated in a general manner in the UDHR, international law regulations adopted following the Second World War dealt primarily with the specific aspect of this right relating to the avoidance of the statelessness of children.

Article 24(3) ICCPR, which stipulates that every child has a right to acquire a nationality, is an important norm in this legal area. It will be expedient to note that from the perspective of the provisions of ICCPR, children are accorded privileged treatment as the only group vested with a right to acquire the nationality of some state. This norm is an expression of the general principle of children being given special care and protection by state authorities. The aforementioned provision requires the states to introduce procedural and substantive regulations to guarantee that a child will acquire some nationality at birth. According to the General Comment no. 17 of the Human Rights Committee, the goal of Article 24 ICCPR is to protect a child from receiving less protection from the state and society on account of statelessness. However, that does not translate into an obligation for the state to confer its nationality on all children born in its territory. Nonetheless, states have the obligation to adopt such measures, both internally and in collaboration with other states, as may be necessary to ensure that every child is assigned some nationality or other upon birth. Accordingly, any discrimination by domestic law with regard to the acquisition of nationality, for example consisting in the application of different rules to marital and extramarital children, is forbidden.[467]

The right of a child to acquire the nationality of some state is also stipulated by the provisions of the Convention on the Rights of the Child. In the CRC, the obligation established by Article 24(3) finds more concrete expression.[468] Article 7(1) CRC states that every child has a right to acquire a nationality upon birth.

467 CCPR General Comment No. 17: Article 24 (Rights of the Child), 7 April 1989, § 8.

468 G.-R. de Groot, *Children, their right to a nationality and child statelessness* [in:] A. Edwards and L. van Waas (eds.), *Nationality and Statelessness under International Law*, Cambridge 2014, p. 146.

Article 7(2) CRC, in turn, binds the states to guarantee the implementation of this right especially in cases when the absence of the relevant regulations would leave the child stateless.[469] Article 8(1) provides that the states party must take action to ensure that the child's right to preserve its identity, including nationality, is respected.

Neither from the ICCPR nor the CRC does it occur what nationality it is the child's right to acquire at birth. Nor do their provisions imply the existence of any unconditional duty to confer the state's nationality on all children born in its territory. In particular, the solutions adopted by the CRC do not oblige the states to follow the principle of *ius soli* with regard to nationality. Rather, the point is that all steps should be taken to protect a child from a situation in which it ends up not being assigned the nationality of any state whatsoever.[470]

The right of a stateless child to a nationality is a norm of customary international law. It is especially important to appreciate the fact of the ratification of CRC — which proclaims the right of a stateless child to a nationality — by almost all member states of the United Nations, as well as the inclusion of similar provisions in the domestic provisions of many states.[471] Consequently, it must be concluded that the standard accepted at present by the states is that every person should acquire the nationality of some state at birth.

What is crucial, however, is how the rights of children in respect of the counteraction of statelessness are given effect. The provisions of the 1961 Convention and of the ECN dealing with this matter often embrace a high level of detail, and there is a great diversity of domestic regulatory landscapes. I discuss these topics below, beginning with statelessness reduction (section 4) and then moving on to prevention mechanisms (section 5).

---

469 Article 7 CRC: '1. The child shall be registered immediately after birth and shall have the right from birth to a name, the right to acquire a nationality and, as far as possible, the right to know and be cared for by his or her parents. 2. States Parties shall ensure the implementation of these rights in accordance with their national law and their obligations under the relevant international instruments in this field, in particular where the child would otherwise be stateless.'

470 J.E. Doek, *The CRC and the right to acquire and to reserve a nationality*, 3 (25) Refugee Survey Quarterly 2006, p. 28.

471 J.-F. Flauss, *L'influence du droit international des droits de l'homme sur la nationalité* [in:] E. Cadeau (ed.), *Perspectives du droit public. Études offertes á Jean-Claude Hélin*, Paris 2004, p. 279.

4. Reducing statelessness in children

It is commonly held that the most effective way of counteracting the statelessness arising from conflicts of law is to safeguard the right of every child to acquire a nationality at birth (or shortly thereafter). Existing mechanisms for the reduction of statelessness arising from a conflict of laws deal primarily with the situation of foundlings (section 4.1) and children who fail to acquire the nationality of any state at birth for other reasons (item 4.2).

4.1. Reducing statelessness in foundlings

4.1.1. The international standard

The principle of conferring nationality on foundlings was voiced for the first time by the Hague Convention of 1930. The final part of its Article 14 stipulates: 'A foundling is, until the contrary is proved, presumed to have been born on the territory of the State in which it was found.'[472] The Hague Convention of 1930 also regulates the situation of children whose parents are unknown. The first part of Article 14 provides: 'A child whose parents are both unknown shall have the nationality of the country of birth. If the child's parentage is established, its nationality shall be determined by the rules applicable in cases where the parentage is known.'

As can be seen from the above, the Hague Convention of 1930 deals separately with the child whose place of birth and parentage are unknown (a 'foundling') and with the child whose parents are unknown but the place of birth is known to have been in the territory of the state. Later conventions (adopted after the Second World War) contain provisions on foundlings but without separate treatment of children having unknown parents but a known place of birth. In accordance with Article 2 of the 1961 Convention, a child found in the territory of a member state should, barring contrary evidence, be presumed to have been born in the territory of that state and of parents being its nationals. In turn, Article 6(1)(b) ECN provides that the domestic legislation of every state party must guarantee the acquisition of its nationality *ex lege* by such children found in its territory as would otherwise be stateless.

472 The French version uses the term *l'enfant trouvé*, literally meaning 'found child'. The word used in the Polish translation, *podrzutek*, implies a child 'dumped' on someone else, typically left at the doorstep of a private home or of a hospital or church.

In the above light, the first important question arising with regard to foundlings is in what situation a child should be regarded as a foundling. As understood by the Hague Convention of 1930, a foundling is a child having not ties with the state either by birth (unknown place of birth) or through the parents (parents unknown). Accordingly, neither the principle of *ius soli*, nor that of *ius sanguinis* is applicable to such a child. As a result, the child does not acquire the nationality of the state unless there is a legal presumption of birth in the state in the territory of which the child was found.[473]

However, due to the absence from the 1961 Convention and from ECN of any separate provisions on a child whose parents are unknown but whose place of birth is known, it is postulated that such a child should also be regarded as a foundling.[474] The resulting conclusion is that if the child's parents are not known (no one saw them), the child is always a foundling, whether or not its place of birth can be determined. This is logical because given that a child of unknown parents and with an unknown place of birth is granted nationality, all the more so should nationality be acquired by a child born of unknown parents with a known place of birth (located within the territory of the relevant state). The contrary interpretation would leave without any nationality children known to be linked to the state by place of birth while granting it to children whose both parents and place of birth are unknown. What is more problematic is a situation in which the place of birth is known (e.g. a specific hospital) and the mother is in fact known but the child was abandoned immediately upon birth and the parents cannot be identified or the mother gave a so-called confidential birth, which is legal in certain states. In my view, for the purposes of nationality law, such children should be given the same treatment as foundlings. This is also the position expressed in the UNHCR's Guidelines on Statelessness no. 4:[475] 'A child born in the territory of a Contracting State without having a parent, who is legally recognised as such (…), is also to be treated as a foundling and immediately to acquire the nationality of the State of birth.'[476]

---

473 United Nations, *A study of statelessness…*, p. 65.

474 G.-R. de Groot, *Children…*, p. 162.

475 UNHCR, *Guidelines on Statelessness No. 4: Ensuring Every Child's Right to Acquire a Nationality through Articles 1–4 of the 1961 Convention on the Reduction of Statelessness*, December 2012, paragraph 61, hereinafter the 'UNHCR Guidelines on Statelessness no. 4'.

476 UNHCR Guidelines on Statelessness no. 4, paragraph 61. I revisit this topic in a later part of this chapter, dedicated to the registration of births in the context of counteraction of statelessness.

Other than the question of when a child should be regarded as a foundling, another important one is the age of such a child. Firstly, doubts arise as to whether the term can apply to newborns only or to older children also. In the opinion of G.-R. de Groot, the texts of the majority of language versions support the former hypothesis.[477] This, however, leaves a gap in the protection of older children abandoned in the territory of a member state whose parents are unknown and who are in a situation similar to that of newborns. Recommendation CM/Rec(2009)13 and explanatory memorandum of the Committee of Ministers to member states on the nationality of children recommends that — for the purposes of conferring nationality — member states treat children of unknown parentage abandoned in their territories as foundlings to the fullest extent possible.[478] UNHCR Guidelines on Statelessness no. 4 refer to this problem in more detail, observing that, as a minimum, the protection against statelessness accorded to foundlings should extend to all small children who are unable to communicate properly concerning information about their place of birth and the identity of their parents. The above is consistent with the scope and purpose of the 1961 Convention, as well as the principle that every child has a right to acquire a nationality. As is aptly noted: 'A contrary interpretation would leave some children stateless.'[479] If a state decides to set an age limit for foundlings, the child's age at the time it was found should be considered, rather than the date when it came into the authorities' attention.[480]

The third problem at hand is how the states should respond to the subsequent discovery of the child's identity or of the fact that the child was born abroad. Although this is an issue of statelessness prevention, I will discuss it here because of its direct logical consequence for the problem of reduction of statelessness in foundlings. In accordance with Article 2 of the 1961 Convention, the presumption of birth in the territory of the state (and 'of parents possessing the nationality of that State') applies only 'in the absence of proof to the contrary'.[481] The 1961 Convention does not contain any safeguards to protect the child from

477 G.-R. de Groot, *Children…*, p. 161. For example, in the Hague Convention of 1930, the Polish term *podrzutek* referred to a neonate. According to PWN Polish Dictionary, the word means a 'newborn child abandoned by the mother to strangers' https://sjp.pwn.pl/sjp/podrzutek;2502730.html (accessed 10 April 2019).

478 Principle no. 9 of Recommendation CM/Rec(2009)13 of the Committee of Ministers to member states on the nationality of children, CM/REC(2009)13.

479 UNHCR Guidelines on Statelessness no. 4, paragraph 58.

480 UNHCR Guidelines on Statelessness no. 4, paragraph 59.

481 Similarly Article 14 of the Hague Convention of 1930.

statelessness in such a situation. According to the UNHCR Guidelines on Statelessness no. 4, nationality should only be lost in such a situation if the child is proved to have the nationality of another state.[482] Unlike the 1961 Convention, the European Convention on Nationality contains a provision protecting the child from statelessness in such a situation — in Article 7(3), which contains the additional safeguard that nationality may be lost on this account only before coming of age.[483]

4.1.2. Regulatory frameworks in selected domestic jurisdictions

Domestic provisions commonly include mechanisms designed with a view to reducing the statelessness of foundlings. Cypriot regulations mark an exception from this rule.[484] In almost all states enabling the acquisition of their nationalities by foundlings, the acquisition happens *ex lege*. Estonia is an exception here, conferring nationality by court judgement (declaration) at the application of the child's legal guardian.[485]

The practice of the states unveils a wide spectrum of solutions addressing the age of the foundling to whom the provisions of the 1961 Convention can be held to apply. While in some states the acquisition of nationality is limited to very small children only, the majority extend the relevant regulations to older children as well. In some cases that is done all the way to the age of maturity. In the former variant, Austria, for example, imposes a time-limit of six months on the acquisition of its nationality by a foundling.[486] In some countries the child must be a newborn (Ireland,[487] United Kingdom,[488] Malta,[489] Portugal[490] or

482 UNHCR Guidelines on Statelessness no. 4, paragraph 60.

483 Article 7(1)(f) ECN: 'A State Party may not provide in its internal law for the loss of its nationality *ex lege* or at the initiative of the State Party except in the following cases: (...) f. where it is established during the minority of a child that the preconditions laid down by internal law which led to the *ex lege* acquisition of the nationality of the State Party are no longer fulfilled.'

484 GLOBALCIT (2017), *Modes of Acquisition*, mode A03a.

485 Article 5(2) of Estonian Citizenship Act 1995, consolidated text as amended by Act of 15 June 2006 (English translation).

486 Article 8(1) of Austrian Citizenship Act.

487 Article 10 of Irish Nationality Act.

488 Article 1(2) of UK Nationality Act.

489 Article 17(3) of Maltese Nationality Act.

490 Article 1(2) of Organic Law 9/2015: 7th Amendment of the Law 37/81 of 3 October.

Ukraine[491]). This excludes older children who are still small enough to be unable to communicate concerning their identity (which violates the UNHCR guidelines). As for the latter variant, some states apply the framework to minors in general (e.g. Poland,[492] Albania,[493] Bosnia and Herzegovina[494] and Kosovo[495]).

Greek regulations are notable in how a foundling acquires Greek nationality only if it can be proved to have been born in Greece.[496] The Greek provision restricts the right of foundlings to acquire Greek nationality, so that only children of unknown parents with place of birth unknown can do so. This hampers the counteraction of statelessness in foundlings and is incompatible with the above-discussed international standard.

Concerning the possibility of statelessness arising from a foundling's loss of nationality in connection with the subsequent discovery of the child's identity or place of birth, many states' legal systems envisage the loss of the birth nationality in such a situation. Not all such states have safeguards in place against statelessness arising from such a development. One of the states having such safeguards is Switzerland. Under Swiss provisions, the nationality acquired by a foundling will be lost if the child's parentage is subsequently discovered, on condition that the child is still a minor and is not going to become a stateless person as a result.[497] Safeguards also exist in France [498] and Belgium[499]. By contrast, explicit safeguards are missing from the legal systems of states such as Moldova,[500] Germany[501] and Slovenia[502].

491 Article 7 of Ukrainian Nationality Act.

492 Article 15 of Polish Citizenship Act: 'A minor shall acquire Polish citizenship on having been found in the territory of the Republic of Poland with parents being unknown.'

493 Article 8(1) of Law No. 8389 of 5 August 1998 on Albanian Citizenship (as amended by Law No. 8442 of 21 January 1999).

494 Article 7(1) of Law of 27 July 1999 on Citizenship of Bosnia and Herzegovina (consolidated version 2003).

495 Article 7(1) of Law No. 04/L-215 on Citizenship of Kosovo.

496 Article 1(2) of Greek Citizenship Code

497 Article 6(3) of Federal Law of 29 September 1952 on the Acquisition and Loss of Swiss Nationality (consolidated version as amended 30 September 2011).

498 Article 19 of French Citizenship Code.

499 Article 10 *in fine* of Belgian Citizenship Code.

500 Article 11(2) of Law on the Citizenship of the Republic of Moldova, No. 1024-XIV of 2 June 2000; consolidated version as last amended by Law no. 232-XV of 5 June 2003.

501 Article 4(2) of German Nationality Act.

502 Article 9 *in fine* of Slovenian Nationality Act.

4.2. Reducing the statelessness of 'otherwise stateless' children

In international law, regulations designed to reduce statelessness at birth extend not only to foundlings, whose case has been discussed immediately above, but also to children whose statelessness arises from a different cause. This refers to situations in which the children cannot acquire their parents' nationality by 'right of blood' (*iure soli*).[503] International law contains an extensive body of regulation in this area. Provisions of this kind appeared for the first time in the 1961 Convention, followed by the ECN. Their domestic implementations vary.

4.2.1. The convention standard

A. The 1961 Convention on the Reduction of Statelessness

In its Article 1(1), the 1961 Convention stipulates: 'A Contracting State shall grant its nationality to a person born in its territory who would otherwise be stateless.' This is referred to as 'the cornerstone of efforts to prevent statelessness among children'.[504] The essential element here is the 'otherwise statelessness'. This ought to be understood to mean that the child would become stateless if the state to which the child has ties due to having been born in its territory or of its national were not to grant its nationality. The UNHCR Guidelines on Statelessness no. 4 note that a child always becomes a stateless person when the parents are stateless persons and the child is born in the territory of a state that does not confer its nationality *iure soli*. Importantly, however, statelessness can arise for different reasons, for example when the parents have a nationality but are unable to transmit it and the child is born in a state not conferring its nationality by virtue of birth in its territory. Hence, restricting the applicability of Article 1 of the 1961 Convention solely to the children of stateless parents is insufficient and incompatible with the provisions of the Convention. Thus, the circumstance for the domestic authorities to determine should be not whether the child's parents are stateless persons but whether the child itself is a stateless person as a result of acquiring neither a parent's nationality nor that of the country of birth.[505]

The acquisition of nationality by the child in such a situation need not be automatic at birth. In accordance with Article 1(2) of the 1961 Convention, a person who would otherwise become stateless should acquire nationality either *ex lege* at birth, or upon application made by the interested party or on their

---

503 O.W. Vonk, C. Dumbrava, M.P. Vink, G.-R. de Groot, *Benchmarking...*, p. 168.

504 UNHCR Guidelines on Statelessness no. 4, paragraph 2.

505 UNHCR Guidelines on Statelessness no. 4, paragraph 18.

behalf to the competent authorities in keeping with the procedure prescribed by domestic legislation. If a given state requires an application procedure for the acquisition of nationality, such acquisition can be made conditional on certain additional requirements but only such as are permitted by the 1961 Convention.

The first such permitted additional requirement for the acquisition of nationality by a person who would otherwise be stateless is for the application to be submitted within a set time-limit (Article 1(2)(a) of the 1961 Convention). The exact time-limit is for the state to determine, but it must begin not after the child's 18th birthday and end not before their 21st birthday. Thus, the Convention guarantees the existence of a minimum time window of three years in which to file the application. This means that the state cannot, for example, decide to restrict the availability of applications to persons aged twenty or older or demand that the application be filed within five years of birth.[506]

Another requirement that a state may impose is for the person concerned to have been habitually resident in the territory of the state for a specific duration determined by the state, not to exceed five years prior to filing or ten years in all (Article 1(2)(b) of the 1961 Convention). Thus, the state is not allowed to require, for example, uninterrupted habitual residence since birth. It is noted that states deciding to impose such a requirement should opt for the shortest possible duration. A duration of ten or even five years can be regarded as a long one in the light of the principles contained in human-rights instruments adopted subsequently (especially CRC) and from the perspective of the purpose of the 1961 Convention, which is to counteract statelessness.[507] The term 'habitual residence' itself already calls for some commentary. According to the UNHCR, habitual residence should be understood to mean stable, factual residence. States may introduce objective criteria for proving habitual residence, but without prescribing a *numerus clausus* of types of admissible evidence.[508]

---

506 Simultaneously, the provision guarantees the existence of a certain minimum period in which the interested party may file without needing the consent of a parent or guardian, which is relevant in cases in which such persons have omitted to apply on the child's behalf. This additional principle had been important at a time when most states regarded twenty-one years as the age of majority, as opposed to the present general rule of eighteen years. UNHCR Guidelines on Statelessness no. 4, p. 9, paragraph 28.

507 G.-R. de Groot, *Children...*, p. 151.

508 UNHCR, Interpreting the 1961 Statelessness Convention and Preventing Statelessness among Children (hereinafter the 'Dakar Conclusions'), September 2011, paragraphs 30, 40–43.

Most importantly, however, habitual residence is not coterminous with lawful residence.[509]

The third permissible requirement for the acquisition of nationality is for the candidate not to have been convicted of a criminal offence against national security or given a prison sentence of five years or longer as a result of criminal charges (Article 1(2)(c) of the 1961 Convention).[510] However, as the UNHCR Guidelines on Statelessness no. 4 emphasize, criminal liability for unlawful stay in the state's territory may never justify withholding nationality.[511]

The fourth permissible requirement under the 1961 Convention is that the individual concerned have always been a stateless person (Article 1(2)(d) of the 1961 Convention). That means having been a stateless person since birth. Where a state opts to require this, there should be a presumption that the individual has always been a stateless person, with the burden on the authorities to establish the contrary.[512]

For a state to introduce requirements other than mentioned in the 1961 Convention is a violation of the Convention.[513] The *numerus clausus* of permissible requirements for the acquisition of nationality upon request by an 'otherwise stateless' person has the logical consequence of the states not being free to opt for a different outcome of the application procedure if the conditions for the acquisition of nationality are satisfied.[514] This means that the application procedure must be shaped in such a manner as to establish the acquisition of nationality as an individual right.[515]

As for the various procedural aspects of the proceedings initiated by the application of an 'otherwise stateless' person, it has been observed that applications should be accepted without demanding any filing fee,[516] and that any

509 UNHCR Guidelines on Statelessness no. 4, paragraph 41 *in fine*.

510 UNHCR Guidelines on Statelessness no. 4, paragraph 46.

511 UNHCR Guidelines on Statelessness no. 4, paragraph 45.

512 The UNHCR Guidelines on Statelessness no. 4 indicate that the applicant's possession of manifestly false or unlawfully obtained papers from another state does not dislodge the presumption of always having been stateless — UNHCR Guidelines on Statelessness no. 4, paragraph 48.

513 G.-R. de Groot, *Children…*, p. 149.

514 The use of the imperative phrasing in 'nationality shall be granted' indicates that the state has no discretion in the matter — Dakar Conclusions, paragraph 37; UNHCR Guidelines on Statelessness no. 4, paragraph 26.

515 UNHCR Guidelines on Statelessness no. 4, paragraph 37.

516 Dakar conclusions, paragraph 40; UNHCR Guidelines on Statelessness no. 4, paragraph 54.

costs arising from the authentication of documents must not pose a barrier to applicants.[517] States opting for an application procedure should provide detailed information to the parents of otherwise children on the details of the possible acquisition of nationality by the child, the filing method and the conditions to be met. The information should be given directly to the parents themselves (circulation through general campaigns is not sufficient). The states should also allow children to file on their own[518] and should take their wishes (opinions) into account.[519]

A state enabling stateless children to obtain its nationality upon request may also enable *ex lege* acquisition at a certain age and in line with the requirements specified by domestic legislation.[520] This means that the acquisition of nationality by children who satisfy certain specific conditions may be automatic, whereas others may need to file an application. The text of the 1961 Convention contains nothing on the conditions for the automatic acquisition of nationality upon reaching a certain age. Nonetheless, there can be no doubt that the states have a duty to ensure that the conditions do not violate such principles as non-discrimination and the child's best interest.[521]

As can be seen from the above, the 1961 Convention does not place on the states party an absolute obligation to confer nationality on an otherwise stateless child. The introduction of a solution enabling nationality to be acquired by application with some specific conditions attached means that some children may be left in a situation of statelessness for many years.[522] UNHCR Guidelines

517 UNHCR Guidelines on Statelessness no. 4, paragraph 54.

518 UNHCR Guidelines on Statelessness no. 4, paragraphs 53–54.

519 Council of Europe Recommendation CM/REC(2009)13. The recommendation contains general language relating to the consideration of the child's wishes in naturalization procedures affecting their nationality. The above, however, is not limited to situations when the child already holds the nationality of another state. Accordingly, the conclusion is that even in the situation of a stateless child the element of consent should be taken into account in the application procedure. Thus, in the light of the recommendations, reduction of statelessness as the goal does not appear to override the child's own wishes in the matter.

520 UNHCR Guidelines on Statelessness no. 4, paragraph 32.

521 S. Jansen, L. van Waas, *Preventing Childhood Statelessness in Europe. Issues, gaps and good practices*, European Network on Statelessness 2014, p. 10.

522 As a marginal note, it will be expedient to point out that the American Convention (Article 20(2)) and the African Charter on the Rights and Welfare of the Child (Article 6(4)) each provide a fuller guarantee by stipulating that a child acquires the nationality of the state of birth upon birth if the child would otherwise be stateless.

on Statelessness no. 4 emphasize that the principles relating to the reduction of statelessness, according to Articles 1(1) and 1(2) of the 1961 Convention, must be interpreted in the light of subsequently adopted human-rights conventions establishing the right of every child to acquire a nationality. In particular, this includes the principles of a child's right to nationality (Article 7 CRC) and of its best interests (Article 3 CRC); when read in conjunction with Article 1 of the 1961 Convention, these principles demand the conferral of nationality on children either automatically at birth or upon request shortly after birth. Accordingly, where a state opts for an application procedure involving specific requirements (which Article 1(2) of the 1961 Convention allows the states party to do), the effect must not be to leave the child stateless for an extended length of time.[523]

In the 1961 Convention, solutions devised to reduce the statelessness of foundlings and 'otherwise stateless' children prioritize the *ius soli* (Articles 1(1–3) of the 1961 Convention, as discussed above). However, the 1961 Convention addresses conflicts of nationality laws by prescribing the subsidiary application not only of the *ius soli* but also of the *ius sanguinis* (Articles 1(4) and 1(5) and Article 4). The casuistic approach taken by the 1961 Convention bears testimony to the compromise struck between, on the one hand, states conferring nationality *iure soli* and, on the other hand, those adhering to the *ius sanguinis* at the time of drafting. The first case of subsidiary application of the *ius sanguinis* is specified by Article 4 of the 1961 Convention, which seeks to provide a safeguard from statelessness for children born to a national of a state party from the *ius soli* camp, abroad, in the territory of a state not being party to the Convention and not having safeguards in place to protect children in such a situation from statelessness. Such a situation triggers the obligation for the parent's state of nationality to confer its nationality on the child. Accordingly, the obligations of the parent's state of nationality are greater when the child's state of birth, unlike the parent's state of nationality, is not party to the 1961 Convention (and cannot be expected to comply with the standard set by the Convention). The significance of this provision in the European context is not completely minimal. Although all European states follow the *ius sanguinis* as the predominant principle in the acquisition of nationality, some impose restrictions on the transmission of nationality to children born abroad.[524] Another case of subsidiary application of the *ius*

523 UNHCR Guidelines on Statelessness no. 4, paragraph 34.

524 Restrictions of this type are used by Cyprus, Ireland, Malta, Portugal, United Kingdom (i.e. states traditionally adhering to the *ius soli*, attaching more symbolic value to birth within the territory of the state than abroad), Germany and Belgium. Despite such

sanguinis is when a child is born in the territory of a state party to the 1961 Convention and is unable to acquire the nationality of that state (or any other state) owing to failure to meet age or residence requirements allowed by Article 1(2) of the 1961 Convention (as discussed above). In such a situation, the parent's state of nationality ought to confer its nationality on the child (Article 1(4) of the 1961 Convention). In principle, the 1961 Convention no longer facilitates the acquisition of nationality by such persons unless one of their parents is a national of another state party. If so, such a parent's state of nationality ought to confer its nationality on the child either *ex lege* or upon application (which may be denied only on grounds allowed by Article 1(5) of the 1961 Convention). This provision also applies to situations in which the parents are nationals of two different states party to the 1961 Convention, conceding to the states party the choice of whether to enable the child to acquire the mother's or the father's nationality.

In the context of the above-discussed legal frameworks, the question is what will happen if a child is indeed born in the territory of a given state and is a stateless person but is also in a position to acquire a parent's nationality by registration in the relevant state or through a similar procedure (e.g. declaration or option). It has been observed that in such a situation, the state is not required to confer its nationality on a child who would otherwise be a stateless person. Thus, if the acquisition of nationality by birth in the state of origin requires certain formalities to be met (i.e. the nationality is not conferred *ex lege*), such as registration, the child's state of birth is not under an obligation to confer its nationality on the child.[525] This avenue is available if the child can acquire the parent's nationality immediately following birth as a guaranteed individual right, i.e. if the parent's state of nationality is unable to withhold its nationality from the child. A state should confer its nationality on a child whose parents cannot register the child in their state of origin or have reasons against doing so. Whether the individual can be reasonably expected to acquire the nationality of one's country of origin is something to be determined in the light of the circumstances of the individual

restrictions, children born to Belgian or German nationals (whether in the first or a later generation) will be assigned Belgian or German nationality if they would otherwise be stateless — M.P. Vink, G.-R. de Groot, *Birthright*…, pp. 9–10.

525 According to domestic court decisions, such a child might also be denied an immigration permit under the protection regime for stateless persons. See Court of Appeals of the United Kingdom, JM (Zimbabwe), R (on the application of) v. Secretary of State for the Home Department [2018] EWCA Civ 188, available at http://www.bailii.org/ew/cases/EWCA/Civ/2018/188.html (accessed 4 January 2023).

case.[526] This of especial importance in situations when the parents cannot be expected to register their child due to having the status of refugees.[527] In this case, it is self-evident that the formal concept of nationality cannot be decisive to the application of statelessness-reduction mechanisms.

B. European Convention on Nationality

The ECN's principle concerning the acquisition of nationality by otherwise stateless children born in the territory of a state party is identical to the one found in the 1961 Convention.[528] Differences from the 1961 Convention standard can only be seen in the details of the solutions envisaged by the ECN. First and foremost, the requirements a state may impose in the application procedure for an otherwise stateless person to satisfy in order to acquire the state's nationality are phrased differently in the ECN. While the 1961 Convention allows four requirements in the application procedure (which have been discussed above), the ECN permits only one of those, namely residence in the territory of the state for a certain period of time preceding the application, not to exceed five years.[529] However, in line with the ECN, the residence requirement may be set more restrictively, because the ECN mentions the requirement of lawful and habitual residence in the territory of the state (as opposed to only habitual residence under the 1961 Convention). Thus, from the perspective of the number of requirements the state may impose in its domestic legislation, the standard of the 1961 Convention is more restrictive, but when considered individually, the ECN's residence requirement is more difficult for stateless persons to meet. The requirement of lawful residence can have the effect of blocking stateless children

526 UNHCR Guidelines on Statelessness no. 4, paragraphs 24–26.

527 The peculiarities of the situation of child refugees in this context are addressed by paragraphs 27–28 of the UNHCR Guidelines on Statelessness no. 4.

528 In accordance with Article 6(2) ECN, the domestic legislation of every state party must guarantee the acquisition of nationality by such children born in its territory as do not obtain another nationality upon birth. Nationality is conferred either *ex lege* upon birth (Article 6(2)(a)) or at a later time — to children remaining stateless, upon application submitted either by the child itself or on the child's behalf by its guardians to the competent authorities as specified by the domestic legislation of the relevant state party (Article 6(2)(b)).

529 Thus, under the provisions of ECN it is not permissible to deny the application due to failure to meet the conditions specified by the 1961 Convention, such as not having been given a criminal conviction for a criminal offence against national security or a prison term of five years or longer, or of having been a stateless person since birth.

from access to nationality due to frequently irregular nature of their stay in the territory.

Another difference compared to the 1961 Convention is that under the ECN, the acquisition of nationality by a child cannot be delayed until eighteen years of age. The European Convention on Nationality does not explicitly permit the imposition of a time-limit for filing. Its Article 6(2) itself is silent on the timing. However, because the provision refers only to children understood to mean minors (in line with the definition contained in Article 2 ECN, a 'child' means anyone younger than eighteen years of age, except where having reached majority at an earlier time in accordance with the person's proper law), the acquisition of nationality must take place before coming of age.[530] Of course, the ability to acquire nationality as soon as possible is of more benefit to the child, as has been discussed above. Paradoxically, the ECN provision can have the effect of an indirect time-limit with negative impact, in some cases, on the situation of a stateless child. In other words, it is problematic how the ECN fails to guarantee that the state must provide a certain filing window after the child reaches the age of majority, which may be necessary in cases such as when the child's legal guardians neglected the matter or actively opposed the acquisition of nationality.

As has already been mentioned, under the 1961 Convention, the states' obligations arising from the application of the *ius soli* take priority before obligations arising from the *ius sanguinis*. In the ECN's case, it is noteworthy that its Article 6(1)(a) establishes as the general principle governing the acquisition of nationality at birth the principle of *ius sanguinis* (with possible exceptions for children born abroad, which will be discussed in a later part of this book dealing with discrimination). This is not surprising in the light of the ECN's being a regional convention in Europe, where the tradition of *ius sanguinis* holds strong. The selection of one of the principles as the priority principle must be viewed in a positive light due to minimizing the potential for conflict of nationality laws resulting in statelessness. Additionally, the Council of Europe Recommendations

530 ECN Explanatory Report, paragraph 50; with regard to principle 2 of the Council of Europe Recommendation CM/Rec(2009)13, its explanatory memorandum observes that the ideal acquisition of nationality would take place soon after birth, with retroactive effect. However, the language of the principle permits the acquisition to lack retroactivity; see Explanatory memorandum of the Committee of Ministers to member states on the nationality of children, 9 May 2009, CM/Rec(2009)13, paragraph 11.

CM/Rec(2009)/13 note that the states ought to confer nationality on children *iure sanguinis* 'without any restriction which would result in statelessness'.[531]

4.2.2. *Purported modifications of the convention standard by soft law*

We have discussed above the key convention provisions dealing with the conferral of nationality on children who do not acquire the nationality of any other state upon birth. Now, it will be expedient to revisit for a moment the requirement pertaining to the nature of the stay, which states are allowed to impose in those cases in which their nationality is acquired upon application. Soft-law instruments such as Council of Europe Recommendation CM/Rec(2009)/13 and UNHCR Guidelines on Statelessness no. 4 contain guidelines concerning the interpretation of Article 6(2)(b) ECN and Article 1(2) of the 1961 Convention, lowering the standard defined by those provisions. First and foremost, the aforementioned instruments expand the licence to impose the requirement of lawful and habitual residence from the children themselves onto the parents and not only for the purposes of the application procedure but also for *ex lege* acquisition. The explanatory memorandum attached with Council of Europe Recommendation CM/Rec(2009)/13 notes that in order to avoid situations of 'mere accidental birth' in a state's territory conferring a right to its nationality, as well as in order to prevent abuses, the state can subject the acquisition of its nationality at birth by potentially stateless children conditional on the lawful and habitual residence of a parent in the territory of the state. According to the memorandum, in order to comply with Article 6(2) ECN, states imposing such a requirement must also guarantee the availability of the acquisition of nationality by application for all children who do not acquire the nationality of the place of birth automatically by virtue of birth in the territory because of not meeting the requirement of a parent's lawful and habitual residence in the territory.[532] In turn, in accordance with the UNHCR Guidelines on Statelessness no. 4, a member-state may apply

---

531 *With a view to reducing statelessness of children, facilitating their access to a nationality and ensuring their right to a nationality, member states should: (...) 1. provide for the acquisition of nationality by right of blood (jure sanguinis) by children without any restriction which would result in statelessness* (emphasis added) — Recommendation CM/Rec(2009)13 and explanatory memorandum of the Committee of Ministers to member states on the nationality of children, 9 May 2009, Appendix, principle no. 1.

532 Recommendation CM/Rec(2009)13 and explanatory memorandum of the Committee of Ministers to member states on the nationality of children, 9 May 2009, paragraph 12.

different alternative paths and modes of acquisition of nationality depending on the 'level of attachment of an individual to that [s]tate.'[533] Among other possibilities, the state may confer its nationality automatically on otherwise stateless children born in its territory to parents being its habitual or lawful residents. For those children whose parents are not lawful residents, the state may prescribe an application procedure. It is noted that any distinction in the treatment of the different groups of stateless persons must serve a reasonable purpose, must not be discriminatory in nature and must be proportionate.[534]

Thus, the discussed soft-law instruments propose a standard different from the one established by the conventions. This is because the language of the two conventions makes it abundantly clear that a requirement of habitual residence (1961 Convention) or habitual and lawful residence (ECN) is only allowed in a naturalization procedure and only with regard to the child. Thus, it cannot apply, firstly, to acquisition of nationality *ex lege* or, secondly, to the child's parents. Moreover, the UNHCR Guidelines open the window to the use of a categorial approach.

A certain ambivalence in the treatment of stateless children is palpable in the aforementioned soft-law documents. On the one hand, they recognize the need for reduction of statelessness in children; on the other hand, though, the tendency to be wary of potential abuse of the conferral of nationality on stateless children by the parents leads to greenlighting solutions that are not envisaged by the conventions. Thus, considerations from the scope of public order make their presence felt even with regard to this particularly vulnerable group of stateless persons.[535]

The question can be asked if such instruments are capable of limiting the convention standard. In accordance with Article 31(1) of the Vienna Convention on the Law of Treaties, done at Vienna on 23 May 1969,[536] '[a] treaty shall be interpreted in good faith in accordance with the ordinary meaning to be given to the terms of the treaty in their context and in the light of its object and purpose,'

533 Also see Dark Conclusions, paragraph 21.

534 UNHCR Guidelines on Statelessness no. 4, paragraph 33.

535 This is a manifestation of fears more generally linked to the application of the *ius soli*. As observed by L. Volpp, in those states in which the *ius soli* is followed, '(...) *fear is routinely expressed about undesirable women "dropping babies" on the territory in order to anchor citizenship*'; L. Volpp, *Feminist, sexual and queer citizenship* [in:] A. Shachar, R. Bauböck, I. Bloemraad and M.P Vink (eds.), *The Oxford handbook of citizenship*, Oxford 2017, p. 161.

536 United Nations, Treaty Series, vol. 1155, p. 331.

Agreements among the parties may be taken into account for the purpose of the interpretation of the treaty. That, however, is not the nature of the UNHCR documents or of the explanatory memorandum (as they are not protocols to the Convention). To the extent, therefore, that such interpretations purport to modify the convention standard, they are ineffective and have no impact on the scope of the states' obligations.[537] Thus, Council of Europe Recommendations CM/Rec(2009)/13, their explanatory memorandum or the UNHCR Guidelines on Statelessness no. 4 cannot be deemed supplementary to the existing obligations under Article 6(2) ECN and relevant provisions of the 1961 Convention.[538]

4.2.3. Regulatory frameworks in selected domestic jurisdictions

Most European states employ some sort of mechanism of reduction of statelessness consisting in the conferral of nationality on an 'otherwise stateless' child. Only Cyprus, Norway, Switzerland and Romania have no such mechanism in place.[539]

However, out of all European states only fewer than a half confer nationality automatically on an otherwise stateless child born in the territory (without insisting on any other conditions).[540] Examples include Belgium,[541] Finland,[542] Bulgaria,[543] Bosnia and Herzegovina,[544] France, Greece,[545] Ireland,[546] Italy,[547] Kosovo,[548] Slovakia[549] and Spain. By way of illustration, the Spanish provisions dispose of the matter as follows: 'The following persons are Spaniards by birth: (...) (c) those born in Spain of foreign parents if both of them should be without nationality or if the legislation of neither should grant the nationality to

537 My thanks to Dr Wojciech Burek for consultation on this matter.
538 Thus R.-G. de Groot, *Children...*, p. 157.
539 GLOBALCIT (2017), mode A03b (*Born stateless*).
540 O.W. Vonk, C. Dumbrava, M.P. Vink, G.-R. de Groot, *Benchmarking...*, p. 170. Some states provide for the acquisition of nationality either *ex lege* at birth or at a later time, upon application (e.g. Czech Republic).
541 Article 10 of Belgian Nationality Code.
542 Article 9(1)(3) of Finnish Nationality Act.
543 Article 10 of Bulgarian Nationality Act.
544 Article 7(1) of Bosnia and Herzegovina Nationality Act.
545 Article 1(2) of Greek Nationality Code.
546 Article 6(3) of Irish Nationality Act.
547 Article 1(1)(b) of Italian Nationality Act.
548 Articles 7(1) and 7(4) of Kosovo Nationality Act.
549 Articles 5(1)(b) and 5(1)(c) of Slovak Nationality Act.

the child.'[550] In turn, the French statute provides: 'The following shall be a French citizen: (1) a child born in France of stateless parents; (2) a child born in France of foreign parents to whom the foreign nationality regulations do not permit the nationality of either parent to be transmitted in any way.'[551]

Many states attach all sorts of requirements to the acquisition of nationality by otherwise stateless children (whether upon birth or by application). Such restrictive conditions include a filing window (or limit on the child's age); type (nature) of the child's stay; length of the child's stay; lack of criminal record; command of the language and integration; length of statelessness; type (nature) of parents' stay; parents' nationality (e.g. requirement that their nationality be unknown); and parents' marital status.[552]

States such as Croatia, Lithuania, Slovenia or Poland confer their nationality automatically only where both parents are stateless persons or their nationality is unknown (unidentified).[553] In accordance with Article 14(2) of the Act on Polish Citizenship, a minor shall acquire Polish nationality by birth 'if born within the territory of the Republic of Poland of parents unknown or holding no citizenship or holding unspecified citizenship.' This does not extend to children who are stateless persons because their parents, whose nationality is known, are unable to transmit their nationality to the child.

Some states stipulate conditions relating to the nature of the child's stay or that of the parents'. Examples of states imposing requirements concerning the parents' stay include Ukraine (e.g. a child born in Ukraine of stateless parents acquires Ukrainian nationality if the parents are lawfully resident; a child born in Ukraine to foreign parents acquires Ukrainian nationality if the parents are lawfully in and the child does not acquire either of their nationalities)[554] and Czech Republic (a child born of stateless parents acquires Czech nationality if at least one of the parents holds a permit exceeding ninety days and the child would otherwise be stateless).[555] In 2017,

550 Article 17(c) of Spanish Civil Code (nationality legislation) (as amended by Law 52/2007).
551 Article 19-1 of French Civil Code.
552 O.W. Vonk, C. Dumbrava, M. P. Vink, G.-R. de Groot, *Benchmarking…*, p. 169.
553 Globalcit (2017).
554 Second and fourth sentences of Article 7 of Ukrainian Nationality Act, respectively.
555 Article 5 of Act 186/2013 on Citizenship of the Czech Republic.

Moldova amended its legislation, so that lawful stay is now required of the parents.[556]

There are states expecting more requirements to be satisfied cumulatively. For example, Article 2 of German Statelessness Reduction Act of 1977[557] provides that German nationality shall be acquired by a person below twenty-one years of age, stateless since birth, lawfully and habitually resident in Germany for five years and not convicted of a criminal offence for which the upper sentencing limit is five years of imprisonment or higher. Sweden requires the child to have been stateless since birth and resident in Sweden on the basis of a permanent permit.[558] In the Netherlands, the child must have been stateless since birth and resident in the country uninterruptedly for at least three years.[559]

5. Prevention of statelessness in children

5.1. Prevention of statelessness upon loss of nationality due to parentage redetermination or adoption

Adoption or changes to determinations concerning the child's origin affecting its nationality (usually denial of parentage) can, in specific situations, have consequences leading to statelessness.

5.1.1. The international standard

As for the prevention of statelessness in connection with changes to determinations concerning the child's parentage, it must be noted that — in accordance with Article 5(1) of the 1961 Convention — if, in accordance with the state party's legislation, nationality may be lost in consequence of a change in civil status resulting e.g. from marriage, divorce, acknowledgement of parentage, or adoption, any such loss should be made conditional on having or acquiring the nationality of another state. This provision establishes a certain general standard for the various different situations connected with status changes relevant to nationality, without, however, limiting its applicability to children. In the light

556 *Moldova introduces changes to nationality laws which leave children at risk of statelessness*, https://index.statelessness.eu/news/moldova-introduces-changes-nationality-laws-which-leave-children-risk-statelessness (accessed 4 January 2023).

557 German Act on Statelessness Reduction of 1977 (*Gesetz zur Verminderung der Staatenlosigkeit Vom 29. Juni 1977, BGBl. I S. 1101*).

558 Article 6 of Swedish Nationality Act.

559 Art. 6.1(b) of Dutch Nationality Act.

of the 1961 Convention, therefore, the loss of nationality ensuing from a status change must not lead to statelessness.

The European Convention on Nationality, by contrast, contains provisions specifically addressing the child's situation in connection with change in status. The ECN's Article 7(1)(f) — establishing one of the exceptions in which the domestic legislation of a state may provide for the loss of nationality — mandates that such a loss may occur if, prior to the child's coming of age, it is found that the conditions prescribed by domestic legislation on the basis of which the *ex lege* acquisition of nationality occurred are no longer satisfied. Such loss of nationality, however, must not result in statelessness. The ECN standard may be regarded as higher than that of the 1961 Convention, because the findings relevant to the child's nationality must be made before the child comes of age. Moreover, Article 7(1)(g)) ECN provides that a child may lose nationality in connection with adoption, but only 'if the child acquires or possesses the foreign nationality of one or both of the adopting parents.'[560]

Following this general introduction to the international standard, it will be expedient to mention several topics relating to the interpretation of Article 5(1) of the 1961 Convention. The first problem is what type of adoption this provision refers to. It has been submitted that types of adoption not dissolving the legal relationship with one's biological parent or parents must never lead to the loss of nationality by the child. This means that only full adoption is allowed to result in the loss of nationality. Moreover, states providing for the loss of nationality upon full adoption must limit that mode of loss to situations when the child acquires the adoptive parents' nationality *ex lege* in connection with the adoption.[561]

560 The international standard is more developed with regard to adoption. Notably, the principle that adoption must not lead to statelessness had been presented already in the Hague Convention of 1930. Its Article 17 provides: 'If the law of a State recognises that its nationality may be lost as the result of adoption, this loss shall be conditional upon the acquisition by the person adopted of the nationality of the person by whom he is adopted, under the law of the State of which the latter is a national relating to the effect of adoption upon nationality.' This is also addressed by the European Convention on the adoption of children, done at Strasbourg, on 24 April 1967 (ETS No. 058), which provides, in Article 11(2): 'A loss of nationality which could result from an adoption shall be conditional upon possession or acquisition of another nationality.' An analogous solution is stipulated by Article 12(2) of the European Convention on the Adoption of Children (Revised), CETS No. 202).

561 UNHCR, *Expert Meeting — Interpreting the 1961 Statelessness Convention and Avoiding Statelessness resulting from Loss and Deprivation of Nationality (Tunis Conclusions)*, March 2014, hereinafter the 'Tunis Conclusions', paragraph 36.

Article 5(1) of the 1961 explicitly mentions 'recognition', i.e. acknowledgement of parentage.[562] This leads to the question of when the acknowledgement of paternity by the father may have the effect of rendering the child stateless. The resulting statelessness is more understandable in cases of denial of parentage, such as denial of paternity or invalidation of the acknowledgement of paternity. However, it is an imaginable situation (although rare in practice) that a child could be acknowledged by its father after the acquisition of nationality on the basis of a provision for foundlings, having been regarded as a child of undetermined nationality at the time of birth. If the parent is a stateless person or e.g. a foreign national unable to transmit nationality (e.g. a child born out of wedlock of a father whose state of nationality prevents its transmission to extramarital children born abroad),[563] there is a risk that the child will become a stateless person. If that is the case, then, in accordance with the Convention, the state party is forbidden from allowing such a child to lose its nationality on account of such recognition.

In the context of the interpretation of Article 5(1) of the 1961 Convention, it must be noted that the status changes specified in this provision are mere examples, with the result being that other situations may be prohibited on the basis of the same Article 5(1) of the 1961 Convention from resulting in statelessness. With regard to children, such situations could include e.g. denial of paternity (a frequent situation in practice) or invalidation of acknowledgement of paternity. Denial of maternity is also possible in some countries.[564] Writers highlight the probability of the list of situations potentially falling under Article 5(1) of the 1961 Convention becoming longer as a result of developments in the field of reproductive technologies.[565]

Another interesting problem in the context of the interpretation of Article 5(1) of the 1961 Convention from the perspective of the topics covered by this book is whether this provision is applicable to the incorrect registration of the child's parentage. That could include situations in which the parent's identity, which is relevant to the child's acquisition of nationality by birth, was registered incorrectly or the child has acquired nationality through the parent's naturalization but the lack of a family link between the parent and the child is subsequently

562 Sometimes involving legitimation.

563 See the previous part of this chapter.

564 For example, since 2015, this has been available under Polish Act of 25 February 1964 — Family and Guardianship Code (Dz.U.2017.682, as amended), Article 61^{12}.

565 Tunis Conclusions, paragraph 37.

established. The Tunis Conclusions are of the view that Article 5(1) of the 1961 Convention is applicable also to such situations,[566] with the consequence being that the change in the contents of a document relating to personal status may affect the children's nationality only if the child holds the nationality of a different states. An exception from the general principle of counteracting statelessness occurs when the child's recognition as the national of a given state was procured by fraud. This means failure by the child's legal guardian to offer full disclosure of the child's existing family links. However, the Tunis Conclusions observe: '(...) as in all decisions relating to children, in instances of fraud committed by a legal representative, State authorities must take into consideration the best interests of the child. In light of this overriding principle set out in the Convention on the Rights of the Child, a range of other factors will need to be examined (including the ties to country concerned), in light of the general principle of proportionality, and not solely whether the child acquired nationality on the basis of fraud conducted by an adult guardian'.[567]

5.1.2. Regulatory frameworks in selected domestic jurisdictions

A few states explicitly foresee the loss of nationality as a result of denial of parentage by a national. These are Belgium, Finland, Luxembourg, Montenegro, the Netherlands, Norway and Switzerland.[568] Out of all provisions explicitly allowing this to happen, only Belgian law[569] does not include a safeguard against statelessness. However, the majority of states allowing this mode of loss have a solution in place to prevent the child from becoming a stateless person on its account.

Some states do not have explicit safeguards protecting children from statelessness in such situations, but they impose additional conditions to protect the child's interests. For example, the Finnish provision allows a child to lose nationality due to denial of parentage by a Finnish nationality, but the decision will have to consider the full picture of the child's situation. Particularly, the child's age and links to Finland have to be taken into account.[570]

Frequently, the states also impose age limits on the loss of nationality on this ground. For example, the relevant provision of the German statute specifies that

---

566 Tunis Conclusions, paragraph 38.

567 Tunis Conclusions, paragraph 39.

568 G.-R. de Groot, K. Swider, O. Vonk, *Practices and approaches in EU member states to prevent and end statelessness*, Brussels: European Parliament 2015, p. 37.

569 Article 8(4) of Belgian Nationality Code.

570 Article 32 of Finnish Nationality Act.

a person whose German paternity has been invalidated will lose nationality unless aged five or older.[571]

In Poland, Article 6 of Polish Citizenship Act is of particular interest in this regard. Article 6(1) provides that changes concerning the identification of one or both of the child's parents are to be taken into account if they occurred within one year following the child's birth. There are exceptions for paternity changes arising from a court judgment regarding the denial of paternity or invalidation of the acknowledgement of paternity. Such changes will be taken into account in the determination of the minor's nationality unless the minor has come of age in the meantime or completed sixteen years of age; in the latter case, the minor's consent will be required. As a consequence of such changes, the child may lose its nationality with the result of becoming a stateless person (e.g. when the mother is stateless and paternity by a Polish national has been denied).[572] There is no safeguard against statelessness in such a situation.

As for domestic provisions dealing with the effects of adoption, the majority of states do not envisage any consequences for nationality. The assumption followed by the states is that adoption is a type of legal fiction, rather than — as is the case with denial of paternity — the acknowledgement of a specific fact. Fewer than a half of European states have provisions allowing for the loss of nationality by a child through adoption.[573] Such provisions refer to full adoption, which, for the purposes of such situations, is regarded as a special case of severing of the child's legal ties to its birth family simultaneously with the acquisition of the adoptive parents' nationality. The majority of states having such provisions also have safeguards in place to prevent statelessness by making the minor's loss of nationality through adoption conditional on the acquisition of (or already having) the adoptive parent's nationality. For example, under the Dutch statute, a minor will lose Dutch nationality as a result of adoption by a foreigner only if acquiring or already holding the foreign adoptive parent's nationality in the process.[574] This is expressed somewhat differently in Lithuanian or Russian legislation. Namely, Lithuanian nationality will be lost once a Lithuanian national who

571 Article 17(3) of German Nationality Act.

572 The Act does not provide for a separate mode or path for the consideration of such changes and their reflection on the child's nationality. J. Jagielski, *Obywatelstwo polskie. Komentarz do ustawy*, LEX 2016, Commentary on Article 6 (of the Act on Polish Citizenship).

573 Fourteen states; GLOBALCIT 2017 (*Modes of Loss*), mode L13b (*Adoption*).

574 Article 16(1)(a) of Netherlands Nationality Act.

is simultaneously the national of another state — the latter as a result of having been adopted as a minor (before completing eighteen years of age) — reaches the age of twenty-one years without having renounced the other nationality.[575] In the Russian system, in turn, the loss of nationality by the child as a result of adoption may occur only upon application by the adoptive parent or parents.[576]

One of the examples of a state whose legislation does not establish any explicit safeguards against statelessness is North Macedonia. The North Macedonian statute provides that a minor adopted by foreigners will lose North Macedonian nationality, albeit only upon the adopters' application. After the age of fifteen, this mode of loss of nationality requires the minor's consent. Although explicit protection from statelessness is lacking from the legislative text, the administrative practice is to require a guarantee from the child's parents that the child will acquire another nationality.[577]

The loss of nationality upon the termination of adoption is envisaged, for example, by Italian law. If the adoption is revoked due to the adopted child's conduct, the child will lose its Italian nationality, although only on condition of having or acquiring another nationality.[578] In the European regulatory landscape, Romanian legislation stands out as an exception in this regard. Under the Romanian statute, children younger than eighteen lose their Romanian nationality upon termination of the adoption if already living abroad or leaving Romania to settle abroad.[579] In the case of invalidation of adoption of minors younger than eighteen, which is a possibility under Romanian legislation, the treatment of such minors is as though they had never acquired Romanian nationality.[580] As the above examples show, Romanian law does not contain a safeguard against statelessness for children residing abroad.[581]

---

575 Articles 24(8) in conjunction with 7(7) of XI-1196 The Republic of Lithuania Law on Citizenship.

576 Articles 26(1) and 9(2) of Federal Law of 31 May 2002 № 62-FZ, consolidated version 2 November 2004.

577 M. Smilevska, *Ending…*, pp. 9–10.

578 Article 3(3) of Italian Nationality Act.

579 Article 7(2) of the Law on Romanian Citizenship no. 21/1991 (as amended by L. no. 112/2010, 17 June 2010).

580 Article 7(1) of *ibidem* ('annulment'/'cancellation').

581 See also: C. Marin, *Ending childhood statelessness. A study on Romania*, 1 European Network on Statelessness, Working Paper 2015, pp. 13–14.

5.2. Prevention of statelessness in children's loss of nationality triggered by parental loss of nationality

5.2.1. *The international standard*

On the one hand, the majority of people acquire their nationality by transmission from their parents. On the other hand, the loss of nationality by one or both parents may, in specific cases, lead to the loss of nationality by their children. In accordance with the 1961 Convention, the loss of nationality by a child as a consequence of the loss of nationality by a parent should be conditional on the child's having or obtaining another nationality (Article 6).

The ECN, by contrast, allows states party to envisage the loss of nationality by a child as a consequence of the loss of nationality by its parent (either *ex lege* or upon the initiative of the state party) if the other parent is not a national, subject to certain exceptional situations.[582] Outside of such situations, the loss of nationality by a child may be the result of the loss of nationality by the child's parent in other cases in which the Convention permits the deprivation of nationality. In all such scenarios, the ECN has a safeguard against statelessness, except for deprivation of nationality on the grounds of fraud (Article 7(3) ECN). Thus, in situations when a parent is deprived of nationality for fraud (and the other parent is not a national), their child may also lose its nationality, even with the result of becoming a stateless person. Accordingly, it is evident that the ECN's standard for the protection of children from statelessness is lower than that of the 1961 Convention.

5.2.2. *Regulatory frameworks in selected domestic jurisdictions*

In many cases the provisions are not clear on what effect, if any, the loss of nationality by parents may have on the nationality of children.[583] Nevertheless,

582 The child's loss of nationality as a consequence of the loss of nationality by a parent cannot take place in situations when the parent's loss of nationality was a sanction for voluntary service in foreign armed forces or for conduct seriously prejudicial to the vital interests of the state party (Article 7(2) ECN). Moreover, when read in conjunction with Article 8 ECN, the language of Article 7 reveals that the consequent loss of nationality by children may not occur where the parents' loss of nationality is by renunciation. This is in connection with Article 7(2) ECN enumerating the list of cases in which the parent's loss of nationality may trigger the child's. Article 8 ECN does not specify that renunciation by a parent may affect a child's nationality.

583 O. Vonk, M.P. Vink, G.-R. de Groot. *Protection...*, p. 100.

there are abundant examples of states never tolerating the loss of nationality by children as a consequence of the loss of nationality by parents (e.g. Latvia, Malta, Cyprus, Estonia, France and Ireland).[584] Out of all states envisaging the loss of nationality by children in such a situation, only some have a safeguard against statelessness in place. For example, under the law of Iceland, a child's loss of nationality is automatic in certain narrowly defined circumstances. In accordance with Article 12 of the Icelandic statute, a national born abroad who has never been domiciled in Iceland or stayed in Iceland in a manner suggesting the intention to remain a citizen will lose their Icelandic citizenship upon reaching twenty-two years of age. This effect extends to their children. The provision, however, does not apply if it would operate to make a child stateless.[585]

Some states lack any safeguards against the statelessness of children (e.g. Bulgaria, Croatia, Denmark, Macedonia, the Netherlands, Poland, Romania or Slovenia). For example, in accordance with Article 7(1) of the Act on Polish Citizenship, the renunciation of Polish nationality by parents extends to any minors under their parental responsibility.[586] The Act foresees no explicit safeguard against child statelessness in such a situation. Moreover, although applicants are required to enclose a document confirming the nationality or assurance of nationality of another state when requesting approval for their renunciation of Polish nationality,[587] there is no such requirement with regard to documents concerning their children. This is incompatible with the 1961 Convention and ECN, which do not permit a child to lose its nationality as a result of renunciation by its parents. It is noteworthy that in 2014 a Czech amendment repealed the grounds for the loss of nationality by children as a result of the parents' declaration to the effect of renouncing their Czech nationality.[588]

In some of the states, e.g. Germany and Finland, the loss of nationality by a child may occur only in connection with one specific ground of loss of nationality by its parent or parents, being fraud. Neither state extends this mode of loss of nationality to the children automatically. For example, the Finnish

584 Thirteen states, GLOBALCIT 2017 (Loss), mode L11 (*Loss of citizenship by parent*).

585 Article 12 of Act No. 100/1952 Icelandic Nationality Act, consolidated version as amended by Act No. 40/2012).

586 In the case of a minor aged sixteen or older, the minor's consent is required (Article 7 in conjunction with Article 8 of Polish Citizenship Act).

587 Failure to attach such documents (after being given notice to cure defects) has the result of setting the application aside. For a discussion of this topic see Chapter III, section 1.1.

588 GLOBALCIT 2017, mode L11 (*Loss of citizenship by parent*), Czech Republic.

statute provides that the child will lose its nationality if the parent has committed citizenship fraud by procuring nationality for the child in reliance on false or misleading information provided in a declaration or naturalization procedure (where the other parent is not a Finnish national). The child's situation, the parent's culpability, the circumstances in which the fraud was committed, the child's own links to the country, and the child's age all have to be considered. The procedure leading to the child's loss of nationality should be initiated within five years of its acquisition.[589]

The German provisions, in turn, similarly allow the loss of nationality by a child only in the sole exceptional case of fraud, which may involve the use of false or incomplete information or the use of a threat or bribery; however, the child's interests are protected by the requirement of a separate decision being made in consideration of all circumstances and especially of the child's interests.[590] Thus, both of the discussed situations involve the children of naturalized individuals having committed citizenship fraud.

6. Counteraction of statelessness and birth registration

The traditional view holds the registration of birth and acquisition of nationality to be two separate matters.[591] However, the discussion of problems relating to statelessness asks for some attention be paid to the links existing between the two institutions. Topics of registration of birth may be perceived as relating to the counteraction of statelessness[592] due to the fact that term 'stateless person' in the 1954 Convention can be given a broad meaning, also covering individuals whose nationality cannot be established (proved).[593] According to some authors,

589 Articles 33(2) to 33(4) of Finnish Nationality Act.

590 Article 35(5) of German Nationality Act.

591 The separate nature of the two procedures is emphasized especially in those countries in which the acquisition of nationality occurs *ex lege* without requiring birth registration for that purpose.

592 However, I discuss them outside of the dichotomy between reduction and prevention mechanisms, because the nature of this matter is completely different and unrelated to the legal mechanisms for the reduction and prevention of statelessness rooted in the formal concept of nationality (viz., respectively, conferral of nationality in the case of stateless persons and protection of nationals from the loss of nationality).

593 See Chapter I. For example, the dedicated government website of the Grand Duchy of Luxembourg for statelessness-determination procedures notes that statelessness can be the result of the lack of civil registration, or inadequate civil registration, in certain

the fact that the 1961 Convention does not address the registration of births is one of the Convention's shortcomings making it a dated instrument in this regard.[594] One of the key areas of interest for the Committee on the Rights of the Child in the context of the child's right to nationality stipulated in Article 7 CRC is the non-registration of certain categories of children, such as the children of refugees, migrants or minority parents. The reason is that the lack of registration effectively leaves the children stateless through the lack of documents.[595]

The importance of a birth certificate consists in its frequently being needed in order to prove the individual's entitlement to a specific nationality.[596] In other words, although a birth certificate does not — in general terms — constitute proof of nationality, it is a key indication of whether the individual is entitled to the nationality of a given state. The above is relevant, for example, in procedures to confirm nationality. Importantly, birth certificates contain key information such as the child's name and surname, date and place of birth, as well as the parents' names. In those cases in which the legislation governing the state's nationality allows for its acquisition by right of blood (*ius sanguinis*), birth certificates provide the much-needed evidence of parentage. Where, on the other hand, nationality is conferred by virtue of birth in the territory (*ius soli*), birth certificates provide evidence of the place of birth.

Moreover, the importance of a birth certificate is that in cases of acquisition of nationality *ex lege* upon birth, the certificate will be needed by its holder to be issued documents attesting the nationality (i.e. identity papers or passport). In a statelessness-determination procedure, the lack of a birth certificate and the authorities' consequent refusal to issue a passport may be regarded as proof of the individual's not being regarded as a national by the authorities of the relevant state, because of not being able to enjoy the rights annexed to nationality.[597]

---

countries; see https://guichet.public.lu/fr/citoyens/immigration/cas-specifiques/apatride/demande-statut-apatride.html (accessed 29 January 2023).

594 L. van Waas, *Nationality…*, p. 152.

595 J. Doek, *The CRC…*, p. 27. Birth registration and the possession of a birth certificate is also of key importance from the broader perspective of the child's right to identity; see Article 8 CRC.

596 UNHCR, *Ensuring birth registration for the prevention of statelessness*, Good Practices Paper — Action 7, November 2017, p. 3.

597 Here, it will be expedient to note that a child's registration in a foreign state will not always suffice in order to be issued such documents; instead, transcription of the birth certificate is sometimes required. The procedure cannot be automatic in those cases in which there exists a conflict between the contents of a foreign certificate and the legislation of the relevant state. See e.g. Polish cases relating to consuls' refusals to issue

In many countries, birth registration suffers from a plethora of problems.[598] As an instrument of counteraction of statelessness, birth registration is uniquely important in the cases of those children whose nationality is undetermined or has not yet been identified. For example, this includes foundlings — children found in the territory of a given state. Whether such a child will become a national depends on the classification of its parents as unknown during the procedure used for the determination of the contents of the child's birth certificate. If, for example, despite the fact that the child was abandoned at a hospital, its birth certificate discloses the mother's personal information as stated by her orally to medical staff and not verified against any identity documents upon her admission to the hospital, this may have the result of making the child a stateless person.[599] The domestic legislation of some states addresses this problem in an explicit manner. For example, since 2011, the Hungarian Act on Civil Registration, Marriage and Names provides that an abandoned child whose father is unknown and mother did not disclose her identity either at the child's birth or within thirty days thereafter should be regarded as a foundling.[600] As a marginal

passports to children born abroad to Polish nationals in same-sex relationships. For a more extensive discussion of this topic see D. Pudzianowska, P. Korzec, *Citizenship 'on paper'. On the risk of statelessness of Polish children raised in same-sex unions abroad*, 16(2) National Taiwan University Law Review, 2021.

598 UNHCR, *Ensuring birth registration...*, p. 5.

599 An interesting case illustrating this problem involved a female child of Romani origin, who was abandoned by her mother in a Polish hospital in 1998. The information from the hospital's records based on the mother's oral declaration was carried over to the girl's birth certificate. Subsequently, the voivode (chief representative of the central government in a Polish province) declined to attest the child's Polish nationality on the grounds of her having a known mother and identified nationality. Polish authorities regarded the child as a Romanian national, despite their inability to obtain any documents to confirm such a claim. For sixteen years, the girl resided initially in a Polish children's home and subsequently in foster care, while her nationality status remained irregular. When the Helsinki Foundation for Human Rights became involved in the case, not even professional legal counsel appeared to be able to obtain a Romanian passport or any other identity document for the girl, i.e. any such documents as would serve to confirm her Romanian nationality, neither through the consulate nor through the authorities in Romania. As a result of defects of registration, the child remained stateless.

600 Article 9(7) of Law-Decree 17 of 1982 on Civil Registration, Marriage and Names. Also see G. Gyulai, *Nationality...*, pp. 3 and 9.

note, in the 60s of the 20th century,[601] commenting on civil-registration provisions dealing with foundlings born of parents unknown, J. Litwin wrote: 'One ought to regard as a child of parents unknown also such a child as for whom there exist certain, however insufficient, data indicating its origin, e.g. an annotation in the establishment's admission records concerning the mother's personal data, if the mother left the establishment abandoning the child and cannot be found and the data have been entered on the record on the basis of her own statement without producing identity papers.'[602]

The importance of birth registration as a mechanism of counteraction of statelessness is also illustrated by the difficulties experienced by children born to Syrian refugees abroad. Between 2011 and 2016, about 300,000 Syrian children were born abroad. The majority have Syrian nationality, but in some cases problems ensue from the fathers' inability to attend and confirm the children's nationality (one fourth of Syrian families were left without fathers as a result of the armed conflict).[603] In accordance with Syrian legislation, children born abroad acquire Syrian nationality only if their father is a Syrian national.[604] If a child of Syrian origin is not registered and does not have a birth certificate, the consequence is the lack of proof of legal ties to a Syrian-national father. It is emphasized that the documentation of the children's links to Syria and of their Syrian nationality is a key aspect of protecting Syrian refugees' right to nationality.[605]

---

601 Article 41 of Polish Decree of 8 June 1955 — Civil Registry Law (Dz.U.25.151, as amended) dealt with the obligation to notify the authorities upon having found a child; its opening words were: 'Whoever shall have found a child of parents unknown […].'

602 J. Litwin, *Prawo o aktach stanu cywilnego. Komentarz*, Warszawa 1961, commentary on Article 41 on p. 403: *Za dziecko nie znanych rodziców należy również uważać takie, co do którego istnieją pewne, nie wystarczające jednak, dane wskazujące pochodzenie, np. zapisek w księdze ewidencyjnej zakładu dotyczący danych osobowych matki, jeżeli matka opuściła zakład, pozostawiając dziecko, i nie można jej odnaleźć, a dane te zostały wpisane do księgi na podstawie jej oświadczenia bez przedstawienia dowodu osobistego.*

603 UNHCR, *Woman alone. The fight for survival by Syria's refugee women*, 2 July 2014, http://www.refworld.org/docid/53be84aa4.html (accessed 29 January 2023).

604 UNHCR, *In search of solutions. Addressing statelessness in the Middle East and North Africa*, September 2016, p. 4, http://www.refworld.org/docid/57dbdaba4.html (accessed 29 January 2023).

605 'The central question in protecting the right to nationality for refugees from Syria is preserving and documenting their link to Syria and their Syrian nationality' — Z. Albarazi, L. van Waas, *Understanding statelessness in the Syria refugee context. Research Report*, Norwegian Refugee Council & Institute on Statelessness and Inclusion 2016, pp. 17 and 26ff.

The connection between birth registration and counteraction of stateless can also be seen on the example of children born on their migrant parents' way to Europe. It is noted that one of the main problems faced by the European Union as a result of the so-called migration crisis is the large number of children born *en route* from their parents' country of origin or residence to the EU. The majority of states make no specific provisions for the situation of migrant children who were born during their parents' journey to the EU, arriving without a birth certificate and unable to obtain either it or a corresponding document in the receiving country.[606] For example, if the parents reside in Poland and the child is born outside of a medical establishment and no birth card is issued, there is no legal way to obtain a birth certificate for such a child.[607]

7. Protection of stateless children

The 1954 Convention, which governs the protection of stateless persons, does not specifically address the situation of children. Although some of the rights stipulated in the Convention may, of course, be of greater importance to children (e.g. the right to education), the special needs of stateless children are not taken into account. While the UNHCR Final Act of the United Nations Conference of Plenipotentiaries on the Status of Refugees and Stateless Persons of 1951 addressed the situation of child refugees with a recommendation that governments take the necessary steps for the 'protection of refugees who are minors, in particular unaccompanied children (…), with special reference to guardianship and adoption',[608] there is no such recommendation in the corresponding act for the 1954 Convention.

Only in recent years have certain indications begun to surface that the situation of children is given attention as part of the broader problem of protection of stateless persons. Analysis of the various instruments of international law relating to statelessness adopted in recent years permits the conclusion that an approach taking the specific needs of minor stateless persons into account is finally forming. Questions of determination of statelessness are the first illustration of this trend.[609] The UNHCR Handbook places the special needs of children

606 *Statelessness in the EU…*, p. 3.

607 Ministry of the Interior and Administration, Department of Civic Affairs, answer of 10 September 2018, no. DSO-WSC-6000-130/2018, to my inquiry.

608 UNHCR Final Act of the United Nations Conference of Plenipotentiaries on the Status of Refugees and Stateless Persons of 1951 (recommendation IV.B *in fine*).

609 I analyse these topics from a more general perspective in Chapter IV.

in the general context of diversity: 'Certain groups may face particular challenges in establishing their nationality status. Age, gender and diversity considerations may require that some individuals are afforded additional procedural and evidentiary safeguards to ensure that fair statelessness determination decisions are reached.'[610] Specifically with regard to the situation of children, the Handbook asserts: 'Children, especially unaccompanied children, may face acute challenges in communicating basic facts with respect to their nationality. States that establish statelessness determination procedures must follow the principle of pursuing the best interests of the child when considering the nationality status and need for statelessness protection of children.'[611] This general directive is consistent with the principle expressed in Article 3(1) CRC, which provides that in all actions taken in respect of children e.g. by administrative authorities 'the best interests of the child shall be a primary consideration.' Unquestionably, there may be a need for additional procedural and evidentiary safeguards for children in statelessness-determination procedures. Examples of such additional safeguards in procedures involving children may include priority consideration of applications concerning them; appointment of suitably trained counsel, interviewers, translators and interpreters; and such a distribution of the burden of proof as for the brunt of it to be borne by the state.[612]

In turn, the Handbook on Statelessness in the OSCE Area, prepared jointly by the UNHCR and the OSCE in 2017,[613] refers to the UNHCR Handbook for the above-discussed standard. It turns attention to the unique challenges presented by (young) age in the determination of nationality, which is connected with the child's difficulties communicating about the subject. Notably, however, no mention is made on placing the greater part of the burden of proof in procedures involving children on the state. However, it is pointed out that facilitations should apply not only to statelessness-determination procedures but also 'any other immigration, civil registration or nationality verification context'.[614] It is further indicated that interviewers and interpreters should also be trained to

610 UNHCR Handbook, paragraph 118.
611 UNHCR Handbook, paragraph 119.
612 UNHCR Handbook, paragraph 119.
613 OSCE & UNHCR, Handbook on Statelessness in the OSCE Area. International Standards and Good Practices, February 2017, https://www.osce.org/handbook/statelessness-in-the-OSCE-area (accessed 29 January 2023).
614 OSCE & UNHCR, *Handbook on Statelessness…*, p. 17.

be aware of and responsive to any cultural or religious sensitivities or personal factors such as age and education level.[615]

In accordance with the Recommendation of the Committee of Ministers of the Council of Europe of 2009 on the nationality of children, states should co-operate closely on matters relating to the statelessness of children, including the exchange of information on their domestic nationality legislation and public policy, as well as details relating to nationality in individual cases (in compliance with the applicable data-protection regulations; principle no. 6). Moreover, the registration of children as having unknown parents or undetermined nationality or nationality 'pending determination' should only be maintained for as short a time as possible (principle no. 8).

On the domestic level, states having statelessness-determination procedures in place do not envisage any special procedures (or procedural facilitations) for children — in particular unaccompanied minor children — such as would take their special vulnerability into account. The majority of EU member states with a defined procedure for the determination of statelessness apply the same principles to children as they do to adults, without any special accommodations. The sole exception is that children are usually assigned a guardian in the procedure, and — in states having established statelessness-identification procedures — provided with guaranteed access to legal assistance (except for Lithuania and the United Kingdom). The distribution of the burden of proof in the procedures, however, does not change when the party is a minor.[616] Germany is an exception here, with the authorities given a margin of discretion in their determinations relating to statelessness. The lack of evidence with regard to a minor has to be given consideration taking the child's best interests into account.[617]

Topics of children as a special group of stateless persons also appear in the UNHCR Handbook's in the context of detention. A stateless person faces an elevated risk of prolonged unlawful and arbitrary detention because of the typical lack of identity documents. Decisions concerning the detention of a stateless person have to take their individual situation into account, and the lack of documents alone does not warrant detention. The UN High Commissioner for Refugees notes that the general principles relating to the detention of stateless persons apply *a fortiori* to children, who, in principle, must not be detained under any circumstances whatsoever.[618]

---

615 OSCE & UNHCR, *Handbook on Statelessness…*, p. 18.

616 *Statelessness in the EU…*, p. 3.

617 *Statelessness in the EU…*, p. 15.

618 UNHCR Handbook, paragraph 113 *in fine*.

Although the 1954 Convention does not address the reunification of families, the matter is discussed briefly by the UNHCR Guidelines on Statelessness no. 4. The Guidelines encourage the states party to facilitate the reunification of individuals recognized as stateless persons with their dependants.[619]

8. Conclusions

As the above remarks demonstrate, provisions dealing with the reduction and prevention of statelessness in children are grounded in a historical context (the first ones were introduced already with the Hague Convention of 1930). They are also somewhat extensive and often address the highly specific circumstances that children's statelessness may involve. Nonetheless, the mechanisms for the counteraction of statelessness of children are not completely 'waterproof', since they do permit new cases of statelessness to arise. The fact that it has not been possible to eradicate statelessness to this date is not a mystery or enigma, as some authors claim,[620] but a concrete example of a compromise struck by the contracting states.

It is remarkable how even with regard to this particularly vulnerable category of stateless persons the states' approaches are marked with ambivalence. It is not rare for the availability of safeguards against statelessness arising upon birth to be made conditional on the status of their parents (e.g. lawful stay in the territory). Moreover, instruments of international law themselves permit the consequences of parents' conduct — such as naturalization fraud — to affect their children's nationality, which may have the consequence of rendering the children stateless.

While instruments adopted with a view to the reduction and prevention of the statelessness of children tend to be extensive and detailed, the international standard and the practice of the states with regard to matters of protection (including identification) of stateless children through the relevant procedures almost completely fail to address the special needs of this category of individuals. This illustrates the existence of a more general problem relating to how the accent is placed on the reduction of statelessness and not on the protection of stateless persons.

619 UNHCR Handbook, paragraph 151.

620 See the thesis of W.E. Conklin discussed in the Introduction.

Chapter VII The Category of Individuals Distinguished on the Grounds of Public Interest

The international order and domestic legal orders are, in principle, founded on the assumption of the necessity of preventing statelessness, reducing the number of its existing cases and offering protection to stateless persons. However, as I will demonstrate in this chapter, international law permits the exclusion of certain categories of persons from the scope of prevention, reduction and protection mechanisms, on a variety of grounds relating to the broadly understood protection of public interest. This may involve aspects such as national safety and security (protection of a constitutional interest), public safety (protection of life and health from unlawful infringement), public order, or risks to national defence.

1. Preventing statelessness

In principle, both the 1961 Convention and ECN prohibit states party from the use of deprivation of nationality with resulting statelessness. Simultaneously, however, both Conventions make an exception for persons guilty of naturalization fraud[621] (section 1.1) and — in the case of the 1961 Convention — conduct disloyal to the state of nationality (section 1.2).

Admitting exceptions from the application of statelessness-prevention mechanisms was the product of a lowering of aspirations with regard to the originally held assumption that the complete elimination of statelessness is possible.[622] In the negotiation process leading up to the 1961 Convention, there existed an alternative draft prepared by the International Law Commission — the Draft Convention on the Elimination of Future Statelessness.[623] Its Article 8 stipulated that a state party: 'may not deprive its nationals of their nationality by way of penalty

---

621 In the broadest terms possible, naturalization is a process of acquisition of nationality by which the state confers it on a natural person who has already been born. It is in this sense that I use the term 'naturalization procedures'. This may refer to detailed modes of acquisition of nationality regulated differently in different jurisdictions.

622 A. Harvey, *Recent developments on deprivation of nationality on grounds of national security and terrorism resulting in statelessness*, 28(4) Journal of Immigration, Asylum and Nationality Law 2014, p. 337.

623 On this topic see Chapter I, section 5.3.2.

or on any other ground if such deprivation renders them stateless'. It was not possible for the states, however, to reach the consensus necessary for the adoption of an absolute prohibition of deprivation of nationality resulting in statelessness.

1.1. Preventing statelessness in denaturalization for fraud

1.1.1. The international standard

Article 8(2) of the 1961 Convention provides that an individual may be deprived of nationality by the state — even with the result of becoming a stateless person — due to having acquired it by fraud or on the basis of false information submitted by the applicant (Article 8(2)(b)[624]). At the same time, in line with the Convention, a state party should not exercise its right to denaturalize a national on this ground except in accordance with the law and with guarantees of a fair hearing before a court of law or some other independent body (Article 8(4) of the 1961 Convention). The European Convention on Nationality also permits this ground of deprivation of nationality. Pursuant to its Article 7(1)(b) in conjunction with Article 7(3), a state's domestic legislation may provide for the loss of a nationality obtained by fraud or culpable misrepresentation or concealment, even with the result of making the affected individual a stateless person.[625] This is the sole exception from the principle stated in Article 7(3) ECN, which is that a state's domestic legislation may not permit the deprivation of nationality on grounds allowed by the Convention (specified in Articles 7(1) and 7(2) ECN) if statelessness would be the result.

Although the above-cited provisions of the Convention use the term 'fraud' in its narrow sense, in comparative studies it is understood broadly; the latter is the meaning I will use throughout this chapter.[626] For the purposes of the analysis, I

---

624 Article 8(2) of the 1961 Convention: 'Notwithstanding the provisions of paragraph 1 of this Article, a person may be deprived of the nationality of a Contracting State: (…) (b) where the nationality has been obtained by misrepresentation or fraud.'

625 '(1) A State Party may not provide in its internal law for the loss of its nationality *ex lege* or at the initiative of the State Party except in the following cases: (…) (b) acquisition of the nationality of the State Party by means of fraudulent conduct, false information or concealment of any relevant fact attributable to the applicant (emphasis added); (…) (3) A State Party may not provide in its internal law for the loss of its nationality under paragraphs 1 and 2 of this article if the person concerned would thereby become stateless, with the exception of the cases mentioned in paragraph 1, sub-paragraph b, of this article.'

626 On this topic see Chapter III, section 1.2.2.

distinguish two types of situations permitted to incur the loss of nationality for naturalization fraud. Firstly, misleading the naturalization authority, which can be achieved in a number of different ways. This may involve submitting false information or documents, failing to disclose certain specific circumstances (such as conviction of a serious crime, possession of nationality of another state, or bigamy)[627] or misrepresenting one's identity (e.g. name and surname) or age. The misrepresentation could be either oral or written. Secondly, fraud includes exerting wrongful influence on the decision-making body. As stated in the explanatory report, the ECN's provisions apply not only to the acquisition of nationality by providing false or incomplete information or submitting false documents, but also to threat, bribery or other dishonest conduct.[628]

It should also be noted that fraud does not include situations when the applicant was merely mistaken (fell in error). On the contrary, having knowingly and deliberately misled the authorities in order to obtain the new nationality must be the case.[629] Furthermore, the conduct has to be related to a circumstance relevant to the acquisition of nationality. As the ECN explanatory report also asserts, the fraudulent conduct has to be the 'result of a deliberate act or omission by the applicant which was a significant factor in the acquisition of nationality.'[630] There is no reason for believing that the conduct needs to constitute a criminal offence in the meaning of criminal law; rather, it refers to an autonomous category of conduct with its own meaning in nationality law.[631] The provisions at hand refer to a broader category of human acts. For example, a threat need not be criminal

627 The last three examples provided here are discussed in the ECN explanatory report, paragraph 61. As an example of fraud by misrepresentation (misleading conduct), the ECN explanatory report cites a situation when the applicant obtains the nationality of a state party on condition of renouncing the original nationality, which the new citizen subsequently deliberately fails to do. There can be some doubt, however, as to whether the subsequent breach of such a promise may qualify as fraud; thus: G.-R. de Groot and M.P. Vink, *Loss of citizenship. Trends and regulations in Europe*, Comparative Report, 4 EUDO Citizenship Observatory, June 2010, RSCAS/EUDO-CIT-Comp., pp. 13–14.

628 CETS 166 — Explanatory Report to the European Convention on Nationality, paragraph 62.

629 R. Bauböck, V. Paskalev, *Citizenship deprivation. A normative analysis*, 82 Centre of European Policy Studies. Papers in Liberty and Security March 2015, p. 20.

630 CETS 166 — Explanatory Report to the European Convention on Nationality, paragraph 61.

631 R. Baubock, V. Paskalev, *Citizenship*..., pp. 20–21.

— suffice for it to be simply unlawful in a wider sense (wrongful, illegal, etc.), that of conduct calculated on compelling the state official to perform a specific action against their will.

The 1961 Convention and ECN permit the deprivation of nationality for fraud, even with the result of rendering the affected individual stateless, subject to no additional preconditions whatsoever. Certain restrictions on domestic jurisdictions envisaging denaturalization for citizenship fraud even with resulting statelessness can be found in the Council of Europe's soft laws and in EU law. In the most general terms, this comes down to the requirement of a proportionality test to precede each and every denaturalization leading to statelessness. However, the criteria of such a test are defined somewhat differently.

Concerning the standard developed by the Council of Europe, attention should be drawn primarily to the guidelines included in Recommendation No. R (99) 18 of the Committee of Ministers to member States on the avoidance and reduction of statelessness, which make the following suggestion: 'In order to avoid, as far as possible, situations of statelessness, a State should not necessarily deprive of its nationality persons who have acquired its nationality by fraudulent conduct, false information or concealment of any relevant fact. To this effect, the gravity of the facts, as well as other relevant circumstances, such as the genuine and effective link of these persons with the state concerned, should be taken into account' (emphasis added).[632] Thus, according to the Recommendation, the deprivation of nationality in cases leading to statelessness should not be automatic but additional circumstances must be taken into account. As noted by G.-R. de Groot and M.P Vink, the Recommendation implies the existence of a need for the imposition of specific time-limits in domestic law after which denaturalization due to fraud will no longer be possible.[633] The question of temporal limits relates to the fact that after the passage of a certain length of time the individual can be assumed to have formed a 'genuine and effective link' with their state of nationality, with the result that depriving them of that nationality should no longer be possible. As I will show later in this chapter, such time-limits can be found in certain jurisdictions.

As for the EU standard, an important role with regard to the problems discussed in this chapter belongs to the principles expounded by the CJEU in its

632 Paragraph 1.II.C (c).

633 G.-R. de Groot, M. P. Vink, *Loss of citizenship*..., p. 8.

judgment in *C-135/08, Janko Rottmann v. Freistaat Bayern*, of 2 March 2010.[634] There, the Court found that whenever statelessness with the resulting loss of EU citizenship is at play, national courts must subject the denationalization decision to a proportionality test in the light of the fundamental significance of EU citizenship and in the light of national law. The proportionality test has the following components: (1) consequences of the deprivation of nationality for the affected individual and their family members; (2) gravity of the offence; (3) time elapsed between the naturalization decision and denaturalization; and (4) options available for the resumption of the original nationality.

Furthermore, the national court must examine whether the principle of proportionality does not perhaps require that the individual whose nationality is being withdrawn be given a reasonable time for the resumption of their original nationality.[635]

1.1.2. Selected domestic jurisdictions

The vast majority of European states envisage the loss of nationality as a consequence of naturalization fraud. Only Iceland, Sweden, Croatia and Poland do not.[636] By contrast, the majority of states foreseeing this mode of loss of nationality allow it even where it leads to statelessness.[637] Below, I discuss examples

---

634 Dr Janko Rottmann was born an Austrian citizen in Graz. In 1995, he was investigated for a crime relating to the exercise of his profession. Shortly thereafter, he left for Germany (Munich) and in 1998 applied for naturalization there, which he obtained in 1999. During the procedure, he did not disclose the criminal proceedings pending against him or the outstanding arrest warrant. When the German authorities learned of those circumstances, they decided to withdraw Dr Rottmann's German citizenship, rendering him a stateless person (he had lost his original Austrian citizenship automatically with the acquisition of German nationality) and consequently depriving him also of his status of EU citizen.

635 For a more extensive discussion of this case see D. Pudzianowska, *Warunki nabycia i utraty obywatelstwa Unii Europejskiej. Czy dochodzi do autonomizacji pojęcia obywatelstwa Unii?* [in:] G. Baranowska, A. Gliszczyńska-Grabias and A. Bodnar (eds.), *Ochrona praw obywatelek i obywateli Unii Europejskiej. 20 lat — osiągnięcia i wyzwania na przyszłość*, Warszawa 2015, pp. 141–154.

636 GLOBALCIT 2017 (Modes of Loss), data for all European states (Europe), L09 (Fraudulent acquisitions). In the case of Poland, there are some doubts as to the correct interpretation of the applicable law, which I will address towards the end of this part of the chapter.

637 Thirty-five out of forty-two European states compared in GLOBALCIT 2017 (Modes of Loss).

taken from those countries in which the deprivation of nationality is permitted to have the effect of rendering the affected individual stateless.

Interestingly, even states having undergone a political and constitutional transformation and prohibited the deprivation of nationality in their constitutions still allow this mode of loss. Although Article 12(b) of the Constitution of the Czech Republic of 16 December 1992 prohibits involuntary deprivation of nationality, an amendment enacted in 2014 enabled the reopening of naturalization proceedings on the grounds of citizenship fraud. Pursuant to Article G(3) of Hungarian Constitution of 18 April 2011, no one may be stripped of Hungarian nationality acquired at birth or lawfully obtained at a later time.[638] Ordinary statutes, however, permit the denaturalization of unlawfully naturalized individuals, especially those whose conduct in the naturalization procedure was aimed at misleading the authorities by providing false information or concealing any data or information whatsoever.[639]

The level of detail of statutory frameworks relating to broadly understood fraud differs from one country to the next. The legislation adopted by some states is fairly concise. For example, in accordance with the Romanian statute: 'Romanian citizenship may be withdrawn from a person who [...] has obtained Romanian citizenship by fraudulent means.'[640] Usually, however, the specific conduct warranting deprivation of nationality is defined in more detail. There is typically a list of behaviours such as the provision of false or misleading facts, circumstances or data.[641] Other frequent items on such lists include the submission of forged documents[642] and concealment of important circumstances.[643] Some

638 'No person may be deprived of Hungarian citizenship established by birth or acquired in a lawful manner.' English translation of Hungarian Constitution: https://www.constituteproject.org/constitution/Hungary_2011.pdf (accessed 23 January 2023).

639 Article 9(1) of Hungarian Nationality Act. Denaturalization decisions are issued by the President at the application of the competent minister (Article 9(3)).

640 Article 25(1) of Romanian Citizenship Act.

641 Russia, Albania, Belarus, Belgium, Denmark, Cyprus, Estonia, France, Hungary, Ireland, Kosovo, Latvia, Liechtenstein, Luxembourg, North Macedonia, Malta, the Netherlands, Norway, Portugal, Serbia, Slovenia, Spain, Switzerland, Ukraine, the United Kingdom and Finland — GLOBALCIT 2017 (Modes of Loss), mode L09.

642 Albania, Belarus, Belgium, Lithuania, Macedonia, Moldova, Russia, Spain and Ukraine — GLOBALCIT 2017 (Modes of Loss), mode L09.

643 Belgium, Bosnia and Herzegovina, Ireland, Kosovo, Malta, Moldova, Norway, Serbia, Slovenia, Switzerland, Ukraine and the United Kingdom — GLOBALCIT 2017 (Modes of Loss), mode L09.

statutes explicitly mention identity fraud; for example, Slovak legislation provides that a naturalization decision may be declared null and void if the applicant was not the individual whose documents were submitted.[644]

It is rarer for statutes to refer to the circumstance that the acquisition of nationality was procured by unlawful influence on the decision-making authority. One such example is the German provision whereby a naturalized person may lose nationality not only if the decision conferring it was procured by fraud or submission of false or incomplete information but also by a threat or bribery.[645] In accordance with the Slovak statute, in turn: 'the nationality of the Slovak Republic shall not arise [if] the issue of deed was reached by a criminal action'.[646]

In some legal systems, the fraud must relate to circumstances relevant or material to the outcome of the case. In other words, there must exist a causation chain between the fraud and the acquisition of nationality. For example, in the Estonian statute, citizenship may be stripped from an individual who 'when acquiring Estonian citizenship or in relation to the restoration to him or her of Estonian citizenship, submits false information to conceal facts that would have precluded the grant or restoration of Estonian citizenship to him or her' (emphasis added).[647] The Danish statute provides that an individual may be denaturalized for having deliberately provided false or misleading information or failed to disclose information that was of decisive importance to the acquisition of nationality.[648] Despite differences in the wordings of the various countries' specific provisions, which sometimes stipulate the necessity of the existence of a causation chain and sometimes do not, the majority view causation as relevant, albeit in some the matter is not so clear.[649] Sometimes, the legislation states clearly that the conduct must be culpable. For example, the already cited Danish provision stipulates that the conduct must be deliberate. The Norwegian statute takes a similar approach.[650]

---

644 Article 8(1)(b) of Slovak Nationality Act.

645 Article 35(1) of German Nationality Act.

646 Article 8b(1) of Slovak Nationality Act.

647 § 28(1)(4) of Estonian Nationality Act.

648 Article 8A of Danish Nationality Act.

649 G.-R. de Groot, M.P Vink, *A comparative analysis of regulations on involuntary loss of nationality in the European Union*, 75 Centre of European Policy Studies. Paper in Liberty and Security in Europe, December 2014, pp. 15–16.

650 Article 26 (2) of Act No. 51/2005 on Norwegian Citizenship, as amended by Act No. 36 of 30 June 2006.

The matter of culpability can be regarded as a component of the proportionality test. The most elaborate exposition of the proportionality test for denationalization decisions is found in the Finnish statute, which requires the analysis of culpability and of the circumstances of the act, as well as the individual's ties to Finland. For minors, moreover, age has to be taken into account.[651]

With regard to the proportionality of decisions, it should be noted that many states (although not all) impose time-bars on the loss of nationality for naturalization fraud. As discussed above, doing so is consistent with the directive of taking the links forming between the person and the state over time into account in the proportionality test. In France, for example, if the naturalization decision was influenced by a falsehood or obtained by fraud, nationality can be forfeited within two years of the circumstance coming into light. There are states in which this time-limit is longer, such as five years (Belgium, Finland), ten (Hungary, Latvia),[652] twelve (the Netherlands) or fifteen (Spain) after the acquisition of nationality. Portugal is an example of a country whose time-limit has been developed by jurisprudence; it is a long one, of twenty years.[653] There are, however, states in which there are no time-limits (e.g. the United Kingdom, Ireland and Denmark), and the loss of nationality for naturalization fraud will always remain possible.[654]

Last but not least, in some states deprivation of nationality for fraud is not expressly envisaged by the provisions of nationality law but has a basis in other

---

651 Article 33(3) of Finnish Nationality Act.

652 Latvia permits an exception from the time-limit for individuals convicted of any of the 'most serious crimes of concern to the international community as a whole' listed by Article 5 of the Rome Statute of the International Criminal Court, done at Rome on 17 July 1998, i.e. genocide, crimes against humanity, war crimes or crime of aggression (Article 24(4)(1) of Latvian Nationality Act) or nationals of a state whose nationality is incompatible with Latvian nationality (Article 24(4)(2)). As for the last-mentioned exception, Latvia permits dual nationality only with regard to a closed list of states. Those include the member states of the EU, EFTA and NATO, as well as Australia, Brazil, New Zealand, and any state with which Latvia has a bilateral agreement. For a more extensive discussion of this topic see K. Kruma, *Country report on citizenship law. Latvia*, 6 EUDO Citizenship Observatory, January 2015, RSCAS/EUDO-CIT-CR, p. 13.

653 Court of Appeals in Lisbon (*Acórdão do Tribunal da Relação de Lisboa*), *8640/2003-6*, judgment, 29 January 2004, cited after G.-R de Groot, N.C Luk, *Twenty years of CJEU jurisprudence on citizenship*, 15(5) German Law Journal 2014, p. 13.

654 Data concerning time-limits cited after G.-R. de Groot, M. P. Vink, *Loss of citizenship…*, table on pp. 14–15.

provisions. For example, an individual having acquired Greek nationality by providing false information or by fraud may lose it by a decision issued on the basis of the general provisions governing administrative procedures.[655] The Polish case is similar. Naturalization decisions issued by voivodes (chief representatives of the central government in a province) are not excluded from the applicability of the Code of Administrative Procedures, which contains provisions relating to a decision obtained by fraudulent means. While Article 34(2) of Polish Constitution proclaims that a Polish citizen cannot forfeit nationality other than by voluntary renunciation, there is a risk that in cases of a declaration of nullity of the administrative decision granting naturalization, the authorities will argue that the affected individual had never become a Polish citizen.[656]

1.2. Statelessness prevention in cases of conduct disloyal to the state of nationality

1.2.1. The international standard

Apart from the above-discussed case of fraud, the 1961 Convention envisages several more cases in which an individual may be deprived of nationality, even with the result of rendering them stateless. The international standard is not uniform in this regard, because the ECN does not permit the deprivation of nationality with resulting statelessness on any grounds other than those of fraud.[657] Generally speaking, the additional grounds foreseen by the 1961 Convention

655 GLOBALCIT 2017, mode L09. This refers to Article 1 of Act no. 261/1968 concerning the declaration of nullity of administrative acts issued in violation of the law. (My thanks for this explanation to Dr A. Petropoulou). Concerning this provision see also: M. Ioannidis, S.-I.G. Koutnatzis, *Evolution and gestalt of the Greek State* [in:] S. Cassese, A. von Bogdandy and P.M. Huber (eds.), *The Max Planck Handbooks in European Public Law*, vol. 1, *The administrative state*, Oxford 2017, p. 282.

656 From the information available to me, no voivodes have to this date initiated any such procedures in matters relating to nationality. Also see the response of the Mazovia Voivodeship Office (*Mazowiecki Urząd Wojewódzki*), Department for Foreigners, *WSC-4.1331.5.2018*, of 22 August 2018. At the same time, however, the queried authorities did not appear to consider such an outcome to be prevented by the constitutional provision.

657 While ECN does provide that states may deprive their nationals for service in foreign armed forces or for conduct seriously prejudicial to the vital interests of the state, any such withdrawal must not result in statelessness. Accordingly, the ECN standard in this category of cases is higher with regard to the prevention of statelessness.

apply to different scenarios of broadly understood disloyalty to the state of nationality.

The first such scenario is of an individual having — again, in violation of the duty of loyalty to their state of nationality and in disregard of a clear prohibition issued by that state — provided or not ceased to provide services to another state or received any emoluments from a foreign state (Article 8(3)(a) i of the 1961 Convention). The second one refers to an individual having — as in the preceding cases, in violation of the duty of loyalty to one's state of nationality — engaged in conduct seriously prejudicial to the vital interests of the state (Article 8(3)(a)(ii) of the 1961 Convention). The last one concerns, in general terms, the situation of an individual who — in violation of the duty of loyalty to the state of nationality — has sworn an oath or made a formal declaration or given some other proof of loyalty to another state (Article 8(3)(b) of the 1961 Convention).

The authorization to maintain the above-discussed solutions in domestic jurisdictions is conditional on having — at the time of signature, ratification or accession to the 1961 Convention — reserved the right to withdraw nationality on such grounds if they were already present in the domestic legal order at the time of accession to the 1961 Convention (the first sentence of Article 8(3)). This is the example of a 'stand-still clause', making the acceding state unable to pass amendments for the purpose of the ratification of the Convention, let alone at a later time; only provisions existing at the time of accession may be retained.[658] Simultaneously, the 1961 Convention stipulates the applicability of its Article 8(4) on procedural guarantees to such grounds, similarly to the previously discussed case of fraud.

In the analysis of the above cases in which the 1961 Convention allows — depending on the fulfilment of specific conditions by the states party — for the loss of nationality, one can distinguish several key aspects. First of all, in accordance with Article 8(3)(a)(i) of the 1961 Convention, the services provided to a foreign state may be either military or non-military in nature. The *ratio* is not for any services provided to a foreign state to incur the loss of nationality (with the possible result of statelessness) but only services violating the duty of loyalty to one's own state. There certainly exist examples of services to a foreign state that do not warrant the loss of nationality, such as humanitarian activities. Neither should services rendered to a foreign state incur the loss of nationality

658 Tunis Conclusions, paragraph 65. Only a small number of states party to the Convention have used the option to make such a reservation. Out of all European states, these are: Austria, Belgium, Georgia, Ireland, Lithuania and the United Kingdom.

if their provision was linked to force majeure or if the affected person cannot be held fully accountable for their actions, for example because of an intellectual or mental disability.[659]

As for the grounds stipulated in Article 8(3)(a)(ii) of the 1961 Convention, i.e. breach of duty of loyalty to one's state of nationality by conduct seriously prejudicial to the vital interests of that state, UNHRC documents state that such interests must be the interests of the individual's state of nationality and not the interests of whatever states with which it might be in friendly relations.[660] It is especially important that this exception from the 1961 Convention's general prohibition of deprivation of nationality with resulting statelessness sets the bar high with regard to the conduct warranting such deprivation. According to the Tunis Conclusions, the conduct 'must threaten the foundations and organization of the [s]tate whose nationality is at issue'[661] and not simply be detrimental to its interests. Accordingly, ordinary criminal offences will not suffice; something of a more serious calibre is required. For example: 'acts of treason, espionage and — depending on their interpretation in domestic law — "terrorist acts" may be considered to fall within the scope of this paragraph.'[662] The view taken by S. Jayaraman suggests that some terrorist acts can fail to meet the threshold of conduct seriously prejudicial to the state's vital interests. In his opinion, the court interpreting the provision may be required to ponder whether acts of terrorism committed abroad — under examination as possible grounds of deprivation of nationality — sufficiently engage the 'vital interests' of the state.[663]

The permissibility of deprivation of nationality on the grounds of breach of the duty of loyalty in situations envisaged by the 1961 Convention is linked to the question of the connection between the provision at hand and the prohibition of deprivation of nationality on political grounds in Article 9 of the Convention[664].

---

659 See Summary Record of the 20th Plenary Meeting, A/CONF.9/ SR.20 (23-8-1961), cited after O.W. Vonk, M.P. Vink, G.-R. de Groot, *Protection…*, p. 79.

660 This is attested by the language of the chapeau of Article 8(3)(a): 'inconsistently with [the] duty of loyalty to the Contracting State'.

661 Tunis Conclusions, paragraph 68.

662 Tunis Conclusions, paragraph 68.

663 S. Jayaraman, *International terrorism and statelessness. Revoking the citizenship of ISIL foreign fighters*, 17(1) Chicago Journal of International Law 2016, Article 6.

664 Article 9 of the 1961 Convention prohibits the divestment of an individual or group of individuals of nationality on religious, ethnic or political grounds. This provision implements Article 15 UDHR (especially Article 15 (2) UDHR) and is in itself supplemented by the relevant provisions of the International Convention on the Elimination of All Forms of Racial Discrimination opened for signatures in New York on

The line between the deprivation of nationality on political grounds and its divestment on grounds of breach of duty of loyalty will not always be perfectly sharp. However, the consequence of Article 9 of the 1961 Convention is that in each and every case of deprivation of nationality — whether resulting in statelessness or not — the state is bound to establish that the decision is not being made on political grounds (or any other discriminatory grounds mentioned by Article 9 of the Convention). Especially conduct consistent with the freedom of speech or assembly or with other rights guaranteed by the international system of human rights can never be grounds for deprivation of nationality.[665] Without question, any provisions foreseeing the deprivation of nationality on the grounds of holding specific political views are incompatible with Article 9 of the 1961 Convention.

1.2.2. Selected domestic legal frameworks

In the domestic legal systems of several states, non-military service to a foreign state may be grounds for deprivation of nationality even if the result would be to make the affected individual stateless. These states are: Austria, Estonia, France, Greece, Italy, Lithuania and Spain.[666] Details vary from one state to the next. In particular, different states define service to a foreign state differently. This can be defined broadly as 'being in the service of another state' (e.g. Lithuania)[667] or more narrowly as employment in the public service (e.g. France,[668] Italy[669] or Greece[670]) or in the security services of a foreign state (e.g. Estonia)[671]. Deprivation of nationality can be the consequence of failure to obtain the authorization

7 March 1966 (United Nations, Treaty Series, vol. 660, p. 195), CEDAW and the UN Convention on the Rights of Persons with Disabilities of 13 December 2006 (A/RES/ 61/106).

665 Tunis Conclusions, paragraph 71.

666 GLOBALCIT 2017 (Modes of Loss), data for all European states, including Turkey, mode L04 (Other service for foreign country). Out of all these states, only Lithuania and Austria are parties to the 1961 Convention, and only Austria submitted the declaration required by the first sentence of Article 8(3) of the 1961 Convention. None is party to the ECN, which does not allow this mode of loss of nationality.

667 Article 24(4) of Lithuanian Nationality Act.

668 First paragraph of Article 23–8 of French Civil Code.

669 Article 12(1) of Italian Nationality Act.

670 Article 17(1)(a) of Greek Nationality Code.

671 § 28(1)(2) of Estonian Nationality Act.

of one's government (e.g. Estonia[672] or Lithuania[673]), of violation of the government's clear prohibition (Spain)[674] or failure to resign from the foreign service when ordered to do so by one's state of nationality (e.g. Italy[675] and France[676]). The applicability of the sanction can be dependent on whether the citizen's actions in the service of another state infringe on the interests and reputation of the state of nationality (Austria)[677]. In most states, the deprivation is not automatic (*ex lege*) but requires a specific decision to be issued by state authorities.[678]

In some of the above-listed countries, non-military service to a foreign state may be grounds for deprivation of nationality only in the case of naturalized citizens; for example, in Spain[679] and Estonia[680].

More states envisage the loss of nationality on the grounds of foreign military service. This features in the domestic legislation of 17 European states,[681] of which the following have no safeguards against statelessness: Cyprus, Estonia, France, Greece, Italy, Latvia, Lithuania, Romania, Spain and Austria.[682]

Similarly to the case of non-military services rendered to a foreign state, it can once again be noticed that certain states restrict the applicability of this mode of loss of nationality to naturalized citizens only (Cyprus,[683] Spain[684] and Estonia[685]). In the majority of states the loss of citizenship does not occur *ex lege* but requires a decision to be issued by the authorities.[686] The Austrian statute is

672 Joining the public service of a foreign state without leave of the government of the Republic of Estonia; see § 28(1)(1) of Estonian Nationality Act.
673 Providing services to a foreign state without the authorization of the government of the Republic of Lithuania; see Article 24(4) of Lithuanian Nationality Act.
674 Article 25(1)(b) of Spanish Civil Code.
675 Article 12(1) of Italian Nationality Act.
676 First paragraph of Article 23–8 of French Civil Code.
677 Article 33 of Austrian Citizenship Act.
678 GLOBALCIT 2017 (Modes of Loss), mode L04 (Other service for foreign country).
679 Article 25(1)(b) of Spanish Civil Code.
680 § 28(3) of Estonian Nationality Act.
681 GLOBALCIT 2017 (Modes of Loss), mode L03 (service in foreign army).
682 GLOBALCIT 2017 (Modes of Loss), mode L03 (Service in foreign army); O.W. Vonk, M.P. Vink, G.-R. de Groot, *Protection…*, table on pp. 77–78.
683 Article 113(3) of Cypriot Civil Registry Law.
684 Article 25(1)(b) of Spanish Civil Code.
685 § 28(3) of Estonian Nationality Act.
686 GLOBALCIT 2017 (Modes of Loss), mode L03 (service in foreign army).

exceptional in providing for the automatic loss of Austrian nationality upon the voluntary acceptance of military service in a foreign state.[687]

There can be no doubt that military service in a foreign state has lost its relevance as a ground of deprivation of nationality due to the abolishment of conscription in many European states. Thus, the risk of statelessness arising on this ground is less than it used to be. Still, it will be expedient to note that in the Netherlands and Germany, for example, loss of nationality on this ground was initially abolished and subsequently reintroduced at the beginning of the 21st century (Netherlands — 2003, Germany — 2000).[688]

When it comes to the breach of duty of loyalty to one's state of nationality — for example by conduct seriously prejudicial to the vital interests of the state — as many as nineteen European states retain this mode of loss of nationality.[689] In ten, it is possible in cases resulting in statelessness (Belgium, Cyprus, Estonia, Greece, Ireland, Lithuania, Malta, Romania, Slovenia[690] and the United Kingdom[691]).

The drafting of the majority of provisions dealing with this mode of loss of nationality is vague and unclear.[692] For example, the Irish statute proclaims that a certificate of naturalization may be revoked if the competent minister is satisfied that the recipient 'has, by any overt act, shown himself to have failed in his duty of fidelity to the nation and loyalty to the State'.[693] The Greek statute provides that nationality may be lost by an individual residing abroad and acting contrary to the interests of the Greek state.[694] Romanian legislation contains similar provisions.[695] In accordance with Estonian law, a naturalized citizen attempting to change country's political system by the use of force may be denaturalized.[696]

The majority of states allowing the loss of nationality on this ground when leading to statelessness restrict its applicability to naturalized citizens only

687 Article 32 of Austrian Citizenship Act.

688 G.-R. de Groot, M.P. Vink, *Loss of citizenship…*, p. 21. In both countries, the loss of nationality on this ground is not possible if it would lead to statelessness.

689 GLOBALCIT 2017 (Modes of Loss), mode L07 (Disloyalty or treason).

690 O.W. Vonk, M.P. Vink, G.-R. de Groot, *Protection…*, pp. 80–81.

691 S. Mantu, *'Terrorist' citizens and the human right to nationality*, 26(1) Journal of Contemporary European Studies 2018, p. 34.

692 G.-R. de Groot, M.P. Vink, *Loss of citizenship…*, p. 26.

693 Article 19(1)(b) of Irish Nationality Act.

694 Article 17(1)(b) of Greek Nationality Code.

695 Article 25(1)(a) of Romanian Nationality Act.

696 § 28(1)(3) of Estonian Nationality Act.

(Belgium, Cyprus, Estonia, Ireland, Lithuania, Malta and the United Kingdom). In those states, nationality is lost on this ground not *ex lege* but through a specific action taken by the state.[697]

Notably, discussions are currently underway in many states as to the deprivation of nationality on the grounds of commission of acts of terrorism, which, as noted beforehand, may fall within the scope of conduct seriously prejudicial to the vital interests of the state (Article 8(3)(a)(ii) of the 1961 Convention). There are also states explicitly providing for the loss of nationality as a sanction imposed for a criminal offence of terrorist nature, even if the effect is to render the individual stateless. In the United Kingdom, for example, a naturalized citizen may be denaturalized because '[i]t is conducive to the public good because the person, while having that citizenship status, has conducted him or herself in a manner which is seriously prejudicial to the vital interests of the United Kingdom'.[698] In practice, as some observe, this may lead to statelessness because there is no safeguard requiring the existence of a guarantee that the affected person will obtain the nationality of another state.[699] The only requirement is that of '[r]easonable grounds for believing that the person is able, under the law of a country or territory outside the United Kingdom, to become a national of such a country or territory.'[700] In 2013, Belgium introduced an amendment allowing the deprivation of nationality with regard to those convicted of a terrorist crime.[701] Romania envisages the deprivation of nationality of an individual having ties to a terrorist organization or having provided such an organization with any form of support or committed other acts posing a threat to national security.[702]

In some states, even ordinary criminal offences may be grounds for deprivation of nationality. This is the case in several European states, but only in Cyprus

697 GLOBALCIT 2017 (Modes of Loss), mode L07 (Disloyalty or treason).

698 Article 40 (4A)(b) of UK Nationality Act.

699 S. Mantu, *Terrorist...*, p. 34.

700 Article 40 (4A)(c) of UK Nationality Act. The majority of those stripped of UK nationality are located outside the country's borders. Investigative journalists have established that out of eighteen identified individuals divested in 2006, fifteen were outside of the borders of the United Kingdom; S. Leo, *Graphic detail. How UK government has used its powers of banishment*, The Bureau of Investigative Journalism, February 27, 2013 https://www.thebureauinvestigates.com/stories/2013-02-27/graphic-detail-how-uk-government-has-used-its-powers-of-banishment (accessed 23 January 2023).

701 Art. 23/1 of Belgian Nationality Code; M.-C. Foblets, Z. Yanasmayan, P. Wautelet, *Country report: Belgium*, EUDO Citizenship Observatory 2013, p. 14, footnote 44.

702 Article 25(1)(d) of Romanian Nationality Act.

and Lithuania is it allowed to have the effect of leaving the affected individual a stateless person. In both of the countries, the relevant provisions apply only to nationals other than by birth. For example, the Cypriot statute provides that a naturalized citizen convicted within five years in any state of a criminal offence for which the upper sentencing limit exceeds twelve months may be deprived of nationality.[703]

With regard to the aforementioned problem of the relationship between Article 8(3) of the 1961 Convention, which permits denationalization for disloyalty, and Article 9 of the Convention, which prohibits loss of nationality on political grounds, it should be noted that no European state has any legislation permitting the deprivation of nationality on political grounds.[704] Similarly, European countries do not envisage the loss of nationality on grounds such as race, religion or disability.[705]

2. Exclusions from protection mechanisms

2.1. Exclusions: Overview

The 1954 Convention distinguishes a specific category of individuals on the grounds of public interest. In accordance with its Article 1(2), the protection offered by the Convention does not apply e.g. to persons undeserving of it on account of their conduct.[706] Article 1(2)(iii) excludes three categories of individuals

703 Article 113(3)(c) of Cypriot Civil Registry Law.

704 Outside of the European context, an example of this can be found in the Egyptian nationality statute, which provides that a citizen may be deprived of nationality 'if, at any time, he is assumed to be a Zionist' — Article 16(7), Law No. 26 Concerning Egyptian Nationality, 1975.

705 Outside of Europe, the provisions in the Kingdom of Mauritania allow the government to oppose a naturalization within one year on grounds of, among several other possibilities, 'serious physical or mental incapacity' — Article 14, Law no. 1961-112 Mauritanian Nationality Code. In Kuwait, in turn, the citizenship of a natural person may be declared void 'if the naturalized person expressly renounces Islam or if he behaves in such a manner as clearly indicates his intention to abandon Islam' — Article 4(5) of Kuwait Nationality Law, 1959 (English translation: https://www.refworld.org/docid, accessed 18 February 2023). In Oman, under the 1962 Nationality Law, it was possible to forfeit nationality for atheism or membership in an 'anti-religious group' — Article 13(2); cited after L. van Waas, *A comparative analysis of nationality laws in the MENA Region, Social Science Research Network*, 9 September 2014, p. 21.

706 The term 'persons undeserving of protection' appears in UNHCR, Guidelines on International Protection No. 5. Application of the Exclusion Clauses. Article 1F of the

from the protection of the Convention.[707] The first category comprises those suspected of a crime against peace, war crime, or crime against humanity within the meaning of the international instruments establishing those crimes (Article 1(2)(iii)(a) of the 1954 Convention). The second one refers to those suspected of a serious criminal offence not political in nature outside of the host country before entering it; (Article 1(2)(iii)(b) of the 1954 Convention). The third category covers the suspected perpetrators of 'acts contrary to the purposes and principles of the United Nations' (Article 1(2)(iii)(c) of the 1954 Convention).

In the process of interpretation of Article 1(2)(iii) of the 1954 Convention, it will be fitting to take a look at interpretations of Article 1F of the 1951 Geneva Convention. This is because the wording of the two provisions is essentially identical.[708] Ever since the adoption of the 1954 Convention, interpreters have noted the possibility of interpreting Article 1(2)(iii) of the 1954 Convention in reliance on existing interpretations of Article 1F of the Geneva Convention of 1951.[709] This includes both the purpose of the provision and the detailed interpretation of its so-called exclusion clauses. Accordingly, the analysis that follows below is largely based on material referring to the Geneva Convention of 1951.

Similarly to the case of the Geneva Convention of 1951, the main *ratio* for the exclusion clauses specified in Article 1(2)(iii) of the 1954 Convention was the belief that the states would be unwilling to bind themselves to the Convention if it were to force them to protect serious criminals. Therefore, the insertion of exclusion clauses was deemed a necessity in order to maximize the number of ratifications of the 1954 Convention. Thus, their purpose is mainly

---

1951 Convention relating to the Status of Refugees, 4 September 2003, HCR/GIP/03/05, paragraph 4, p. 3.

707 Article 1(2)(iii) of the 1954 Convention: 'This Convention shall not apply: (…) (iii) To persons with respect to whom there are serious reasons for considering that: (a) They have committed a crime against peace, a war crime, or a crime against humanity, as defined in the international instruments drawn up to make provisions in respect of such crimes; (b) They have committed a serious non-political crime outside the country of their residence prior to their admission to that country; (c) They have been guilty of acts contrary to the purposes and principles of the United Nations.'

708 Article 1(2)(iii) of the 1954 Convention uses the plural rather than the singular, refers to a stateless person rather than a refugee and replaces the phrase 'outside the country of refuge prior to his admission to that country as a refugee' with 'outside the country of their residence prior to their admission to that country' (Article 1(2)(iii)(b).

709 N. Robinson, *Convention…*, p. 12. For a discussion of the close links arising at the time of the drafting of the two Conventions, see Chapter I, section 5.2.

instrumental, aimed to preserve the credibility of the protection system.[710] The purpose of the provisions goes beyond protecting the interests of any specific state or guaranteeing that justice is served on any specific individuals.[711] That last-mentioned purpose is achieved primarily by Article 31(1) of the 1954 Convention, which deals with the expulsion of a stateless person on grounds of national security and public order.

The power of exclusion from protection on the basis of Article 1(2) of the 1954 Convention is simultaneously an obligation, as is evidenced by the imperative language: 'This Convention shall not apply'.[712] This means that the states are not in a position to make any individual evaluations of their own concerning the admission of an individual who qualifies for exclusion.

The exclusion clauses must be given a strict interpretation.[713] Firstly, one should not lose sight of the fact that the overarching purpose of the 1954 Convention is to provide stateless persons with international protection. Secondly, this involves an exception being made from human-rights guarantees, where the exclusion of an individual from protection has very serious implications. Thirdly, as for Article 1(2)(iii)(c) of the 1954 Convention (referencing 'acts contrary to the purposes and principles of the United Nations'), the need for a narrow interpretation is also prompted by the ambiguity of the language with the resulting susceptibility to abuse. Simultaneously, emphasis is placed on the need to give

---

710 J.C. Hathaway, M. Foster, *The law of refugee status*, Cambridge 2014, pp. 525–526.

711 J. Bond, *Principled exclusions. A revised approach to article 1(F)(A) of the Refugee Convention*, 35(1) Michigan Journal of International Law 2013, p. 13.

712 This was debated at the stage immediately preceding the adoption of the 1951 Convention. For example, the preference voiced by the US delegates was for the exclusion of criminals to be made optional.

713 In reference to the Geneva Convention of 1951 see E. Kwakwa, *Article 1F(c). Acts contrary to the purposes and principles of the United Nations*, 12 International Journal of Refugee Law 2000, Special Supplementary Issue, p. 80: '*every accepted canon of interpretation would seem to suggest that the relevant provisions on exclusion should be interpreted as restrictively as possible*'. Also see G. Geoff, *Exclusion and evidentiary assessment* [in:] G. Noll (ed.), *Proof, evidentiary assessment and credibility in asylum procedures*, Leiden–Boston 2005, p. 162; M. Bliss, *"Serious reasons for considering". Minimum standards of procedural fairness in the application of the article 1 F exclusion clauses*, 12 International Journal of Refugee Law 2000, Special Supplementary Issue, p. 98; differently D. McKeever, *Evolving interpretation of multilateral treaties. "Acts contrary to the purposes and principles of the United Nations" in the Refugee Convention*, 64(2) International and Comparative Law Quarterly, April 2015, pp. 421–425 (an isolated position).

exclusion clauses an interpretation reflecting modern developments in international law.[714] This directive of dynamic interpretation should be favourably received, even though to some extent it does conflict with the previously discussed directive of strict interpretation of the exclusion clauses.[715] For example, such interpretation entails, as I will demonstrate below, a broader scope of the terms 'war crimes' and 'crimes against humanity'. In principle, therefore, the overall interpretative directive should be formulated as follows: the provisions must be interpreted in a manner that is as strict as possible but also reflective of the present state (stage) of development of international law.

The burden of proving that a stateless person qualifies for exclusion under Article 1(2)(iii) of the 1954 Convention rests upon the state.[716] The above is a different standard of proof than the one used for determinations of statelessness (where the burden is split between the state and the applicant).[717] This applies to all elements of this provision. Thus, for example, in the case of Article 1(2)(iii)(b) of the 1954 Convention, it is for the state to prove that the nature of the crime is both serious and non-political (rather than for the applicant to prove that the crime is a political one).[718] As the UNHCR observes, the burden may shift only in exceptional cases, such as when the individual is wanted by an international criminal court or has been the member of a government manifestly engaged in activities falling under the exclusion clauses.[719]

The assessment of the applicability of exclusion grounds should in principle be part of SDP. Neither in the 1954 Convention nor in any soft law are there any guidelines as to how the exclusion grounds should be applied to stateless persons. It must be assumed that, as a minimum, the standards of procedural fairness should apply.[720] Procedures involving exclusion clauses pose a challenge to domestic authorities due to the need for the application of certain institutions of criminal law (e.g. presumption of innocence) and the need, in many cases, to consider the various aspects of the individual's criminal liability (e.g. the *iter*

714 E. Kwakwa, *Article 1F(c)...*, p. 86.
715 D. McKeever, *Evolving...*, p. 413.
716 By analogy, for Article 1 F of the Geneva Convention of 1951 see G. Geoff, *Exclusion...*, p. 168; UNHCR, *Guidelines on International Protection No. 5...*, paragraph 34, p. 9.
717 See Chapter IV, section 2.
718 G. Geoff, *Exclusion...*, p. 168.
719 UNHCR, *Guidelines on Statelessness No. 5...*, paragraphs 34 and 19, pp. 9 and 6.
720 For a more detailed discussion of this topic see M. Bliss, "*Serious reasons...*, p. 93.

criminis, principals, aiders and abettors, accessories, justifications, excuses, spent convictions and statutes of limitations).[721]

It must be emphasized that the applicability of Article 1(2)(iii) of the 1954 Convention is not conditional on the individual's prosecution or conviction in relation to the crime. The language of the provision only requires the existence of 'serious reasons for considering' that the individual has committed the specified act. This is an idiosyncratic evidentiary standard, unknown to the majority of legal systems. In itself, it does not constitute a clear and precise standard of proof.[722] Most writers agree that it is lower than the standard required for a criminal conviction in common law.[723] Other than the above, it is not clear what the standard exactly is supposed to be.[724] It must be assumed to be higher than what is needed to present a suspect with criminal charges under common law.[725] As a result, it falls somewhere between the standard needed for an indictment and the one needed for a conviction in common-law systems. It should be interpreted as demanding the existence of 'clear and convincing evidence', which in turn requires the existence of evidence meeting the description. Accordingly, the evidence gathered should be detailed and specific, as well as 'credible and reliable in nature'. The *ratio* for the imposition of such a high evidentiary standard is found in the serious consequences of the decision to exclude an individual from

---

721 Concerning this topic and other detailed aspects of criminal liability, procedural guarantees and evidentiary matters with regard to exclusion clauses (under Article 1 F of the Geneva Convention of 1951) see G. Geoff, *Exclusion…*, pp. 163ff; K. Przybysławska, *Niepożądani uchodźcy. Granice ochrony i zasady wykluczenia w świetle prawa międzynarodowego*, Warszawa 2009, pp. 61–72; UNHCR, *Guidelines on International Protection No. 5…*, pp. 6–7.

722 M. Bliss, *Serious reasons…*, p. 115.

723 That would be proof beyond a reasonable doubt; thus e.g. M. Bliss, *Serious reasons…*, p. 115. Proof beyond a reasonable doubt is the evidence standard, used especially in criminal cases, requiring proof that the existence of any other reasonable hypothesis is excluded — R. Bujalski, *Angielsko-polski słownik orzecznictwa sądów europejskich*, Warszawa 2009, p. 51.

724 The UNHCR guidelines issued in relation to Article 1 F of the Geneva Convention of 1951 do not purport to give any explanation of this standard. As noted by M. Bliss, *Serious reasons…*, p. 115, the analysis of the *travaux preparatoires* of the Geneva Convention 1951 does not cast much light in this regard.

725 Referred to as the 'balance of probabilities'. As observed by P. Wiliński and H. Kuczyńska [in:] P. Wiliński (ed.), *Rzetelny proces karny w orzecznictwie sądów polskich i międzynarodowych*, Warszawa 2009, p. 209, 'in principle, it corresponded to by the *intime conviction* standard in the civil-law tradition'.

protection, as well as the exceptional nature of any such exclusion and the generally protective purpose of the 1954 Convention.[726]

2.2. Individuals excluded from protection by Article 1(2)(iii)(a) of the 1954 Convention

As for the specific subcategories of individuals mentioned in Article 1(2)(iii) of the 1954 Convention, Article 1(2)(iii)(a) excludes those guilty of a crime against the peace, war crime or crime against humanity from the protection of the Convention. This provision makes a general reference to the meaning attributed to these crimes by international treaties ('as defined in the international instruments drawn up to make provisions in respect of such crime'). Without a doubt, the interpretation of Article 1(2)(iii)(a) must take heed of international instruments adopted prior to the 1954 Convention, such as the Charter of the International Military Tribunal (Annex to the Agreement for the prosecution and punishment of the major war criminals of the European Axis, 8 August 1945), Convention on the Prevention and Punishment of the Crime of Genocide of 9 December 1948 (UNTS, vol. 78, p. 277) and the four Geneva Conventions of 1949 relating to the protection of victims of armed conflicts (and two additional protocols of 1977). Moreover, the language of the provision indicates that the intention of the 1954 Convention's drafters was for its interpretation to reflect subsequent developments in international criminal law. As a result, instruments enacted on later dates, especially the Rome Statute of the International Criminal Court of 17 July 1998, should be given effect in the interpretation of the exclusion clauses.[727] Although such a possibility had been considered, the decision was ultimately made against including a list of treaties to be taken into account in the interpretative process. In a similar way, the decision was made against the incorporation of existing definitions of the crimes mentioned in Article 1(2)(iii)(a) of the 1954 Convention.[728]

Here, it will be expedient to give a concise description of the offences mentioned by Article 1(2)(iii)(a) of the 1954 Convention. As far as crimes against peace are concerned, Article 1(2)(iii)(a) partially overlaps with Article 1(2)(iii)

726 Lawyers Committee for Human Rights, *Safeguarding the rights of refugees under the exclusion clauses. Summary findings of the Project and a Lawyers Committee for Human Rights Perspective*, 12 International Journal of Refugee Law, Special Supplementary Issue, pp. 328–329.

727 UNHCR, *Guidelines on Statelessness No. 5…*, paragraph 10.

728 J. Bond, *Principled…*, p. 14.

(c) — which refers to the 'purposes and principles of the United Nations' — due to the maintenance of peace being the most important purpose of the United Nations. The interpretation of both of these provisions involves the problem of the definition of a crime against peace.[729] The only definition to date is provided by the Nuremberg Charter. Pursuant to its Article 6(a), a crime against peace is the 'planning, preparation, initiation or waging of a war of aggression, or a war in violation of international treaties, agreements or assurances, or participation in a common plan or conspiracy for the accomplishment of any of the foregoing'.

As opposed to crimes against peace, war crimes have been defined by numerous international instruments. In the day of the adoption of the 1954 Convention, the term 'war crimes' was interpreted as referring to serious violations of international humanitarian law, especially of the Nuremberg Charter or of the Geneva Conventions of 1949. Since then, however, the term has been developed further by the additional protocols to the Geneva Conventions of 1977, the Statute of the International Criminal Tribunal for the Former Yugoslavia and the Statute of the International Criminal Tribunal for Rwanda. The main difference in the approach seen through the Rome Statute of the International Criminal Court in 1998 is that, at present, war crimes are considered to include certain acts committed in an internal conflict. Examples of war crimes include the deliberate killing and torturing of civilians, as well as mass attacks on the civilian population.[730]

The concept of crimes against humanity has also evolved over time. Unlike the Nuremberg Charter — which in 1954 was the most important instrument defining the term — the present understanding of a crime against humanity does not presuppose the existence of an armed conflict.[731] For this reason, crimes against humanity are broadest of the categories mentioned by Article 1(2)(iii)(a) of the 1954 Convention.[732] In accordance with Article 7 of the Rome Statute of the International Criminal Court, examples of crimes against humanity include murder, extermination, enslavement, deportation or forcible transfer of population, and rape, if — which is a constitutive characteristic of a crime against humanity — the acts are 'committed as part of a widespread or systematic attack directed against any civilian population'.

---

729 European Council on Refugees Exiles, *Position on exclusion from refugee status*, March 2004, paragraph 16, p. 11.

730 UNHCR, *Guidelines on Statelessness No. 5…*, paragraph 12.

731 D. McKeever, *Evolving…*, p. 413.

732 UNHCR, *Guidelines on Statelessness No. 5…*, paragraph 13.

As for the personal scope of Article 1(2)(iii)(a) of the 1954 Convention, with regard to crimes against peace it must be noted that, due to their nature, they can only be committed by individuals in high positions of authority, representing a state or state-like entity.[733] Crimes against humanity and war crimes, by contrast, can be committed by individuals not having any such special relationship with a state or state-like entity, for example by rebels, guerrilla fighters or members of militias.

2.3. Individuals excluded by Article 1(2)(iii)(b) of the 1954 Convention

Stateless persons guilty of serious non-political crimes are also excluded from the protection offered by the 1954 Convention. In the first place, it should be noted that whether a criminal offence is of serious nature must be decided primarily on the basis of international rather than local (domestic) standards. The assessment of the 'seriousness' of the crime should include elements such as the nature of the crime, the harm done, the path of prosecution, the nature of the penalty, and whether the relevant offence is regarded as a serious crime by the majority of the world's legal systems. According to UNHCR guidelines, murder, rape or armed robbery have this nature, but petty theft does not.[734]

Not any serious crime excludes its perpetrator from the protection of the Convention but only a serious crime that is not political in nature. Therefore, the basis for the exclusion of a stateless person from protection may be found in the commission of a serious common crime. As is emphasized by writers in this context, the term 'political crime' is taken from extradition law,[735] but outside of a narrow handful of treaty instruments there is no single commonly accepted definition of the term. In the process of application of Article 1(2)(iii)(b) of the 1954 Convention, state authorities should refer for interpretative purposes to extradition law, and with it to international law, rather than to the concepts and terminology of the domestic system of criminal law. As noted by UNHCR documents, the circumstance that a crime is defined in an extradition treaty as being non-political in nature is relevant but not decisive.[736]

---

733 UNHCR, *Background Note on the Application of the Exclusion Clauses. Article 1F of the 1951 Convention relating to the Status of Refugees*, September 2003, paragraph 28.

734 UNHCR, *Guidelines on Statelessness No. 5...*, paragraph 14.

735 J.C. Hathaway, M. Foster, *The law of refugee...*, p. 554.

736 UNHCR, *Guidelines on Statelessness No. 5...*, paragraph 15.

Before we move on to the matter of the definition of a political crime, it will be necessary to explain briefly the reasons for the privileged treatment conceded to political criminals by the 1954 Convention. In other words, the reasons why stateless persons guilty of serious political crimes are not excluded from the protection. The literature on this subject appreciates the exceptional nature of political crimes. Idealization of the political criminal's motives was the prevalent concept in the 19th century. It was believed that a political criminal is, in principle, motivated by the common good and not by a desire for personal gain.[737] That is only partially true, because a political criminal's motivation can be a complex one, and it can incorporate the desire for revenge or for some form of material gain. At the current stage of development of international law, an explanation anchored in the need to protect individual rights is put to the fore instead. As noted by B. Wierzbicki: '(...) a criminal attacking the political organization of a state and its organs or acting contrary to its external interests is in no position to expect in that state the full guarantees of human rights'.[738]

Moving on to the definitional aspects, one should note that extradition law distinguishes two basic types of political crimes: purely (absolutely) political crimes and mixed (relatively political) crimes.[739] This distinction corresponds, in principle, to the distinction between the objective and subjective concepts of political crime followed, for example, by Polish writers on the subject.[740] International law is also familiar with a third concept, one using the criterion of the act's

737 B. Wierzbicki, *Pojęcie przestępstwa politycznego w prawie międzynarodowym*, Warszawa 1979, p. 142–143.

738 B. Wierzbicki, *Pojęcie przestępstwa...*, p. 145. This aspect is heavily emphasized by K. Przybysławska in her analysis of the provisions of the Refugee Convention. In her opinion, the purpose of the exclusion clauses is not to protect political criminals while visiting condemnation on common criminals; instead, one should rather speak of a 'general aspiration to protect those accused of "political" acts from vulnerability to political persecution' — K. Przybysławska, *Niepożądani uchodźcy...*, p. 32.

739 This distinction (absolute/purely political offences vs relative/related political offences) was proposed by B.L. Ingraham and K. Tokoro in 1969 in their article titled *Political crime in the United States and Japan. A comparative study*, 4(2) Issues in Criminology 1969, pp. 145–170, cited after J.I. Ross, *An introduction to political crime*, Bristol 2012, p. 32.

740 See T. Gardocka, 60(2) *Przesłanki ekstradycyjne w prawie polskim*, Studia Prawnicze 1979, p. 94; L. Gardocki, *Zarys prawa karnego międzynarodowego*, Warszawa 1985, pp. 172–173.

connections with political developments, which derives from the common-law tradition (the *delits connexes*).[741]

Purely political crimes are criminal offences aimed directly against the state, its sovereignty and its political organization. Decisive to the political nature of the crime is the nature of the protected interest being infringed. Definitions of political crimes of this type are usually provided in the domestic criminal codes of the various states.[742] Usually, this group includes treason, espionage, membership in outlawed political parties, or coup d'état. For such offences extradition is not available, nor should they serve as grounds for the exclusion of stateless persons from protection.[743]

The two categories of relative crimes and crimes connected with (related to) political crimes (*delits connexes*) expand the list considerably. Relative political crimes denote ordinary offences committed out of a political motivation for the purpose of altering the balance of political power in the state.[744] In this case, the subjective elements of the crime are decisive to its political nature, especially the inspiration, motivation or purpose of the perpetrator's conduct.[745] This group of crimes may include the killing of a politician or the taking of hostages for the purpose of forcing political concessions.[746] On the other hand, connected crimes are ordinary crimes in a certain relation to purely (absolutely) or relatively political crimes. They can precede a political crime for the purpose of its commission, or they can be committed simultaneously with it, to assist with the achievement of its goal or to prevent prosecution, or they can occur subsequently to it for the purpose of protecting the offenders.[747] Examples include the theft of weapons by individuals preparing a political coup, or the harbouring of an individual guilty of a political crime.[748]

---

741 'Connected political offences'.

742 J.I. Ross, *An introduction...*, p. 1.

743 European Council on Refugees and Exiles, *Position on exclusion...*, p. 13, paragraph 21.

744 W. Kälin, J. Künzli, *Article 1F(b). Freedom fighters, terrorists, and the notion of serious non-political crimes*, 12 International Journal of Refugee Law 2000, Special Supplementary Issue, p. 65.

745 P. Kardas, *Przestępstwo polityczne w prawie polskim. Próba analizy teoretycznej na tle obowiązującego stanu prawnego*, 1–2 Czasopismo Prawa Karnego i Nauk Penalnych 1998, p. 171.

746 L. Gardocki, *Zarys...*, p. 173.

747 W. Kälin, J. Künzli, *Article 1F(b)...*, p. 65.

748 L. Gardocki, *Zarys...*, p. 173.

Relative political crimes and connected crimes are regarded as purely political if the political nature of the act prevails over its nature of an ordinary crime.[749] In other words, it is a *sine qua non* condition for the recognition of a specific act as a political crime that its political element must predominate its criminal element. The term 'non-political crime' used in Article 1(2)(iii)(b) of the 1954 Convention should, therefore, be interpreted in line with the theory of predominance (alternatively: prevalence, preponderance). Pursuant to that theory, a crime is political in nature where the perpetrator's political motivation preponderates (though it need not be their sole motivation). Moreover, for an act to be regarded as political, the political motives must be compatible with the principles of human rights.[750] Furthermore, the act must be committed as part of a struggle for political power and must have constituted means realistically capable of contributing to the intended purpose. Thus, it must be the direct means to a political goal. Last but not least, it is important for the perpetrator to maintain the proportion between the purpose of the act and the means used, especially where crimes against life or health are involved.[751]

In the above light, the nature of a serious criminal offence is not political where motives other than political preponderate in the characterization of the crime. Non-political elements preponderate where the perpetrator's motives are not mainly political or there is no clear and close connection between the crime and the alleged political motive or the conduct is disproportionate to it.[752] This approach makes it possible to exclude persons guilty of terrorist acts, because their conduct will in principle fail the preponderance test due to being wholly out of proportion to any political goal.[753]

Crimes providing grounds for exclusion from the protection of the Convention must be committed outside of the territory of the host state. Stateless persons committing serious non-political crimes in the territory of the host state are subject to the ordinary regime of criminal liability in that state. In the last case,

---

749 W. Kälin, J. Künzli, *Article 1F(b)...*, p. 65.

750 UNHCR, *Guidelines on Statelessness No. 5...*, paragraph 15, p. 5.

751 Thus, the principle of proportionality is applicable to this provision; according to the UNHCR, the importance of this principle is limited with regard to Articles 1(2)(iii)(a) and 1(2)(iii)(c) due to the exceptionally serious nature of the crimes. UNHCR, *Guidelines on International Protection No. 5...*, p. 7, paragraph 24. For a more extensive discussion of this topic see UNHCR, *Background...*, paragraphs 76–78, pp. 27–29.

752 UNHCR, *Guidelines on Statelessness No. 5...*, p. 5, paragraph 15.

753 W. Kälin, J. Künzli, *Article 1F(b)...*, p. 77.

criminal liability and conviction may lead to the application of Article 31(1) of the 1954 Convention.[754]

2.4. Individuals excluded from protection by Article 1(2)(iii)(c) of the 1954 Convention

The principles and purposes mentioned in Article 1(2)(iii)(c) of the Convention are expounded by the preamble and Articles 1 and 2 of the UN Charter. Pursuant to Article 1 of the Charter, the purposes are to maintain international peace and security; develop amicable relations among the nations on the basis of respecting the principles of equality and self-determination of all nations; resolve international problems of social, cultural or humanitarian nature in a collaborative manner; support and encourage respect for human rights; be a centre for harmonizing the nations' actions taken in order to achieve these common goals. As provided by Article 2, in turn, the principles include the sovereign equality of all states, compliance in good faith with the obligations assumed in accordance with the Charter, peaceful resolution of international disputes, as well as abandonment of the use of force or threat of the use force against the territorial integrity or political independence of any state or in any other manner contrary to the purposes of the United Nations.

As one can see from the above, the purposes and principles of the United Nations referenced by Article 1(2)(iii)(c) of the 1954 Convention are described in a general manner with no international instruments defining or narrowing their exact scope.[755] The result is that, in respect of the category of conduct falling under it, this provision has the least clarity of all exclusion clauses. As already noted, the argument of a need for restrictive interpretation of the entire Article 1(2)(iii) of the 1954 Convention is further reinforced in this case on account of the highly ambiguous and imprecise language of Article 1(2)(iii)(c).[756] The directive of giving this provision a restrictive interpretation is prompted, in particular, by concerns over its susceptibility to abuse.[757] It has been aptly observed

754 In reference, *mutatis mutandis*, to the Geneva Convention of 1951 see UNHCR, *Guidelines on International Protection No. 5…*, paragraph 16, p. 5; European Council on Refugees and Exiles, *Position…*, pp. 23–24, paragraph 57.

755 This is despite the fact that the same language had seen earlier use; see Article 14(2) UDHR.

756 UNHCR, *Guidelines on Statelessness No. 5…*, paragraph 17, p. 5.

757 A. Grahl-Madsen, *The status of refugees in international law*, vol. 1, Leiden 1972, pp. 282–283.

that the use of any other interpretation could expand the applicability of the imprecisely worded provision beyond any limits.[758]

Restrictive interpretation of Article 1(2)(iii)(c) of the 1954 Convention implies that the provision should be applicable to exceptional cases in which the very foundations of the international community's co-existence are undermined. Such exceptions will include crimes violating the international peace and security and peaceful relations among the states, as well as persistent and serious violations of human rights.[759]

The scope of the vaguely worded exclusion clause of Article 1(2)(iii)(c) partially overlaps with the exclusion clauses of Articles 1(2)(iii)(a) and 1(2)(iii)(b). Crimes against peace, war crimes and crimes against humanity (Article 1(2)(iii)(a)) are acts contrary to the purposes and principles of the United Nations, as are serious non-political crimes having an international dimension (Article 1(2)(iii)(b)). Accordingly, in many cases in which the purposes and principles of the United Nations are infringed, the provisions of Articles 1(2)(iii)(a) and 1(2)(iii)(b) will be applicable. These provisions should be given priority of invocation due to their more precise drafting and greater clarity of interpretation.

The nature of the activities falling within the ambit of Article 1(2)(iii)(c) must be criminal. As noted by the UNHCR, although this is not expressly stated in the provision — for Article 1(2)(iii)(c) refers to persons 'guilty of acts', rather than those who 'have committed a crime' as in Articles 1(2)(iii)(a) and 1(2)(iii)(b) — acts falling within the scope of this provision need to be criminal in nature, similarly to those referred to in Articles 1(2)(iii)(a) and 1(2)(iii)(b).[760] However, the fact alone that the conduct constitutes a criminal offence will not be sufficient to trigger the applicability of Article 1(2)(iii)(c). It will also be necessary for clear indications to exist that the international community regards the relevant criminal offence as being contrary to the 'purposes and principles of the United Nations'. This means that criminal offences not falling within the scope of Articles 1(2)(iii)(a) and 1(2)(iii)(b) of the 1954 Convention can automatically be classified under Article 1(2)(iii)(c). This last leg of Article 1(2)(iii) should

---

758 M.K. Nyinah, *Exclusion under article 1F. Some reflections on context, principles and practice*, 12 International Journal of Refugee Law Issue suppl_1, July 2000, p. 309.

759 UNHCR, *Guidelines on Statelessness No. 5…*, paragraph 17, p. 5.

760 UNHCR, *Handbook on Procedures and Criteria for Determining Refugee Status under the 1951 Convention and the 1967 Protocol relating to the Status of Refugees*, HCR/IP/4/Eng/REV.1 Re-edited, Geneva, January 1992, 1979; similarly: UNHCR, *Guidelines on International Protection No. 5…*, paragraph 18, p. 6. For a different, isolated, position see D. McKeever, *Evolving…*, pp. 426–430.

not become, as Article 1F(c) of the Geneva Convention of 1951 has once been graphically described, a 'ravenous omnivore'[761]. For example, in the case of the cross-border crime of drug trafficking, the application of Article 1(2)(iii)(b) may be precluded by the limited territorial applicability of the provision.[762] There are, however, no indications that the international community regards drug trafficking as an action contrary to the purposes and principles of the United Nations.[763] By contrast, certain acts have had such a character explicitly attributed to them. For example, resolutions of the UN Security Council expressly include international terrorism among acts contrary to the purposes and principles of the United Nations.[764]

As for who can commit acts falling with the ambit of Article 1(2)(iii)(c) of the 1954 Convention, the view has evolved over time. Initially, it was assumed that — because the preamble and Articles 1 and 2 of the UN Charter enumerate core principles to be followed by the member states in relations among themselves and vis-à-vis the international community as a whole — only persons in positions of power in a state or state-like entity were capable of the commission of such acts.[765] Thus, heads of state and other high-level officials. At present, however, it is more widely appreciated that the developments in international law — especially in the context of terrorism — have rendered obsolete the belief

761 J.C. Hathaway, M. Foster, *The law of refugee…*, p. 594. When it comes to Article 1F(c) of the Geneva Convention of 1951, Canada has been identified as a forge of innovative ways of application of this provision. It has been applied by Canadian authorities to a broad range of acts, including drug crimes, minelaying, abductions, hostage taking, human trafficking and electoral fraud; D. McKeever, *Evolving…*, p. 416.

762 M.K. Nyinah, *Exclusion…*, p. 309.

763 Nevertheless, in the celebrated case of Pushpanathan, the Supreme Court of Canada ruled that while drug trafficking was a very serious problem indeed, in the absence of clear indications of the international community regarding it as an act contrary to the purposes and principles of the United Nations, individuals should not on its account be deprived of the basic protection offered by the Convention — Pushpanathan v. Canada (Minister of Citizenship and Immigration), [1998] 1 S.C.R. 982, Canada: Supreme Court, 4 June 1998.

764 See e.g. Security Council Resolution 1373, 28 September 2001, S/RES/1373 (2001): 'acts, methods, and practices of terrorism are contrary to the purposes and principles of the United Nations and that knowingly financing, planning and inciting terrorist acts are also contrary to the purposes and principles of the United Nations' — (paragraph 5).

765 UNHCR, *Guidelines on Statelessness No. 5…*, p. 6; UNHCR, *Handbook on Procedures…*, paragraph 163; UNHCR, *Background…*, pp. 47–49.

that only holders of public office are in a position to commit acts contrary to the purposes and principles of the United Nations, as opposed to 'ordinary' individuals.[766]

As can be seen from the above, the interpretation of Article 1(2)(iii) of the 1954 Convention (with recourse being taken to Article 1F of the Geneva Convention of 1951) reveals that the purpose of this provision is to exclude the perpetrators of the most serious crimes from protection. It should be emphasized that the purpose is not to judge the applicants' moral character or attitude and reserve the protection only to those of good character with no history of conflict with the law.[767]

2.5. Selected domestic regulatory frameworks and court decisions

When the European states having ratified the 1954 Convention introduce the definition of statelessness to their domestic legal orders, they also introduce the exclusion clauses.[768] However, domestic practice with regard to the application of the exclusion clauses of the 1954 Convention is scarce, with virtually no information available on the subject. Some of what precious little is available comes from the decisions of Belgian courts. In one of the Belgian cases, the Court of Appeals in Antwerp withheld protection from a stateless person on the grounds of information received from the immigration authorities about the discovery of a criminal conviction for drug trafficking. That, in the opinion of the court, constituted a serious crime of non-political nature, with the effect of excluding the applicant from the protection of the 1954 Convention.[769] In a different Belgian case, the Tribunal of First Instance in Brussels dealt with the matter of a stateless person of Kurdish origin having refused military service in Turkish armed forces, which the authorities in Turkey interpreted as a threat to the public order

766 A. Zimmermann, P. Wennholz, *Article 1F 1951 Convention* [in:] A. Zimmermann (ed.), *The 1951 Convention relating to the status of refugees and its 1967 Protocol. A commentary*, Oxford 2011, pp. 596 and 603; D. McKeever, *Evolving…*, p. 83; J.C. Hathaway, M. Foster, *The law of refugee…*, p. 589.

767 J. Bond, *Principled…*, p. 12; M. Nyinah, *Exclusion…*, p. 297.

768 Information according to data available for states listed in the *Statelessness Index Survey*, see footnote 148.

769 Court of Appeals in Antwerp, unpublished judgement of 2 June 2004, cited after C. Rustom and Q. Schoonvae, *Mapping Statelessness in Belgium*, UNHCR, October 2012, p. 56.

and grounds for deprivation of nationality. The tribunal ruled that the exclusion clause of Article 1(2)(iii) of the 1954 Convention did not apply.[770]

The domestic legal orders of various states have been confronted with the question of whether an individual whose conduct may qualify for the exclusion clauses is still a stateless person. In the legal system of the United Kingdom, for example, the categories of individuals excluded from protection on the basis of the exclusion clauses are treated as not being stateless persons. In other words, the exclusions of Article 1(2) of the 1954 Convention form part of the very definition of a stateless person in the United Kingdom. According to § 401 of UK Immigration Rules, a stateless person is deemed to be one who has satisfied the conditions set out by Article 1(1) of the 1954 Convention, is present within the territory of the United Kingdom and is not ineligible for recognition as a stateless person in the light of § 402 (which copies the language of the exclusion clauses). From the perspective of the definitional aspects discussed in Chapter II,[771] that is not an adequate solution. It falls short because Article 1(2) of the 1954 Convention identifies the categories of individuals excluded from the protection afforded by the provisions of that particular treaty and does not constitute an element of the definition of a stateless person.

2.6. *Ex-post* exclusion

In the light of the 1954 Convention, further categories of persons who are undeserving of protection on the grounds of public interest may be distinguished subsequently to recognition as a stateless person (i.e. *ex post*), pursuant to Article 31(1) of the 1954 Convention, which deals with grounds for expulsion (section 2.6.1) or withdrawal or cancellation of the protection status (section 2.6.2).

2.6.1. *Expulsion of a stateless person*

Article 31(1) of the 1954 Convention provides the basis for the expulsion of a stateless person who presents a threat to the 'national security or public order'. This mechanism is applicable to stateless persons rightly granted protection under Article 1 of the 1954 Convention whose subsequent behaviour has become problematic in the light of 'national security or public order'. For example, a stateless person who is guilty of a serious criminal offence committed while already in

770 Tribunal of First Instance in Brussels, judgment of 8 April 1998, cited after C. Rustom and Q. Schoonvae, *Mapping…*, p. 56.

771 Chapter II, section 2.

possession of the protection status is not liable to exclusion from protection on the grounds of Article 1(2)(iii)(b) of the 1954 Convention because of the territorial limitations of its applicability. However, such an individual's conduct may be assessed from the perspective of Article 31(1) of the 1954 Convention.

In practice, the applicability of Article 31(1) of the 1954 Convention to stateless persons will be limited due to the scarcity of options available to the state for their expulsion. Firstly, often no state will be under an obligation to receive them. Secondly, expulsion may be impossible due to the application of provisions relating to the protection of human rights. Although the 1954 Convention has no provision on *non-refoulement*, an individual excluded from protection may continue to be entitled to protection from expulsion to a state in which their live or health would be placed in danger, on the basis of the general instruments of protection of human rights such as Article ECHR, Article 3(1) of the Convention Against Torture and Other Cruel, Inhuman or Degrading Treatment or Punishment adopted by the UN General Assembly on 10 December 1984,[772] Article 7 ICCPR or Article 37(a) CRC, among many other examples.

2.6.2. Withdrawal or cancellation of stateless status

The 1954 Convention does not contain any provisions enabling the state authorities to respond to situations of stateless persons rightly given protection subsequently committing acts falling under Articles 1(2)(iii)(a) or 1(2)(iii)(c) of the 1954 Convention.[773] States whose SIP envisages the grant of a specific status to the individual must be assumed to be free to adopt suitable provisions in this regard. As in the case of refugee protection,[774] solutions may be adopted involving the withdrawal of the status (with the effect of terminating the protection *ex nunc*).

In the same vein, neither does the 1954 Convention contain any provisions dealing with those stateless persons who have been accorded a specific status by the state — through the application of SIP — that should never have been granted to them. By analogy to refugee law, the states should be assumed to have the option to cancel the status (with the effect of removing the protection *ex tunc*) when the holder does not meet the conditions legally prescribed for the

772 United Nations, Treaty Series, vol. 1465, p. 85.

773 Article 1(2)(iii)(b) of the 1954 Convention, however, will not be applicable, because of the territorial limitations of the applicability of the middle leg of Article 1(2)(iii) (as discussed above).

774 See UNHCR, *Note on the Cancellation of Refugee Status*, 22 November 2004, paragraph 1; UNHCR, *Guidelines on International Protection No. 5…*, paragraph 6, p. 3.

grant.[775] This includes SIP fraud (or, more precisely speaking, misleading the determination authority or exerting unlawful influence on its decision-making process), which involves two scenarios. In the first one, there is competent evidence that the individual does not meet the positive conditions of recognition as a stateless person from Article 1(1) of the 1954 Convention. In the second one, the individual is affected by circumstances warranting the application of the exclusion clauses of Articles 1(2)(iii)(a-c) of the 1954 Convention at the time of the making of the determinations concerning statelessness and recognition, but the authorities become aware of this only at a later time. This may involve misrepresentation of circumstances relevant to the determination of statelessness (such as providing false personal information or concealing the citizenship of another state) or concealment of circumstances suggesting the commission of one or more of the acts mentioned in Articles 1(2)(iii)(a–c) of the 1954 Convention.

Any withdrawal or cancellation must have a sufficient basis backed by competent evidence. All guarantees of procedural fairness must be respected. Most importantly, the decision must be proportionate to its basis.[776]

Currently made proposals of provisions governing the protection of stateless persons include withdrawal and cancellation of the status. The relevant provision of the Draft Articles on the Protection of Stateless Persons and the Facilities for their Naturalisation (designed for the specific domestic regulatory needs of Latin American states) stipulates that the state authority shall withdraw the status of a stateless person where there are serious reasons for believing that the recipient has engaged in any conduct falling under the exclusion clauses of Articles 1(2)(iii)(a) and 1(2)(iii)(c) of the 1954 Convention. The provision on cancellation stipulates that the domestic authority shall review the grant of statelessness status where there are serious reasons for believing that the individual has deliberately failed to disclose, or has tampered with, such information or documents as would have led to the application being denied on the grounds of ineligibility or exclusion, had they been known to the authorities at the time.[777]

---

775 Concerning status cancellation in the procedure for refugees: UNHCR, Handbook on Procedures and Criteria for Determining Refugee Status, Geneva 1992, paragraph 117 and p. 39; UNHCR, *Note on the Cancellation…*, paragraph 1; UNHCR, *Guidelines on International Protection No. 5…*, paragraph 6.

776 UNHCR, *Note on the Cancellation…*, paragraphs 8–9.

777 UNHCR, *Draft Articles…*, p. 15.

2.7. The individual's situation following exclusion

In the light of the above-discussed matter of the exclusions from protection stipulated by the 1954 Convention, the practical problem emerges of what the treatment of a stateless person excluded from protection should be. An individual who is excluded from protection cannot be given the protection of the 1954 Convention or the protection and support of the UNHCR.[778] However, the 1954 Convention does not contain any provisions requiring the state to take any specific actions following the exclusion.

In the post-exclusion situation, different scenarios can apply. The consequences of the exclusion will differ depending on the stateless person's individual situation (e.g. whether lawfully in the territory or not) and the domestic laws and regulations of the host state. In some situations, the stateless person can be expelled and the domestic authorities are desirous to enter on that path. In others, a re-admission treaty may be applicable, such as when having habitual residence in another state or having entered the current host state unlawfully.

However, as I have noted above, in the usual case, the stateless person cannot be expelled lawfully. A stateless person excluded from protection will either remain in an irregular situation for as long as they remain in the host state, or they will be given an immigration status on some other basis regulated by the law on foreigners. This leads to a very serious problem from the perspective of the protection of human rights. Namely, the 1954 Convention does not require the states to accord any specific minimum of rights to a stateless person — i.e. an individual satisfying the criteria of Article 1(1) — who is also liable to the exclusion clauses of Article 1(2)(iii). The obligation to issue identity papers must be regarded as belonging to such a minimum, as they are the *sine qua non* condition of the individual's ability to gain access to the protective solutions of the international law of human rights.[779]

3. Reducing statelessness

Pursuant to the various instruments of international law, states have an obligation to facilitate the naturalization of stateless persons. Provisions regulating facilitated naturalization serve as a mechanism for the reduction of statelessness. In particular, in accordance with Article 32 of the 1954 Convention, a stateless person should be given the option to acquire the nationality of the host state

778 UNHCR, *Background...*, paragraph 21, p. 8.
779 I address this topic also in Chapter I.

through a facilitated procedure. Similarly, the facilitated naturalization of stateless persons lawfully and habitually resident in the territory of a given state is foreseen by Article 6(4)(g) ECN. Soft-law documents from the United Nations and from the Council of Europe formulate the same directive.[780]

Nonetheless, because of the need to protect the public interest as it is perceived by the states, not all stateless persons will be in a position to apply for naturalization procedures. Similarly to other foreigners, stateless persons may fall under one of the bars to naturalization — 'negative conditions' — of which the purpose is to prevent the acquisition of nationality by individuals whom states deem undeserving according to a variety of criteria. All European states impose some sort of positive or negative conditions on naturalization, restricting foreigners' access to the acquisition of their nationality. The applicant's moral or social qualities are among the aspects typically considered.[781] Naturalization requirements frequently include good character or, more precisely, lack of a criminal record. The purpose is to make sure that the candidate 'has not been engaged in activities undermining public safety, public order, health or morality, or the rights and freedoms or honour or reputation of others.'[782] There is a consensus that the inclusion of conditions relating to public safety is a justified exercise of the states' powers in this area. States are free to decide that the admission of a new individual in the ranks of their citizens must not have a negative impact on safety, security and defence or that the applicant should not have a track record of activities detrimental to national security.[783]

Writers on this subject argue that, when it comes to the application of naturalization bars, stateless persons should be given preferential treatment due to the greater gravity of the consequences of rejection for them. The suggestion offered by the Committee of Ministers of the Council of Europe is to 'ensure that offences, when they are relevant for the decision concerning the acquisition of nationality, do not unreasonably prevent stateless persons seeking the nationality

---

780 For a more extensive discussion of this topic see Chapter III, section 2.

781 Typically used requirements can be divided into three categories. The first one refers to residence, e.g. type and length of stay; the second one to the command of the language and to cultural assimilation; third, which I discuss more extensively in this chapter, to the applicant's moral and social character. I discuss this topic more extensively in D. Pudzianowska, *Obywatelstwo…*, pp. 89–92.

782 Committee of Experts on Nationality, *Report on Conditions for the Acquisition and Loss of Nationality*, Strasbourg, 14 January 2003, paragraph 32.

783 Committee of Experts on Nationality, *Report…*, paragraph 38.

of a State.'[784] It has been suggested that in the case of stateless persons petty crime should not pose an impediment to naturalization. According to some authors, for example, in their case the bar should attach to activities 'endangering the core principles of the state'.[785] In my view — although this is somewhat of a theoretical consideration, as the circumstances here at play are usually verified by the states at the earlier permit stage — a stateless applicant for naturalization should not receive any preferential treatment in considerations of national security, provided the availability of the minimum of rights prescribed by the 1954 Convention. However, the proposal of making the past commission of less serious crimes by stateless persons only a relative obstacle to naturalization should be met with support. To that end, states could prescribe 'qualifying periods' after which the stateless applicant would be able to re-apply.[786]

As can be seen from the above, for the purposes of exclusion from statelessness-reduction mechanisms, often the applicant's qualities — such as good character — are evaluated rather than concrete actions. Moreover, criminal offences committed after entering the territory of the host state are also taken into account. Thus, an individual could successfully obtain protection under the 1954 Convention but fail to qualify for the host state's statelessness-reduction mechanisms, for example because of a bar to naturalization posed by the individual's criminal record (not necessarily serious crime).

4. Conclusions

In the law of statelessness, there exists an inherent categorization of cases that arises from the need to protect the public interest. This is not an adventitious categorization but rather one that is grounded in the international community's consensus that certain categories of individuals should be excluded from the applicability of statelessness-counteraction and stateless-protection mechanisms.

As far as statelessness-prevention mechanisms are concerned, naturalization fraud and broadly understood disloyalty to the state of nationality, including the commission of various criminal offences (treason, espionage or terrorist acts), may incur the sanction of loss of nationality, even with the result of making the

784 Recommendation R(1999)18 on the Avoidance and Reduction of Statelessness, Section II.B (d).

785 E. Mrekajova, *Naturalization of stateless persons. Solution of statelessness?*, Tilburg 2012, p. 41.

786 E. Mrekajova, *Naturalization…*, pp. 36 and 59.

affected individual a stateless person. As for reduction mechanisms, naturalization procedures often incorporate the assessment of the applicant's 'good character'. When it comes to protection mechanisms, in turn, the 1954 Convention stipulates exclusions primarily for those guilty of exceptionally serious crimes. Moreover, similarly to refugee law, mechanisms for the withdrawal or cancellation of stateless status may apply. Lastly, the 1954 Convention contains provisions for the expulsion of stateless persons who pose a threat to national security and public order.

The state — by devising different solutions for different cases of statelessness — may provide for exclusions from reduction, protection and prevention mechanisms, subject to the potential applicability of any higher standard foreseen by domestic legislation (such as constitutional prohibitions of denationalization in certain domestic systems). Whenever a state opts for exceptions from the protection of stateless persons, it becomes important to regulate the treatment of a stateless person finding themselves in the resulting situation (which is not addressed by the 1954 Convention). Often, expulsion is not available for objective reasons, as a result of which the individual must remain in the territory of a host state unwilling to grant protection. As a minimum, the state should have the obligation to provide such an individual with identity papers in order to enable them to take advantage of the various instruments of human-rights protection.

Chapter VIII The Category of Individuals Distinguished on Account of 'Voluntarity'

In international law and in the domestic legal systems of certain states, a special approach is taken to voluntary statelessness. Examination of this aspect of statelessness will first call for answering the question of what voluntary statelessness is and what individuals may be regarded as voluntary stateless persons (section 1). Answering this will make it possible to discuss solutions for the protection of voluntary stateless persons (section 2) and for the reduction of statelessness in such cases (section 3). In the last part, I will discuss the relevant topics of statelessness prevention (section 4).

1. The concept of 'voluntary stateless persons'

At first glance, it might appear that voluntary stateless persons are those who have renounced their original nationality. However, voluntary statelessness is not necessarily tied to any particular source of statelessness. The diversity and complexity of voluntary statelessness in its different scenarios is best reflected by the umbrella term 'biographic circumstance', often unique to the individual concerned. This approach provides the most extensive view of the category of voluntary stateless persons, from which we can move on to the analysis of what legal qualifications this characteristic is assigned in domestic legal systems and the diversity of treatment of voluntary stateless persons.

The category of 'voluntary stateless persons' includes two basic subcategories of stateless persons. The former is people who have become stateless by their own conduct. The source of their statelessness is of principal importance here. The category of 'voluntary stateless persons' will not necessarily be united by a common 'voluntary' source of statelessness. Secondly, therefore, one has to regard as voluntary stateless persons those individuals who have become stateless by some other cause, independent of any action on their part, such as territorial changes or conflicts of nationality laws, but who are subsequently unwilling to acquire — despite being entitled to it — the nationality of the state to which they have ties. Due to the existence of options for reintegration, the continued statelessness of such persons is the effect not of compulsion but of an informed choice. With regard to the former group, one could speak of 'voluntary statelessness through the individual's own conduct', and with regard to the latter 'voluntary statelessness through the individual's inaction' (passive voluntary statelessness). Following in the footsteps of K. Swider, I will use the terms 'active voluntary statelessness' and 'passive voluntary statelessness', respectively, to refer to these two situations.[787]

The distinction between active and passive voluntary statelessness may be the point of departure for the identification of a diverse range of cases of voluntary statelessness. As I will demonstrate below, the two types of voluntary statelessness — active and passive — can refer to two different subcategories of voluntary stateless persons. It is, however, possible for an individual to be a simultaneously actively and passively stateless person (there is no mutual exclusion between the two). Furthermore, passive voluntary statelessness can be 'selective' in the sense that the intention (choice) to remain stateless can refer exclusively to the previous state of nationality or the current host state. The existence of a 'subjective element', i.e. intention to become stateless or lack of intention to obtain the host state's nationality or resume the original nationality, is key to distinguishing the different types of voluntary statelessness. When discussing the different types of statelessness, I will take a closer look at the reasons for which individuals renounce nationality with the effect of becoming stateless or for which they intend to remain so. This is because — as I will subsequently demonstrate during the analysis of the position of voluntary stateless persons in the perspective of international law and domestic legal orders — the individual stateless persons' reasons and motivations are relevant to the assessment of their situation and application of instruments for their protection.

Firstly, one could be both an active and a passive stateless person by having lost one's nationality through one's own conduct and, despite the opportunity to do so, not subsequently obtaining the nationality of any other state (subcategory 1). Such a situation of 'pure' voluntary statelessness seldom occurs. For example, some citizens of the United States become stateless through the surrender of US citizenship, which the law of their country allows them to do,[788] and afterwards they live the life of a stateless person elsewhere, for example in the European Union. Their reasons for surrendering the citizenship and for having the

---

787 K. Swider, *A rights-based…*, p. 160.

788 In the United States the ability to renounce citizenship (expatriation) is a fundamental individual right. In 1868, Congress adopted The Expatriation Act, which provides that 'the right of expatriation is a natural and inherent right of all people'. For a more extensive discussion of the problem of renunciation of citizenship in American law see *Formal Renunciation of United States Citizenship to Avoid Criminal Liability under Selective Service Law Constitutes a Voluntary Relinquishment of Nationality within the Meaning of Afroyim v. Rusk*, 71(8) Columbia Law Review, December 1971.

intention to be stateless vary. One of the prominent cases is that of Mike Gogulski, having renounced US nationality in 2008 at the embassy in Bratislava and residing as a stateless person in Slovakia. His motives for expatriation could be described as ideological or political,[789] similarly to those of other publicly active individuals such as Gareth Sol Davis[790] or Clark Hanjian[791]. Such individuals, albeit not interested in the acquisition of any nationality whatsoever, may still apply for the status of a stateless person in their state of residence (or some form of residence permit).

Secondly, one could be both actively and 'selectively' passively stateless by having lost one's nationality through one's own conduct and subsequently remaining voluntarily stateless only with regard to their original state of nationality (subcategory 2). This means that, although entitled to do so, the person does not intend to resume their original nationality, but, if they could, they would be willing to acquire the nationality of the state of residence (barring that possibility,

---

789 M. Mendoza, *Stateless in Slovakia. What if you renounce US citizenship…*, Global Post, 6 December 2011.

790 Davis renounced his US citizenship in 1948 and remained a stateless person until his death in 2013. His free decision to become stateless was rooted in the experience of the Second World War, in which he served as a pilot. In his memoir, published initially in 1968 as *The World Is my Country* and re-issued as *My Country Is the World*, he asked himself: 'How many bombs had I dropped? How many men, women and children had I murdered? Wasn't there another way, I kept asking myself.' He dedicated his life to the ideal of world citizenship. His activities were well-known and had the support of pre-eminent political figures; for example, Eleanor Roosevelt backed his efforts for the creation of an international global government. In 1949, Davis founded the International Registry of World Citizens, on which several hundred thousand people continue to remain to this day. In 1953 this was followed by a World Government of World Citizens, issuing several hundred thousand passports recognized by a couple of countries in the world (e.g. Ecuador and Tanzania). M. Fox, *Garry Davis, man of no nation who saw one world of no war, dies at 91*, The New York Times, 28 July 2013.

791 Hanjian renounced his US citizenship in 1985 and has remained stateless ever since. He gives the following reasons for his voluntary statelessness in his book: 'The demands of state membership often conflict with principles I struggle to live by — nonviolence, compassion, forgiveness, personal responsibility, consensus-based decision making, and fairness. In a nutshell, I cannot uphold a political system which effectively abandons the opinions and concerns of many minority factions. I cannot support military and police force, which are essential ingredients of most states. (…) Because my conscience is troubled by these ingredients of citizenship, I cannot in good faith maintain status as a citizen.' — C. Hanjian, *The Sovrien. An exploration of the right to be stateless*, Vineyard Haven, Massachusetts: Polyspire, 2003, p. viii.

they would apply for the status of a stateless person or look for other avenues to remain in the host state). Accordingly, this applies to those individuals who for various reasons do not want to be the nationals of specific states. At present, this particular group not infrequently includes immigrants renouncing their nationality in a search for ways of being allowed to remain in the state in which they are currently staying. This happens, for example, when an individual first unsuccessfully applies for international protection in a European state and then renounces their nationality to avoid expulsion to the state of origin. Such persons' motives can vary, from a mere desire for better living conditions in another state (an economic motivation) to, in some cases, a justified fear of returning to the state of origin.[792]

Thirdly, one could be an active voluntary stateless person by having lost nationality through one's own conduct and subsequently desiring to recover it but being prevented by objective difficulties created by the original state of nationality (subcategory 3). This may involve a situation in which the individual renounces their original nationality because that is what needed in order to qualify for naturalization in another state, which, however, does not happen, and neither is there any way for the now-stateless person to recover their original nationality. In Europe, such situations are rare, because the vast majority of states make provisions for the reintegration.[793] However, stateless persons belonging to this subcategory can originally come from non-European states. One of the examples of this subcategory of voluntary stateless persons could be the situation of several thousand female citizens of Vietnam having renounced their nationality prior to 2008 in the hope of acquiring that of their foreign husbands from Taiwan, as a result of which the women became stateless persons.[794]

---

792 Historical examples include Albert Einstein, who renounced his German citizenship and became stateless in 1896. As for his reasons for doing so, biographers on the one hand point toward his pacifist beliefs and the profound contempt he had for the authoritarian education system and militant atmosphere in Germany during the period, and on the other hand a more practical reason linked to avoidance of conscription into the German army. Five years later, Einstein acquired Swiss nationality, which he kept for the remainder of his life. W. Isaacson, *Einstein. Jego życie, jego wszechświat*, original title: *Einstein. His life and universe*, transl. by J. Skowroński, Warszawa 2010, p. 45; T. Levenson, *Einstein in Berlin*, New York 2003, p. 13.

793 GLOBALCIT 2017 (Modes of Acquisition), data for all European states (Europe), mode A16.

794 The Taiwanese procedure required the renunciation of Vietnamese nationality. However, Taiwanese nationality was often not eventually acquired due to separation or divorce occurring prior to naturalization. Vietnamese law, on the other hand, did not

In the fourth subcategory, one could be a passive voluntary stateless person by having lost one's nationality through no initiative of one's own but subsequently preferring to remain stateless (subcategory 4). This is an exceedingly rare occurrence. Historians describing the situation of Poles residing in the United Kingdom who were stripped of Polish citizenship by the communist authorities after 1945 note that some of those preferred to remain stateless for patriotic or sentimental reasons.[795] Another illustrative case is that of Russian cellist Mstislav Rostropovich and his wife, who were divested of Soviet citizenship in 1978 and never applied for the nationality of their states of residence (France and the USA).[796]

In the fifth subcategory, a person could be only 'selectively' passively stateless (subcategory 5) by having lost nationality by omission, subsequently either being unwilling to naturalize in the host state out of preference to wait for an opportunity to recover their original nationality (subcategory 5.1) or, on the contrary, not resuming the original nationality despite qualifying for reintegration (subcategory 5.2). An example of the former (5.1) is the celebrated case of the former president of Georgia, Mikheil Saakashvili, who became a stateless person following loss of Ukrainian nationality (he had previously been deprived of Georgian nationality) and preferred to remain stateless until such time as the reinstatement of his Ukrainian nationality might be possible, rather than acquiring the Lithuanian citizenship that he claims had been 'offered' to him.[797] A historical example of 'selective' passive voluntary statelessness could be found in the case of the Nobel Prize winner, Aleksandr Solzhenitsyn, whose Soviet citizenship was revoked in 1974 and who, over many years of émigré life in the USA,

---

envisage reintegration (reinstatement of previously lost nationality). Approximately three thousand women became stateless in this manner. In 2008, in order to resolve this situation, Vietnam introduced an amendment allowing reintegration. For a more extensive discussion of this topic see Chapter IV and the literature cited therein.

795 K. Sword, N. Davies and J.M. Ciechanowski, *The formation of the Polish community in Great Britain 1939–1950*, School of Slavonic and East European Studies, University of London, London 1989, p. 138.

796 In 1990, their Russian nationality was restored. J. Kilner, *Rostropovich, cellist who fought for artistic freedom*, Reuters 28 April 2007.

797 *Saakashvili doesn't plan to seek Lithuanian citizenship*, The Baltic Course, Vilnius 9 August 2017, http://www.baltic-course.com/eng/legislation/?doc=132034 (accessed 29 January 2023); *Auštrevičius proponuje nadać obywatelstwo Litwy Saakaszwilemu*, ZW.lt 28 July 2017, http://zw.lt/litwa/austrevicius-proponuje-nadac-obywatelstwo-litwy-saakaszwilemu/ (accessed 29 January 2023).

never accepted American citizenship, waiting instead for the political system in Russia to change and for his original nationality to be reinstated.[798] The latter situation (5.2) can be exemplified by Syrian Kurds having lost their nationality in the past but, despite qualifying for Syrian citizenship since 2011, not always being willing to avail themselves of the opportunity, preferring to apply for the status of a stateless person in European countries instead.[799] The case of Kazakh citizens deprived of nationality for having, without a justified reason, failed to register at a consulate for three years while staying abroad could be seen in a similar light.[800] In practice, failure to comply with this particular formality rendered such individuals stateless, and they were not always inclined to pursue reintegration, as opposed to applying for the status of a stateless person in, for example, Belgium.[801]

The above categories do not exhaust all possible scenarios of voluntary statelessness. Their purpose is to illustrate the diversity of factual circumstances (as broad a spectrum of situations as possible) as a point of departure to show how the condition of being a voluntary stateless person is qualified legally in order to exclude or limit protection and restrict the applicability of statelessness-reduction mechanisms.

2. Legal qualification of 'voluntarity' in the context of protection

In international law and in the domestic legal systems of certain states, the condition of being a voluntary stateless person is a relevant characteristic in the application of the protective regime for stateless persons. At the same time, every case of voluntary stateless persons being accorded different treatment compared

798 According to Solzhenitsyn's biographer, on the authority of the novelist's wife, for the entire duration of his residence in the USA he could not imagine himself as a citizen of any state other than Russia (not the USSR). He decided to remain stateless pending the change of political system in the USSR, which he always hoped would eventually come; J. Pearce, *Sołżenicyn. Dusza na wygnaniu*, original title: Solzhenitsyn: A Soul in Exile, transl. by W. Fladziński, Warszawa 2004, pp. 204–205.

799 See the decisions of Swiss courts concerning *Ajanib* Kurds from Syria, discussed later in this book.

800 Law No. 1017-XII of 20.12.91 of the Republic of Kazakhstan, On Citizenship of the Republic of Kazakhstan, last amended 2002, 1 March 1992, Article 21 (4); available at https://www.refworld.org/docid/3ae6b56a14.html (accessed 29 January 2023).

801 C. Rustom, Q. Schoonvae, *Mapping…*, p. 52.

to other stateless persons involves the legal qualification of the 'voluntarity' of their statelessness.

2.1. The international standard

The definition of a stateless person in Article 1(1) of the 1954 Convention, established for the purposes of the application of the protection regime created by the Convention, makes no mention of the manner in which the individual became stateless or whether their statelessness is voluntary. It only mentions the factual situation of a 'person who is not considered as a national by any [s]tate under the operation of its law'. According to the UNHCR Handbook: 'The treaty's object and purpose, of facilitating the enjoyment by stateless persons of their human rights, is equally relevant in cases of voluntary as well as involuntary withdrawal of nationality.'[802] A similar position is taken by the Prato Conclusions: 'The definition in Article 1(1) refers to a factual situation, not to the manner in which a person became stateless. Voluntary renunciation of nationality does not preclude an individual from satisfying the requirements of Article 1(1) as there is no basis for reading in such an implied condition to the definition of "stateless person".'[803]

As can be seen from the above, in the light of UNHCR documents, the fact of voluntary renunciation of nationality cannot have any bearing on the recognition of an individual as a stateless person in the light of Article 1(1) of the 1954 Convention. However, both documents authorize the offering of different terms of protection to such individuals. Thus, while the international definition of a stateless person has nothing to say about those stateless persons who are voluntarily so, the UNHCR's soft law does not regard this characteristic as irrelevant.

UNHCR documents embark on the legal qualification of voluntary statelessness, delineating the scope in which individuals affected by it may be accorded different (i.e. worse) treatment from the perspective of protection. According to the UNHCR Handbook, it is permitted for the fact of having become stateless voluntarily to influence one's treatment by the host state. First and foremost, the UNHCR Handbook specifies that the voluntary nature of renunciation may be relevant to the treatment received by a stateless person already after the

802 It appears that the UNHCR's taking of a position on this matter was prompted by the practice of the states confronted with the challenge. In the Handbook's paragraph 51, we read: 'In some States voluntary renunciation of nationality is treated as grounds for excluding an individual from the coverage of Article 1(1). However, this is not permitted by the 1954 Convention.'

803 Prato Conclusions, paragraph 20.

recognition of their stateless status.[804] A similar directive is included in the Prato Conclusions: 'the manner in which an individual became stateless may be relevant to his or her treatment following recognition and for determining the most appropriate solution.'[805]

In the same spirit, the UNHCR Handbook envisages the possibility of differentiating the treatment accorded to voluntary stateless persons, as opposed to those whose statelessness is involuntary. There is, however, no uniform standard for the treatment of voluntary stateless persons. This is because the UNHCR Handbook draws a distinction between a voluntary renunciation 'in good faith' and 'voluntary renunciation of nationality as a matter of convenience or choice',[806] foreseeing a difference in the standards of treatment accorded to these two subcategories of active voluntary stateless persons. In the above manner, the UNHCR documents embark on the legal qualification of voluntary statelessness to specify the scope in which individuals affected by it may be accorded different (i.e. worse) treatment from the perspective of protection.

Voluntary statelessness 'in good faith' refers to persons having deliberately renounced their previous nationality with the intention of obtaining that of another state, when doing so was required for the acquisition of the new nationality.[807] As observed by the UNHCR Handbook, the preferred solution in such cases is for the individuals to recover their previous nationality. Hence, if the finding made by the authorities of the state in which such a stateless person is staying is that the individual has an opportunity to recover their original nationality, the authorities will not be required to grant the residence permit generally recommended by the UNHCR in cases of recognizing a stateless person (i.e. renewable residence permit valid for at least two years and giving access to a broad spectrum of rights envisaged by the 1954 Convention).[808] They will

804 UNHCR Handbook, paragraph 51.

805 Prato Conclusions, paragraph 20.

806 UNHCR Handbook, paragraph 158, 161.

807 As the UNHCR Handbook explains (paragraph 158): 'In some cases, on account of poorly drafted nationality laws such individuals must renounce their nationality in order to apply for another but are then unable to acquire the second nationality and are left stateless.'

808 As discussed in Chapter I, the 1954 Convention does not require the states party to grant permits to individuals recognized as stateless persons. However, according to the UNHCR Handbook, such a permit 'would fulfil the object and purpose of the treaty' (paragraph 147). For this reason, the Handbook recommends that (paragraph 148) 'States grant persons recognised as stateless a residence permit valid for at least two years, although permits for a longer duration, such as five years, are preferable in

only have the obligation to grant a form of temporary immigration status allowing the individual to stay in the territory for the purpose of taking the necessary steps to resettle to their original state of nationality.[809] Such a temporary permit may be awarded for a period as short as a couple of months, and the rights enabled by it are not required to be coextensive with the rights guaranteed by the 1954 Convention. The host state may extend the duration of such a temporary permit if the individual, through no fault of their own, is prevented either from resuming their original nationality or from resettling to their state of origin. Where the permit has expired and the individual, due to their own fault, still has not achieved reinstatement in their previous nationality and cannot enter the territory of their state of origin despite their efforts, the host state is required to grant them such status as is generally awarded to those recognized as a stateless person.[810] Granting interim status will only be justified if the procedure for the acquisition of nationality of the state of origin satisfies certain conditions of accessibility. According to the UNHCR Handbook, this means that a fast and simple non-discretionary procedure must be available. The procedure must be easily accessible and uncomplicated in its procedural aspects and evidentiary requirements. Access to naturalization procedures in which the authorities are free to choose the outcome after the individual satisfies the conditions will be insufficient. Access to a procedure involving the assessment of imprecisely worded regulatory conditions for the acquisition of nationality or in which the individual has to be physically present in the country of their previous nationality but legal entry and stay are not guaranteed will not suffice, either.[811] Thus, this must be a procedure in which the administrative authorities have no discretion with regard to the outcome of the decision and no margin of appreciation is left to them.

Different standards apply to those having renounced their nationality to become stateless persons 'as a matter of convenience or choice'. According to the UNHCR Handbook, this means persons who 'voluntarily renounce a nationality because they do not wish to be nationals of a particular [s]tate or in the belief

the interests of stability. Such permits are to be renewable, providing the possibility of facilitated naturalization as prescribed by Article 32 of the 1954 Convention.'

809 UNHCR Handbook, paragraphs 153, 159.

810 UNHCR Handbook, paragraph 160.

811 UNHCR Handbook, paragraphs 154–156. The Handbook specifies that such requirements are satisfied, for example, by a procedure in which former nationals are readmitted by submitting a declaration to the consul along with their birth certificate (footnote 102).

that this will lead to grant of a protection status in another country.'[812] In contrast to the category discussed beforehand, this refers to those active voluntary stateless persons who could be viewed as being 'in bad faith' from the perspective of the protection mechanism. Similarly to the case of the last-mentioned category, the UNHCR Handbook notes that the best solution here is resettlement to the previous state of nationality (re-admission) together with re-acquisition (restoration) of nationality. If the individual does not co-operate with this objective, the authorities of the host state are entitled to enter into talks with the individual's previous state of nationality in order to secure their re-admission.[813] The host state is under no obligation to grant any permit to the individual in such a situation. What is important in this context is that according to the UNHRC Handbook, with regard to such persons expulsion is not off-limits.[814]

As can be seen from the above, the limitations contemplated by the UNHCR Handbook with regard to the protection of persons who are stateless voluntarily are applicable only to active voluntary stateless persons (subcategories 1 to 3). They do not apply, by contrast, to persons who are merely passive voluntary stateless (subcategories 4 to 5). Therefore, the worse treatment of voluntary stateless persons relative to those who are stateless involuntarily is applicable only to a certain range of individuals who could be regarded as being voluntarily stateless on account of their specific biographic circumstances. Simultaneously, the UNHCR Handbook provides for the different treatment of individuals depending on the causes of (or reasons for) their active voluntary statelessness, distinguishing within that group between those who are in 'good faith' and those who are in 'bad faith'.[815] Accordingly, in the light of the UNHCR's guidelines, the reasons for the individual's renunciation of nationality may have a bearing on the level of protection granted (i.e. they may constitute additional factors to be taken into account).

812 UNHCR Handbook, paragraph 161.

813 It has been observed that such a situation engages other international obligations of the state of the individual's previous nationality, such as in the area of prevention of stateless in the event of renunciation of nationality, as well as the prohibition against arbitrary deprivation of the right of entry to one's own country, which is mandated by Article 12(4) ICCPR.

814 UNHCR Handbook, paragraph 162.

815 Those who are categorized as active voluntary stateless persons within my subcategory 3 are the 'good-faith' stateless persons, whereas those in subcategories 1 and 2 are the 'bad-faith' stateless.

2.2. Selected domestic regulatory frameworks and court decisions

In some states, domestic regulations or the decisions of domestic courts and other bodies distinguish a category of individuals who are voluntary stateless persons and who are to be given different treatment from the perspective of protection mechanisms. The very concept of voluntary statelessness is subjected to legal qualification in domestic legal systems and is understood differently from one state to the next. The following analysis of legal provisions and decisions of courts of law and administrative authorities in a selection of states is provided by way of example to illustrate the diversity of approaches taken to voluntary stateless persons from the perspective of the scope of protection to be accorded to them.

In some states, voluntary stateless persons are excluded from protection as a consequence of the adoption of special provisions. Such is the case, for example, in Hungary, where certain active voluntary stateless persons are left without access to statelessness-identification procedures.[816] In accordance with the Hungarian provision, an application for the recognition of statelessness status will be rejected in cases in which the applicant has renounced a previous nationality deliberately with the intention of qualifying for the status of a stateless person.[817] The objective sought, therefore, is to exclude some active voluntary stateless persons from the identification procedure (and, consequently, from protection), namely those who have renounced their previous nationality with a specific goal in mind. The drafting of the Hungarian provision falls short of the ideal, primarily because it is not clear what the 'intention of qualifying for the status of a stateless person' is supposed to mean. For this reason, in concrete factual configurations, the individual's intention will be either difficult or outright impossible to assess unequivocally. As for previously identified subcategories, difficulties can arise with distinguishing among the situations of persons in subcategories 1 to 3.[818]

816 For a more extensive discussion of statelessness-identification procedures see Chapter IV.

817 Hungarian Act II of 2007 on the Admission and Right of Residence of Third-Country Nationals and the Government Decree 114/2007 (V. 24), section 78(1)(b).

818 For example, if an individual renounces their original nationality with the intention of naturalizing in the host state but, through their own fault, fails to meet the naturalization conditions, it will be difficult to achieve clarity as to whether their intention included the acquisition of stateless status.

In certain other European states, the exclusion of voluntary stateless persons from protection is the product of judicial or administrative practice. Such individuals are not excluded from the procedure itself (as in the Hungarian case), but they cannot achieve recognition as stateless persons in the existing procedures, as a result of which they are excluded from the protection mechanisms. Examples include Switzerland and France. In those countries, the criteria for the qualification of such individuals as voluntary stateless persons and the standard of treatment accorded to them are the outcome of judicial decision-making.

According to the settled line of Swiss administrative courts, Article 1(1) of the 1954 Convention must be interpreted in such a way as for the term 'stateless person' to be understood to mean those who have lost nationality through no initiative of their own and have no way of re-acquiring it. *A contrario:* „The Convention does not apply to those persons who renounce their nationality voluntarily (loss of nationality by own initiative) or, for no worthy reasons, refuse its restoration when offered to them (loss of nationality by omission), where their sole goal is to obtain the status of a stateless person.'[819] According to the decisions of Swiss courts, the status of a stateless person may only be granted if there are 'objective reasons'[820] — meaning reasons that are important and justified — for failure to acquire (re-acquire) the nationality of a state to which the individual has ties. In such cases, Swiss administrative courts consider whether the applicants have taken 'such actions as could be reasonably expected of them'[821] with a view to having their original nationality reinstated.[822] Subjective motivations or psychological problems are not such objective reasons.[823]

---

819 *A contrario, cette convention n'est pas applicable aux personnes qui abandonnent volontairement leur nationalité (perte de la nationalité par action) ou refusent, sans raisons valables, de la recouvrer alors qu'ils ont la possibilité de le faire (perte de la nationalité par omission), dans le seul but d'obtenir le statut d'apatride* — Federal Administrative Court, *C-4959/2007*, judgment, 12 November 2008; see also judgments in: *2C_1/2008*, 28 February 2008; *2A.153/2005*, 17 March 2005; *2A.388/2004*, 6 October 2004; *2A.221/2003*, 19 May 2003; *2A.147/2002*, 27 June 2002; *2A.78/2000*, 23 May 2000; *2A.373/1993*, 4 July 1994.

820 French: *raisons objectives*; German: *triftige Gründe.*

821 French: *démarches raisonablement exigibles d'elles.*

822 *Article F4: La demande de reconnaissance du statut d'apatride* [in:] *Manuel Asile et retour*, Département fédéral de justice et police, Secrétariat d'Etat aux migrations (SEM), p. 11, https://www.sem.admin.ch/dam/data/sem/asyl/verfahren/hb/f/hb-f5-f.pdf (version of 2019; accessed 7 April 2019).

823 Swiss Federal Administrative Court, *E-3562/2013*, judgment of 17 December 2014, SEM, p. 13.

The existence of 'objective reasons' for not applying for the nationality of one's state of origin is something for Swiss courts to determine on a case-by-case basis. This can be illustrated on the example of three cases involving stateless Kurds before administrative courts in Switzerland. The first one featured a stateless Kurd from Syria. Syrian Kurds referred to as *Ajanib*[824] lost their Syrian nationality upon failure to comply with registration requirements in the census conducted by the authorities in 1962. The Swiss Federal Administrative Court found that while the applicant was eligible to have his Syrian nationality reinstated to him in accordance with a decree issued by the Syrian government in 2011, doing so would require him to return to Syria (for the purpose of submitting the application personally). In the case of *Ajanib* Kurds, however, the court was of the opinion that there were important reasons for them not to return to Syria for the purpose of submitting an application for the reinstatement of Syrian nationality because of the situation in the country and the fact that travelling without documents would require them to cross state borders illegally. As a result, the court held that the applicant ought to be recognized as a stateless person and granted the corresponding status.[825] The second case also involved an *Ajanib* Kurd from Syria,[826] but the facts of the case were viewed by the court in a different light with regard to the existence of 'objective reasons'. In this case, the stateless Kurd initially applied for the restoration of his Syrian nationality in reliance on the aforementioned 2011 decree while staying in Syria and then left without waiting for the decision. In its judgment, the Swiss court held that his reasons for leaving Syria were not relevant in the procedure for applying for the status of a stateless person, and, accordingly, the necessary conclusion was that he could have waited in Syria for the authorities' decision concerning his citizenship and was thus not

824 The history of stateless Kurds from Syria goes back to a census held in 1962 in the majority-Kurdish province of al-Hasakah. Pursuant to the then-government's Decree no. 93, the Kurds were required to register and produce, among other things, a document confirming that they had resided in the region in 1945. As a result, the Kurdish inhabitants were divided into three groups: (1) those who satisfied the registration requirements and remained Syrian nationals; (2) those having made an attempt to register but failed to satisfy the requirements and lost their Syrian nationality, subsequently issued residence permits for foreigners (*Ajanib* means 'foreigners'); and (3) those never having made any attempt to register, consequently removed from the population register (the *Maktoumeen*) – Z. Albarazi, *The Stateless…*, pp. 15–16.

825 Federal Administrative Court, *C-1873/2013*, cited after SEM, p. 13.

826 Swiss Federal Administrative Court, *F-1672/2015*, judgment of 22 September 2016, SEM, p. 14.

entitled to stateless status in Switzerland. The court emphasized that, because of how high the bar was set with regard to efforts to acquire the nationality of one's state of origin, the objective reasons (*raisons objectives*, *triftige Gründe*) for failing to acquire the nationality of the state of origin had to be interpreted strictly. In the cases of *Ajanib* Kurds having left Syria after 2011, the position of Swiss courts is that their reasons for failing to re-acquire the nationality after the enactment of the 2011 decree are for the court to consider in each individual case, so as to determine whether they satisfy the criteria of objectivity.[827] The third case involved the situation of a stateless Kurd from Turkey having lost his Turkish nationality in the past as a consequence of his refusal of military service.[828] The court decided that his efforts for the reinstatement of his original nationality had been insufficient because the Turkish authorities' lack of response to his application did not in itself warrant the conclusion that it was denied. In the face of the inaction of the competent Turkish authority, the applicant — in the court's opinion — should have 'insisted on the Turkish authorities in this case, which he failed to do with sufficient insistence',[829] for which reason he was not eligible for the status of a stateless person.[830]

As can be seen from the above, individuals who are active voluntary stateless persons cannot be recognized as stateless persons in Switzerland, nor can the majority of those who are passive voluntary stateless persons. Only those who are passive voluntary stateless persons and, although eligible for the reinstatement of their original nationality, do not seek it for 'objective reasons' (because certain actions cannot be reasonably expected of them) can obtain protection. Thus, out of all scenarios of voluntary statelessness situations falling within my subcategories 1 to 5 above, only part of those who are voluntary stateless persons within subcategory 5.2 can be recognized as stateless persons in Switzerland — if their reasons for not applying for a nationality are judged to be 'objective'. Almost

827 Swiss Federal Administrative Court, *E-3562/2013*, judgment of 17 December 2014, SEM, p. 13.

828 This mode of loss of nationality was prescribed by Turkish Law No. 403/1964 on Turkish Citizenship. One of the most important changes introduced by the new nationality law of 2009 was the abolishment of this mode of loss. For a more detailed discussion of this topic see Z. Kadirbeyoglu, *Country Report: Turkey*, 31 EUDO Citizenship Observatory 2010, p. 1.

829 French: *Le recourant aurait dû insister auprès des autorités turques, ce qu'il a toutefois manqué de faire avec suffisamment d'insistance.*

830 Swiss Federal Administrative Court, *C-346/2010*, judgment of 21 December 2012, SEM, p. 11.

all subcategories of voluntary stateless persons are thus excluded from protection (all active voluntary stateless persons, i.e. subcategories 1 to 3, as well as passive voluntary stateless persons in subcategories 4 and 5.1).

In their exclusion of nearly all voluntary stateless persons from protection (outside of a narrow subcategory of passive voluntary stateless persons having objective reasons for failing to resume the original nationality), the Swiss courts apply a teleological interpretation of the 1954 Convention. They emphasize that the purpose of the treaty is to assist persons who have found themselves in an unfavourable situation due to fortuitous events, a situation in which one would remain vulnerable but for such protection. The Convention's purpose, by contrast, is not to allow every willing individual to obtain the status of a stateless person, which in some aspects is more advantageous than what is granted to other foreigners, in particular with regard to the scope of assistance provided by the state. Moreover, it is argued that it would be incompatible with the aim pursued by the international community to award the status of a stateless person to an individual having renounced nationality for convenience.[831] According to the position taken by the courts, the legal system cannot approve of conduct that bears the marks of *praeter legem*. Granting nationality to such individuals — especially those having renounced their original nationality during the procedure for refugee status when they saw no chance of obtaining that status and endeavoured to secure the status of a stateless person instead (subcategory 2 on my list) — 'would come down to the favourable reception of abusive conduct.'[832]

Much in a similar way, the courts in France do not recognize as stateless persons those who are stateless voluntarily. However, the French legal qualification of voluntary statelessness is unique to that legal system. Initially, court decisions emphasized that for an individual to be eligible for the status of a stateless person, their statelessness should not derive from their own conduct. The French courts' position withholding recognition as a stateless person from individuals rendered stateless by their own conduct dates back to the first half of the 90s of the 20th century. Here, particularly noteworthy are the judgments of the Administrative Tribunal in Strasbourg in *Dragotel*[833] and the Council of State's *Popescu*[834] and

831 Federal Administrative Court, judgment of 12 November 2008, paragraph 2.3; see also judgment of 28 February 2008, paragraph 3.2; judgment in *TF 2A.78/2000*, of 23 May 2000, paragraph 2b; *2A.373/1993*, judgment of 4 July 1994, paragraph 2b.

832 *Cela reviendrait, en outre, à favoriser un comportement abusif* — Swiss Federal Administrative Court, *E-3562/2.3*, judgment of 12 November 2008 (paragraph 2.3 *in fine*).

833 *Dragotel*, judgment of 31 March 1994, Rec. 1994, tables, p. 950.

834 *Popescu*, judgment of 21 November 1994, Rec. 1994, tables, pp. 940, 947 and 949.

Cucu[835] cases of the same year (1994). In all of these cases, the courts denied the status of a stateless person to former Romanian nationals having, upon failure to obtain refugee status, renounced their nationality in order to prevent their own expulsion from France.[836]

At a later time, French decisions developed another important criterion for the recognition of stateless persons and for the granting of protection. Namely, the courts started to assess not only whether the individual's statelessness is the outcome of their own conduct but also whether such conduct truly represents the individual's will, as opposed to being externally driven. Thus, the position held by the courts is that it is possible for an individual's statelessness to be the consequence of the individual's own conduct while not being the effect of their will. As observed by C.-A. Chassin, the concept of a voluntary act (*acte volontaire*) had been at the centre of judicial disputes involving statelessness in the first decade of the 20th century in France.[837] The most important judgment in this context is *Sarigul*,[838] featuring a Kurd from Turkey stripped of his Turkish

835 *Cucu*, judgment of 21 November 1994, req. 147194, Cucu, *inédit*. In their application to the European Commission of Human Rights, Marius Popescu and Emilia Cucu, stateless persons of Romanian origin, claimed (among other things) that their expulsion from France to Romania would expose them to inhuman and degrading treatment (violation of Article 3 ECHR). Without discussing all of their allegations or of the Commission's reasoning here, as they are not relevant to the subject at hand, it should be noted that the Commission did not dispute the logic of distinguishing voluntary from involuntary statelessness. In its decision, the Commission quotes from the position taken by the French Council of State that the applicants had renounced their nationality voluntarily for the purpose of avoiding the effect of the provisions of the Geneva Convention of 1951. The Commission emphasizes the absence of any evidence to support the conclusion that the applicants had been forced to give up their nationality — decision of non-admissibility of applications no. 28152/95 and 28153/95 brought by Marius Popescu and Emilia Cucu against France, p. 4.

836 As noted by F. Julien-Laferriere when commenting on the aforementioned *Dragotel* case, the applicant had procured his own statelessness by his own conduct for the purposing of circumvention of the OFPRA's decision denying him refugee status. And such a purpose must qualify as fraud (*M. Dragotel s'est donc de son propre fait place en situation d'apatridie dans en but que l'on peut qualifier de frauduleux*) — *Tribunal Administratif 31/03/1994 (Dragotel), D.1994.Somm.comm.246, observations* F. Julien-Laferriere, p. 2.

837 C.-A. Chassin, *Panorama du droit français de l'apatridie*, 2 *Revue Française de Droit Administratif* March-April 2003, p. 328.

838 *Préfet de police c. Sarigul*, judgment of 29 December 2000, req. 216121.

citizenship by the authorities for refusing military service to Turkey. Firstly, the Council of State found him to be a voluntary stateless person because of his loss of Turkish nationality being the consequence of his own conduct consisting in the refusal of military service.[839] Subsequently, however, the court's analysis went one step further, to arrive at the conclusion that, although it was possible for the applicant to re-acquire Turkish nationality in the event of his returning to Turkey, the risk of persecution on account of his Kurdish origin and political involvement would have had the effect of exposing him to inhuman or degrading treatment within the meaning of Article 3 ECHR. For that reason, the Council of State decided he should be recognized as a stateless person. As can be seen, the French cassation court attempted to verify that the individual's conduct was not caused by 'elements external to the individual's will', i.e. fear of persecution.[840]

The justification given for the exclusion of voluntary stateless persons (according to the qualification discussed above) from protection in France relies on a teleological interpretation of the 1954 Convention. Commentators observe that the status of a stateless person was designed as a form of substitute protection (*protection de substitution*) for those excluded from any protection within the international system of states. Therefore, the acquisition of such protection should not be a 'disguised means of migration'[841] under the pretence of statelessness, because that would be incompatible with the assumptions underlying the status of a stateless person, as well as its specific characteristics, and it would have an adverse impact on the situation of involuntary stateless persons. An argument is also made from objection to the legitimization of *praeter legem* conduct: if an individual is free to return to their state of origin and obtain re-admission, that means we are dealing with 'false statelessness' (*fausse apatridie*).[842]

Although the examination of the subjective element (the individual's true will) is a development prompted by the analysis of the situation of active voluntary stateless persons, its application by French courts is wider. Paradoxically, taking into account the individual's true will, on the one hand, allows protection to be granted in specific situations to voluntary stateless persons, but on the other

839 In *Bayram*, the outcome of such verification allowed the court seised of that case to deny the status of a stateless person to an applicant who was able to return to Turkey and obtain re-admission. Administrative Court of Appeals in Bordeaux, *Bayram*, judgment of 19 July 1999, req. 98BX00688, *inédit*, cited after C.-A. Chassin, *Panorama…*, p. 327, footnote 36.

840 C.-A. Chassin, *Panorama…*, p. 328.

841 French: *moyen deguisé d'immigration*.

842 C.-A. Chassin, *Panorama…*, pp. 327–328.

hand it also leads to a broader range of cases of voluntary statelessness being categorized as cases of active statelessness. This is illustrated by the aforementioned *Sarigul* case, in which the situation of an individual from Turkey deprived of nationality by Turkish authorities for his refusal of military service[843] is interpreted to be the result of the individual's own conduct. In the view of the court in *Bayram*, dealing with a similar case, such an individual 'ought to be regarded as having voluntarily placed themselves in the situation of being deprived of their nationality.'[844] Hence, while France does not exclude all voluntary stateless persons *en bloc* from protection, delineation of the scope of those excluded involves the assessment of the reasons for which they are stateless, in particular whether their voluntary statelessness is truly voluntary (conforms to their will) or has been caused by factors external to their will (*extérieurs à la volonté*).

As can be seen from the above analysis, neither in Switzerland, nor in France does the lack of a nationality alone suffice for an individual to be characterized as a stateless person. In each of the two states, court decisions have developed certain criteria for the assessment of whether a given set of facts corresponds to the definition of voluntary statelessness. Referring back to the subcategories of stateless persons introduced at the beginning of this chapter, this can be summarized with the observation that in these two countries individuals who are active voluntary stateless persons are either not protected at all (Switzerland) or given a very narrow scope of protection (France). When it comes to passive voluntary stateless persons, in both countries they can obtain protection, although decisions are made on a case-by-case basis upon detailed analysis of the facts of the case, in which the reasons (causes) behind the individual's statelessness are significant factors. In France, because of the incorporation of an element of true will in the analysis, the situation of such individuals may qualify as active voluntary statelessness, for which protection is granted only on an exceptional basis. In Switzerland, on the other hand, the test is whether there exist objective reasons for not applying for the nationality of the individual's state of origin.

In other countries, too, it is possible to find court decisions excluding voluntary stateless persons from eligibility for recognition and protection. Certain judgments of Belgian and Luxembourgian courts are headed in that direction.

843 That was possible on the basis of Law No. 403/1964 on Turkish Citizenship. See footnote 828 above.

844 *Doit être regardé comme s'étant volontairement placé dans la situation d'être privé de sa nationalité* — judgement in *Bayram*, cited after C.-A. Chassin, *Panorama…*, p. 327, footnote 36.

The judicial practice in those two countries, however, is not uniform, and — as I will demonstrate below — one can also find judgments of higher courts expressing the opinion that individuals who are voluntary stateless persons should be recognized as stateless persons.

In Belgium, the status of applicants having voluntarily renounced their previous nationality is seen as problematic.[845] Belgium ratified the 1954 Convention in 1960, and the definition of a stateless person from this treaty applies in Belgian law; in practice, however, it is subjected to interpretations by courts and tribunals. The judicial decisions do not always follow a consistent line,[846] and it is not possible to identify any homogeneous main trends. In some cases, voluntarily stateless individuals have been recognized as stateless persons with all consequences of such recognition. For example, in a judgment of 1996, the Tribunal of First Instance in Antwerp[847] found that an individual having voluntarily renounced their Romanian nationality did not, as a consequence of their own conduct, hold the nationality of any state. With that, the court found them to meet the criteria of Article 1(1) of the 1954 Convention and ruled that recognition should be given. It did not enter the court's consideration whether the individual was eligible for the nationality (or reinstatement of nationality) of any state.

Sometimes, however, Belgian courts have ruled that an individual having lost their nationality voluntarily cannot be recognized as a stateless person. Different arguments have been made from case to case. And so, for example, in one of its cases,[848] the Court of First Instance in Antwerp, invoking a teleological interpretation, held that the recognition of a stateless person was exceptional in nature and applicable only to those who have been denied nationality against their will. In a different case,[849] the Court of First Instance in Liège argued that in order for an individual to be recognized as a stateless person, the host state must, as a minimum, be able to find merit in their reasons for having renounced the protection of their former state of nationality, provided that a choice motivated solely by

---

845 C. Rustom, Q. Schoonvae, *Mapping…*, p. 54.

846 C. Rustom, Q. Schoonvae, *Mapping…*, p. 55.

847 Tribunal of the First Instance in Antwerp, judgment of 25 November 1996. This and following judgments of Belgian courts are cited after C. Rustom, Q. Schoonvae, *Mapping…*, p. 55.

848 Tribunal of First Instance in Antwerp, judgment of 20 November 1998 (no case number).

849 Tribunal of First Instance in Liège, *2006/RF/38*, judgment of 13 March 2007, unpublished.

'personal convenience' could not be regarded as a sufficient reason. Courts of a higher instance have also taken this approach. For example, the Court of Appeals in Liège [850] has found it impossible to stake a reasonable claim that the 1954 Convention has the purpose of protecting those who voluntarily refuse to acquire or re-acquire the nationality of the state to which they have ties (except out of fear) with the intention of acquiring a status similar to citizenship in their state of residence. Embarking on a systemic interpretation, the Court of Appeals in Brussels found that Article 1 of 1954 had to be interpreted in a manner respectful of the philosophies of the international and domestic instruments governing stateless persons, which have been adopted for the purpose of avoiding statelessness and reducing the number of its existing cases. On the above basis, the court concluded that the status of a stateless person should remain subsidiary or exceptional (*subsidiaire ou exceptionnel*). In the court's opinion, where an individual is eligible for the acquisition or re-acquisition of the nationality of their state of origin, that solution must be given priority before any other, under two conditions, of which the former requires having ties to the state and the latter addresses any justified reasons for refusing to reapply.[851]

Belgian Court of Cassation, however, took a completely different view[852] (on appeal-in-cassation against the previously discussed judgment of the Court of Appeals in Brussels), holding in a judgment issued in 2008 that neither Article 1(1) of the 1954 Convention — which deals with the objective authority of every state to define by its own legislation who its nationals are — nor any other provision allows states to withhold recognition as a stateless person from a foreigner for failure, even voluntary, to take steps for the reinstatement of their original nationality. In consequence, by denying recognition, the judgments of the inferior courts had added to Article 1(1) of the 1954 Convention a condition that was not found in it. In a similar way, the Court of Cassation clarified that an applicant for recognition as a stateless person in Belgium does not have to prove that they are unable to acquire any other nationality.[853]

850 Court of Appeals in Liège, judgment of 13 June 2006 (no case number).

851 Court of Appeals in Brussels, judgment of 29 March 2007 (no case number); opinion cited after the Court of Cassation of Belgium, *C.07.0385.F/1*, judgment of 6 June 2008, which heard the appeal-in-cassation against the former judgment (discussed in the following paragraph).

852 Court of Cassation of Belgium, *C.07.0385.F/1*, judgment of 6 June 2008, available in French at http://www.refworld.org/pdfid/499154412.pdf (accessed 29 January 2023), cited [in:] C. Rustom and Q. Schoonvae, *Mapping...*, p. 55.

853 Ch. Chiurulli, *La protection...*, p. 22.

The existence of certain doubts at the bench can also be traced in Luxembourg. One of the cases coming up before its courts for ruling involved a former citizen of Russian Federation having renounced that nationality. He had previously applied for refugee status in Luxembourg, which was not granted. The Administrative Tribunal in Luxembourg cited the arguments made by the French courts, pointing out that the status of a stateless person should offer 'subsidiary protection' to individuals unable to avail themselves of the protection of any state and should not provide a 'disguised means of migration'. It ought not to be recognized in a 'person whose pretended statelessness results from their own act, in particular the renunciation of previous nationality, at least if such an act was not justified by elements external to the affected individual's will, such as in particular the risk of being subjected to inhuman or degrading treatment in their country of origin.'[854] However, on appeal, the Administrative Court found the applicant to have renounced his Russian citizenship not 'for convenience' (*par commodité*) but out of political conviction, having considered himself a dissident already during the existence of the USSR and thereafter until his departure from Russia in 2005. The Court cited the applicant's argument that, according to the UNHCR guidelines, voluntary renunciation of nationality should not be grounds for exclusion from the applicability of Article 1(1) of the 1954 Convention. The court invoked the aforementioned judgement of Belgian Court of Cassation of 6 June 2008 to demonstrate that the language of Article 1(1) of the 1954 Convention does not leave the states free to withhold recognition as a stateless person on the grounds of the individual's not having attempted to re-acquire their previous nationality, even forfeited in voluntary manner.[855]

As can be seen from the above analysis, in France and Switzerland voluntary stateless persons are excluded from recognition as stateless persons by a consistent judicial practice that does not regard them as stateless persons within the meaning of the 1954 Convention except where special circumstances are at play. Both active and passive voluntary stateless persons may be recognized and protected on condition that, for whatever reasons, their 'voluntary' loss of

---

854 *[I]l ne saurait être reconnu à une personne dont la prétendue apatridie résulte de son propre fait, notamment de la renonciation à la nationalité qui était la sienne, à moins que ce fait ne soit justifié par des éléments extérieurs à la volonté de l'intéressé, tels que notamment le risque de subir des traitements inhumains et dégradants dans son pays d'origine* — Administrative Tribunal of the Grand Duchy of Luxembourg, *35177*, judgment of 9 July 2015, p. 11.

855 Administrative Court of the Grand Duchy of Luxembourg, *36744C*, judgment of 27 October 2015, pp. 7–8.

nationality or continued statelessness thereafter does not reflect their true will. In Hungary, some active voluntary stateless persons are excluded from SIP eligibility. In Belgium and Luxembourg, by contrast, decisions do not follow a consistent line, and the courts of higher instances have taken the position that a voluntarily stateless individual should be recognized as a stateless person and, consequently, given protection.

In those situations in which the decisions withhold protection from some part of voluntary stateless persons, the rationale invokes, among other arguments, the need to penalize conduct intended in circumvention of the law. An important matter here to consider is whether, if the legal system considers the reasons for voluntary statelessness and penalizes *praeter legem* conduct by withholding recognition (and thus protection), this means that whatever stateless persons find themselves in such a situation are left without any rights. It would seem that even individuals excluded from protection in this manner should be accorded a certain minimum of rights, especially the right to be issued identity papers. This is the approach that can be identified in one of the judgments coming from the Netherlands. The Dutch court sat on the case of a voluntary stateless person from Georgia having renounced Georgian nationality for political reasons. The court, invoking the UNHCR guidelines, found that such an individual should be given at least a certain minimum of rights, especially the right to be issued identity papers.[856]

To summarize this part of the discussion, the conclusion should be that both in international law and in certain domestic systems different treatment is accorded to individuals who are stateless voluntarily. In the light of binding norms of international law, voluntary stateless persons ought still to be recognized as stateless persons under Article 1(1) of the 1954 Convention, but they may be accorded different treatment compared to those who are stateless involuntarily. This is the standard developed by UNHCR soft law despite the absence of a clear basis in the text of 1954 Convention. Here, it must be noted that the limitations referring to the treatment of voluntary stateless persons apply only to active voluntary stateless persons. In some states, contrary to the UNHCR guidelines, individuals who are stateless voluntarily are not even recognized as stateless persons at all; moreover, in some cases they are ineligible to initiate statelessness-identification procedures. Who exactly qualifies as a voluntary stateless person differs from

856 District Court of the Hague, *X v. the Mayor of The Hague*, judgment of 19 February 2014, SGR 13/2490, cited after K. Swider, *A rights-based…*, pp. 164–165.

one state to the next, and limitations on the treatment can potentially apply to both active and passive voluntary stateless persons.

3. The legal qualification of 'voluntarity' in the context of statelessness reduction

The topic area of statelessness reduction should be viewed through a dual lens in the case of voluntary stateless persons. Firstly, this will involve the problem of statelessness reduction in the state of residence. Secondly, for this category of individuals, the reduction aspect will apply also to their state of origin and to their eligibility for the acquisition (reinstatement) of its nationality.

In the first aspect, the key question is whether voluntary stateless persons are eligible for facilitated naturalization in the host state as foreseen by the international conventions dealing with stateless persons. As noted before,[857] in accordance with the 1954 Convention, the states party should to the greatest possible extent facilitate the assimilation and naturalization of stateless persons (Article 32). In particular, they should strive to expedite the naturalization of such individuals and, as far as possible, reduce the burdens and costs of any such procedure. The obligation for states to facilitate — through their domestic laws and regulations — the naturalization of stateless persons lawfully and habitually resident in the territory is also stipulated by the European Convention on Nationality (Article 6(4)(g)). However, the latter convention standard is subjected to restrictions and limitations in soft-law documents.

According to the ECN's explanatory report, persons having become stateless voluntarily are not eligible for facilitated naturalization in their state of residence: 'Persons who have deliberately become stateless, in disregard of the principles of this Convention (for example persons originating from a State with an internal law which, contrary to Article 8 of this Convention, permits the renunciation of nationality without the prior acquisition of another nationality) shall not be entitled to acquire nationality in a facilitated manner.'[858] As can be seen, the ECN explanatory report assumes different treatment for voluntary stateless persons. The distinction between passive and active statelessness, however, permits the observation that the limitations on the accessibility of facilitated naturalization mechanisms are applicable not to all voluntary stateless persons but

857 Chapter III, section 2.

858 CETS 166 — Explanatory Report to the European Convention on Nationality, paragraph 57.

only to some, i.e. to those voluntary stateless persons who have become stateless intentionally.

Domestic statelessness-reduction frameworks rarely distinguish the situation of voluntary as opposed to involuntary stateless persons. One of the examples of a state having a statutory distinction in place in this matter is Finland. The Finnish nationality statute distinguishes voluntary stateless persons from those being stateless involuntarily. In line with its provisions, only those who are stateless involuntarily are eligible for facilitated naturalization.[859] A voluntary stateless person means an individual who does not hold the nationality of any state and remains stateless out of their own will or due to the decision of their parent or guardian.[860] It is worth noting that a child who remains stateless due to the decision of their parent or guardian is regarded as a voluntary stateless person by that provision, even though the child is not the individual making the choice to be stateless.[861] In my opinion, the Finnish regulation is problematic on account of the formalistic nature of the criterion used in it. In turn, an involuntary stateless person is deemed to be one who does not hold the nationality of any state whatsoever and remains stateless against their will or that of their parent or guardian.[862]

Concerning the second aspect of reduction of statelessness, dealing with eligibility for restoration of nationality of the state of origin, according to the UNHCR Guidelines on Statelessness no. 4 (as has been discussed above),[863] the state of residence is not required to grant a protection status to those voluntary stateless persons who are in a position to acquire (re-acquire) the nationality of their state of origin. On the contrary, the authorities of the host state may take steps to procure the re-admission of such individuals. The guiding idea behind these solutions is that such individuals should be acquiring the nationality of that state with which they have ties. This demonstrates that the UNHCR prioritizes solutions aimed at the reduction of statelessness (at the expense of protective solutions in the country of residence), provided that this means the reduction of statelessness in the state of origin rather than naturalization in the state of residence.

---

859 Article 20(1) of Finnish Nationality Act.

860 Article 2(1)(4) of Finnish Nationality Act.

861 UNHCR, *Mapping Statelessness in Finland*..., p. 42; available at https://www.refworld.org/docid/546da8744.html (accessed 29 January 2023).

862 Article 2(1)(3) of Finnish Nationality Act.

863 This chapter, section 2 above.

4. Prevention of 'voluntary' statelessness

Voluntary statelessness can be the outcome of the affected individual's own renunciation of nationality (active voluntary statelessness).[864] The important question to ask is how the international order and domestic legal systems regulate statelessness prevention in this type of statelessness. The crucial point is whether there exists an individual right to renounce one's nationality and become a stateless person or there are some limitations in this area.

4.1. The international standard

Under both the 1961 Convention and the ECN, the domestic legislation of a state must not allow the loss of nationality by renunciation to occur if the affected individual is to be rendered stateless by it (the principle of prevention). However, while the principle is absolute under the ECN, the 1961 Convention does admit of an exception. Its Article 7(1)(b) provides for departure from the principle of counteraction of statelessness resulting from the renunciation of nationality if the application of the principle would conflict with the rights specified in Articles 13 and 14 UDHR. This means the right to leave any country, including one's own, and to return to one's home country,[865] and the right to seek and find asylum in a different country in the event of persecution.[866] In the light of the 1961 Convention, therefore, an individual has a right to renounce nationality with the effect of becoming a stateless person if their holding the nationality of a given state interferes with their right to leave the country (or return to it) or right to seek asylum. In other words, the principle that renunciation should not lead to statelessness 'is qualified in the sense that the provision shall not apply where its application would be inconsistent with the principles voiced by Articles 13

864 Here, I am not addressing the situations in which the individual renounces nationality not for the purpose of becoming a stateless person. For a more general discussion of counteracting statelessness in cases of renunciation of nationality, see Chapter III, section 1.1.

865 Article 13 '1. Everyone has the right to freedom of movement and residence within the borders of each state. 2. Everyone has the right to leave any country, including his own, and to return to his country.'

866 Article 14 '1. Everyone has the right to seek and to enjoy in other countries asylum from persecution. 2. This right may not be invoked in the case of prosecutions genuinely arising from non-political crimes or from acts contrary to the purposes and principles of the United Nations.'

and 14 of the Universal Declaration of Human Rights of 1948.'[867] As noted by P. Weis, this provision reflects an 'interesting compromise' between the prevention of statelessness and the reluctance to compel individuals to remain the nationals of a state in cases when — for reasons justified in the light of the UDHR[868] — they would prefer to extricate themselves from the relationship. The provision imposes on the states an obligation not to create new cases of statelessness, but it allows for exceptions to be made if that is the only way for the state to respect certain rights specified in the UDHR.[869]

At present, the exception from statelessness prevention that is explicitly allowed by the 1961 Convention usually is not given much attention. For example, in the Tunis Conclusions it is mentioned in the following way: 'There was a strong consensus that the exceptions to this rule allowed by Article 7(1)(b), which refers to Articles 13 and 14 UDHR, are of limited relevance and that they have largely been superseded by subsequent developments in international law, in particular the right to leave any country including one's own, as set out in ICCPR Article 12 and regional other instruments.'[870] In my opinion, however, the existence of such a provision is important from the perspective of the

867 P. Weis, *The United Nations Convention on the Reduction of Statelessness, 1961*, 11(4) The International and Comparative Law Quarterly, October 1962, pp. 1082 and 1083.

868 As noted by Weis, this marks a departure from the corresponding provision of the Hague Convention of 1930 — P. Weis, *The United…*, pp. 1082 and 1083.

869 As a marginal note, during the discussion on a working draft in the UN forum, attention was drawn to the need for an even broader departure from the principle of preventing new cases of statelessness from arising. For example, Belgian government invoked the following argument, somewhat awkward from a modern perspective: 'Although it may be highly desirable that "renunciation shall not result in loss of nationality unless the person renouncing it has or acquires another nationality", there are cases where it is equally desirable for other considerations to be given precedence. Thus, on the rare occasions when Belgian legislation allows deprivation of nationality, there is a provision permitting the spouse and children of the person deprived of nationality to renounce Belgian nationality without having to prove possession of another nationality. The intention here is to preserve family unity.' — United Nations Conference on the Elimination or Reduction of Future Statelessness. Comments by Governments on the revised Draft Convention on the Elimination of Future Statelessness and the revised Draft Convention on the Reduction of Future Statelessness Prepared by the International Law Commission at its sixth session, A/CONF.9/5, 1959, p. 5, available at https://legal.un.org/diplomaticconferences/1959_statelessness/docs/english/vol_1/a_conf9_5.pdf (accessed 29 January 2023).

870 Tunis Conclusions, paragraph 43.

fundamental observation that international law allows (permits) states to introduce provisions enabling individuals to renounce their nationality with the effect of rendering themselves stateless in certain narrowly defined cases. Because international law tolerates (in a narrow scope) the existence of voluntary statelessness, it is impossible to argue that the concept of voluntary statelessness as such is contrary to the philosophy of the international instruments on statelessness.[871] Moreover, it would appear that the existence of such a provision in the 1961 Convention should protect the individual from the adverse consequences of having renounced their nationality and become stateless through the renunciation. However, according to the above-discussed UNHCR guidelines, such persons will fall within the category of 'bad faith' stateless persons, which seems to be problematic from the perspective of the systemic coherence of instruments on statelessness and treatment of stateless persons. Of course, in a case involving renunciation of nationality with the effect of becoming a stateless person, where that renunciation was linked with the intention of leaving the country or seeking asylum, domestic legal systems will keep the door open to assessing whether the renunciation of nationality truly reflected the individual's will.

4.2. Selected domestic jurisdictions

On the level of domestic jurisdictions in Europe, a consensus exists that renunciation of nationality must not lead to statelessness. Out of all European states permitting the loss of nationality by renunciation, the vast majority stipulate that such an act must not leave the renouncing individual stateless. Therefore, the overwhelming majority of states are in agreement that voluntary statelessness resulting from the renunciation of nationality should not be possible. This can be regarded as a manifestation of the general principle of preventing new cases of statelessness from arising.

Despite the introduction of safeguards against becoming stateless through renunciation of nationality, cases of active voluntary statelessness continue to arise in the practice of European states. This is connected, firstly, with the existence of gaps in statelessness-prevention frameworks. For example, in the domestic legal systems of European states, it is possible for an individual's renunciation of nationality to take effect upon submission of an assurance of a new nationality, which is ultimately not conferred. Not all states employ safeguards to protect

871 For example, see the above-discussed arguments raised by the Court of Appeals in Brussels, 29 March 2007.

individuals from statelessness arising from such situations.[872] Secondly, this will also involve the cases of individuals who are staying in Europe and have renounced their original nationality (becoming stateless persons) because the state of which they had been nationals made that possible. As I noted on a previous occasion, one of the examples of renunciation being regarded as the constitutional right of every individual is the United States.

5. Conclusions

International law permits the adoption of special provisions to address voluntary statelessness. Such a possibility has no basis in the 1954 Convention but is specified by the soft laws created by the UNHCR and the Council of Europe. There is also the faculty to introduce a lower standard of protection with regard to such persons and to exclude the applicability of statelessness-reduction mechanisms in their state of residence. On the protection side, the ability of an individual to return to their state of origin and acquire its nationality (or have it reinstated to them), may be grounds for exclusion from protection. A clear convention standard, by contrast, applies to the aspect of statelessness prevention (under the 1961 Convention and ECN), under which the renunciation of nationality with the effect of statelessness is, in principle, excluded. Different treatment of voluntary stateless persons is also envisaged by certain jurisdictions. Rarely part of the legislative text, it is more often the result of court practice. Attention is drawn to how in some legal systems the non-recognition of such individuals as stateless persons effectively excludes them from protection.

For the purposes of differentiating the treatment of the affected individuals, the characteristic of voluntary statelessness (or of being a voluntary stateless person) is the object of legal qualification by the international legal order and by the various domestic jurisdictions. The 'scenarios' (subcategories) of voluntary statelessness distinguished in this chapter permit the observation that the treatment accorded to voluntary stateless persons is further differentiated in international law and in some internal legal systems on account of the precise nature of the individual's voluntary statelessness (for example, depending on whether passive or active voluntary statelessness is at play). Moreover, the specific individual's reasons for having renounced their original nationality may affect the treatment accorded to them by the legal system. Aspects of internal motivation — such as good faith or bad faith — are taken into account, with a clear tendency

872 More on this topic see Chapter III, section 1.1.

to exclude stateless persons from protection in cases in which their statelessness appears to have been contrived in circumvention of the law.

The situation of voluntary statelessness may justifiably be taken into consideration in the drafting of domestic provisions. At the same time, however, if different treatment is contemplated on account of voluntary statelessness, it becomes necessary to narrow down precisely what kind of voluntary statelessness is being addressed. The solutions should assume the possibility of recognizing such an individual as a stateless person within the meaning of Article 1(1) of the 1954 Convention through statelessness-identification procedures (irrespective of the manner in which they became stateless and of their reasons for remaining so), but with allowance being made for according such individuals different treatment from that prescribed for stateless persons in general.

Afterword

The present book marked an opportunity to make some important conclusions with regard to statelessness. First and foremost, arguments are provided in support of the position that the term 'statelessness' refers both to the actual and to the potential existence of the negative condition consisting in the lack of nationality of any state whatsoever. In this connection, not only do the provisions on statelessness deal with stateless persons themselves (such as their protection or reduction of their number through the application of reduction mechanisms), they also contain preventive mechanisms designed with a view to not allowing new cases of stateless to arise. Taken together, the legal provisions intended for the prevention, reduction and protection of statelessness compose a complex system regulating statelessness. The provisions of the law of statelessness in this meaning include parts of traditionally distinguished disciplines such as nationality law (counteraction of statelessness) and broadly understood law of foreigners (protection of stateless persons).

From the definitional perspective, the identification of stateless persons with foreigners, which is the case e.g. in Poland's legal system, is not correct. Stateless persons can, of course, be regarded as foreigners, but only in the sense of not having the nationality of the relevant state. However, as aptly argued by M. Vichniac already in the 30s of the 20th century: 'one should not confuse stateless persons with foreigners and ignore the fact that, unlike foreigners in general, stateless persons are not the nationals of any state whatsoever.'[873] Failure to distinguish stateless persons, on the definitional level, as a category separate from other non-nationals leaves them with a sort of invisibility that allows the highly specific problems affecting them to escape notice. Theirs is one-of-a-kind situation that needs to be addressed by instruments designed specifically for this purpose. The regulation of the different cases (or scenarios) of statelessness may, however, reflect the internal diversification that exists within the broader category of stateless persons.

The analysis completed on this occasion made it possible to provide examples of this diversification of the various cases of statelessness, which the law of statelessness reflects. In the first part of the book, I demonstrated that certain manifestations of a categorial approach can be traced in the various approaches taken

873 M. Vichniac, *Le statut international...*, p. 136.

to the regulation of statelessness and in the various aspects of the resulting provisions. Firstly, the analysis of the definitional problems relating to the concept of a stateless person in international law shows that, at present, the term 'stateless person' does not denote a homogeneous category of individuals lacking nationality from a formal legal standpoint. The soft law created under the auspices of the United Nations assumes that the personal scope of the definition of a stateless person in Article 1(1) of the 1954 Convention extends to certain categories of persons historically regarded as *de facto* stateless. Secondly, the efforts of the international community and the individual states' willingness to counteract statelessness are not always on par with regard to the various different categories of individuals. The same applies to the protection of stateless persons. For example, the 1954 Convention enumerates a list of rights of stateless persons, but what rights specifically should be accorded to them depends on the closeness of the stateless person's ties to the host state. The closer the ties, the more rights the stateless person has. This means that only some of the rights need to be guaranteed to all stateless persons without distinction. Thirdly, at last, a categorial approach can be seen in the documents of the various international organizations defining the standards for statelessness-determination procedures in situations in which special solutions are foreseen for certain categories of individuals, e.g. minors, women or people with disabilities.

In the second part of the book, I focused on the systematic demonstration — on the example of four categories of individuals — that, although no description of it exists to date, the presence of a categorial paradigm is felt in the approach taken to topics of statelessness on the international level and in domestic legislation. The application of this paradigm has made it possible to discern a certain logic governing the treatment of the different categories of individuals from the perspective of statelessness-counteraction and stateless-protection mechanisms. For example, individuals who might pose a threat to the public interest are treated differently on the planes of prevention (international law permits their denationalization, even resulting in statelessness), protection (derogations from protective instruments) and reduction (they will be denied naturalization in their state of residence, even though they are stateless persons).

The categorial approach is of both theoretical and regulatory utility. On the one hand, it permits the observation that the term 'statelessness' encompasses a broad and diverse range of individuals, not all of whom are in the same situation, which warrants the use of adapted solutions to the various cases (scenarios) of statelessness. In the past, such an approach was met with success in the form of elimination of the statelessness of women arising from the conflict of nationality laws. In a similar way, it successfully reduces the number of stateless children through the introduction of reduction mechanisms intended to apply immediately following birth. It also allows for the special treatment of certain cases (scenarios) of statelessness in respect of which it would be difficult to speak of the existence of a consensus regarding the application of reduction or protection mechanisms. This includes certain situations of voluntary statelessness, as well as cases of e.g. individuals posing a threat to the public order. From this perspective, the categorial approach also serves to maintain the credibility and integrity of the protection system itself.

On the other hand, the categorial approach allows a break from the 'all-or-nothing' paradigm of thinking about protection issues (i.e. the polar opposites of either offering the same level of protection to everyone or no protection to anyone). The categorial approach assumes the modality of the level of protection depending on the characteristics of the individuals who need to be protected. This makes it possible to offer protection to the widest potential circle of individuals while at the same time differentiating the scope of rights accorded to them. This can mean, for example, extending the definition of a stateless person not only to those formally lacking the nationality of any state but also to those who are unable to obtain the attestation of their nationality.[874] In this manner, individuals needing protection are not left without it (after all, the relevant situations are not made to disappear by the absence of suitable, adapted solutions), but not all persons who are protected are given access to the broadest catalogue of rights of stateless persons foreseen by the legal system. In each and every case, however, stateless persons must be guaranteed a certain narrow minimum of rights, the most crucial of which is the right to be issued identity papers. This fundamental entitlement guarantees their 'recognition as a person before the law' stipulated in Article 6 UDHR, as well as effective access to the human-rights system.[875]

The categorial approach permits the comprehensive consideration of the needs of a given category of individuals from the perspective of reduction, prevention and protection. For example, an individual who is naturalized through the application of a reduction mechanism no longer needs a protection status as a stateless person. By contrast, an individual who is excluded from statelessness-prevention and statelessness-reduction mechanisms will need such protection (at least the minimal scope specified above). An approach emphasizing the reduction of statelessness (i.e. one insisting that, in principle, a stateless person

874 See Chapter II, section 2.2.2.
875 See Chapter I, section 5.1.

should be given the nationality of some state)[876] ignores the fact that not all stateless persons are willing to obtain a nationality. Some cases (scenarios) of voluntary statelessness indicate renunciation of nationality for the purpose of acquiring a residence status in a specific state. Placing the emphasis on statelessness reduction also leads to the absence of comprehensive thinking about the different mechanisms of regulation of statelessness with regard to the various different categories of affected individuals. For example, the almost universal accent on the reduction of the statelessness of children has the result of making the states neglect the importance of protection procedures.[877]

However, the problem of statelessness of children continues, and will continue, to exist. This is because the international order tolerates the continued existence of statelessness of children at birth, and some European states do not introduce comprehensive mechanisms for its reduction. Therefore, the situation of this category of stateless persons should be regulated in a holistic manner, taking due account not only of the need to adopt statelessness-reduction and statelessness-prevention mechanisms but also of the need to protect children in those situations in which counteraction mechanisms have failed. The results of not having specific solutions in place to ensure that statelessness-identification procedures involving minors take their needs into account can be such as the analysed case of a girl of Roma origin abandoned in a Polish hospital who was left without any papers and with uncertainty of her status until the sixteenth year of her life.[878]

Despite the attempts undertaken on the international level since the 30s of the 20th century to eliminate statelessness, the goal has not been achieved. The cause of this failure is not a complicated enigma.[879] The complete elimination of statelessness is achievable, but there is simply no consensus, either on the international level or on the level of domestic jurisdictions, as to the pursuit of the complete elimination of statelessness. As I have demonstrated, international law and the domestic provisions of the majority of European states permit the use of denationalization as a penalty. Even with regard to children and causes of statelessness arising at birth, full consensus as to the need for the 'elimination' of this type of statelessness is lacking. At the time of adoption of the 1961 Convention, the states agreed only to the 'reduction' of statelessness (the International Law

876 See Chapter I, section 6.
877 See Chapter VI, section 7.
878 See footnote 599.
879 See the Introduction and the thesis of W.E. Conklin discussed there.

Commission's alternative draft referring to 'elimination' fell through).[880] Moreover, international instruments focus on the reduction of types of statelessness arising from 'traditional' causes, while new causes continue to emerge (e.g. in connection with developments in reproductive technologies or problems with birth registration).

Although the elimination of statelessness, if used as a catchword in the UNHCR's campaigns, can still mobilize the states to action in the field of statelessness,[881] from the research perspective it is an impossible goal to meet. Furthermore, it obfuscates the importance of the fact that the term 'statelessness' refers to a broad and diverse range of individuals. A perspective aimed at the elimination of statelessness ignores the fact that individuals do not always aspire to become the nationals of a state and sometimes of any state whatsoever. Moreover, it ignores the fact that the international community and the individual states do not always have the political will to treat each and every category of stateless person with an equal insistence on the prevention and reduction of statelessness.

880 See Chapter I, section 5.3.2.

881 Since 2014, the UNHCR has conducted an extensive campaign titled #IBelong Campaign to End Statelessness with the goal of eliminating statelessness by 2024.

Court Cases

Domestic courts

Belgium

Tribunal of First Instance in Liège, *2006/RF/38*, judgment of 13 March 2007

Court of Cassation, C.07.0385.F/1, judgment of 6 June 2008

France

Administrative Tribunal in Strasbourg, *Dragotel*, judgment of 31 March 1994, Rec. 1994, tables, p. 950

Council of State, *Popescu*, judgment of 21 November 1994, Rec. 1994, tables, pp. 940, 947 and 949

Council of State, *Cucu*, judgment of 21 November 1994, req. 147194

Council of State, *Sarigul*, judgment of 29 December 2000, req. 216121

Administrative Court of Appeals in Bordeaux, *Bayram*, judgment of 19 July 1999, req. 98BX00688

Netherlands

District Court in the Hague, *X v. the Mayor of The Hague, SGR 13/2490*, judgment of 19 February 2014

Canada

Pushpanathan v. Canada (Minister of Citizenship and Immigration), [1998] 1 S.C.R. 982, Canada: Supreme Court, 4 June 1998

Luxembourg

Administrative Tribunal of the Grand Duchy of Luxembourg, *35177*, judgment of 9 July 2015

Administrative Court of the Grand Duchy of Luxembourg, *36744C*, judgment of 27 October 2015

Poland

Supreme Administrative Court, *II OSK 1155/10*, judgment of 16 June 2011

Supreme Administrative Court, *II OSK 1251/14*, judgment of 26 January 2016

Portugal

Court of Appeals in Lisbon, *8640/2003-6*, judgment of 29 January 2004

Switzerland

Federal Administrative Court, *C-4959/2007*, judgment of 12 November 2008

Federal Administrative Court, *C-346/2010*, judgment of 21 December 2012

Federal Administrative Court, *C-1873/2013*, judgment of 9 May 2014

Federal Administrative Court, *E-3562/2013*, judgment of 17 December 2014

Federal Administrative Court, *F-1672/2015*, judgment of 22 September 2016

Supreme Court, *2A.373/1993*, judgment of 4 July 1994

Supreme Court, *TF 2A.78/2000*, judgment of 23 May 2000

Supreme Court, *2A.147/2002*, judgment of 27 June 2002

Supreme Court, *2A.221/2003*, judgment of 19 May 2003

Supreme Court, *2A.388/2004*, judgment of 6 October 2004

Supreme Court, *2A.153/2005*, judgment of 17 March 2005

Supreme Court, *2C_1/2008*, judgment of 28 February 2008

USA

Shanks v. Dupont, 28 U.S. 242 (1830)

United States v. Wong Kim Ark 169 (US) 649 (1898)

United States v. Thind, 261 U.S. 204 (1923)

Dickson Car Wheel Company (U.S.A.) v. Mexico, US-Mexico General Claims Commission, UN Reports of International Arbitral Awards, vol. IV (1931)

Hungary

Constitutional Court, *6/2015*, judgment of 25 February 2015.

United Kingdom

JM (Zimbabwe), R (on the application of) v Secretary of State for the Home Department [2018] EWCA Civ 188

Italy

Constitution Court, judgment no. 87 of 9 April 1975

European Court of Human Rights

ECtHR, *Genovese v. Malta*, appl. no. 53124/09, judgment of 11 October 2011

ECtHR, *Mennesson v. France*, appl. no. 65192/11, judgment of 26 June 2014

ECtHR, *Labassée v. France*, appl. no. 65941/11, judgement of 26 June 2014

ECtHR, *Kim v. Russia*, appl. no. 44260/13, judgment of 17 July 2014

Court of Justice of the European Union

C-135/08, Janko Rottmann v. Freistaat Bayern, judgment of 2 March 2010, EU:C:2010:104

Legislation

Poland

Constitution of the Polish People's Republic, enacted by the Legislative Sejm on 22 July 1952 (Dz.U.1976.7.36, as amended)

Constitution of the Republic of Poland of 2 April 1997 (Dz.U.78.483, as rectified and amended)

Act of 20 January 1920 on the Citizenship of the Polish State (Dz.U.7.44, as amended)

Regulation of the President of Poland of 13 August 1926 on Foreigners (Dz.U.83.465, as amended)

Act of 8 January 1951 on Polish Citizenship (Dz.U.4.25)

Decree of 8 June 1955 — Civil Registry Law (Dz.U.25.151, as amended)

Act of 14 June 1960 — Code of Administrative Procedure (Dz.U.2018.2096, as amended)

Act of 15 February 1962 on Polish Citizenship (Dz.U.2000.28.353)

Act of 29 March 1963 on Foreigners (Dz.U.1992.7.30, as rectified and amended)

Act of 25 February 1964 — Family and Guardianship Code (Dz.U.2017.682, as amended)

Act of 7 May 1989 on Guarantees of Freedom of Conscience and Belief (Dz.U.2017.1153)

Act of 18 October 1991 amending the Constitution of the Republic of Poland (Dz.U.119.514)

Act of 25 June 1997 on Foreigners (Dz.U.2001.127.1400, as amended)

Act of 2 April 2009 on Polish Citizenship (Dz.U.2018.1829)

Act of 4 April 2011 — Private International Law (Dz.U.2015.1792)

Act of 12 December 2013 on Foreigners (Dz.U.2018.2294, as amended)

Other states

Constitution of North Macedonia of 17 November 1991, as amended on 6 January 1992

Constitution of the Czech Republic of 16 October 1992

Constitution of the Italian Republic of 27 December 1947

Constitution of Hungary of 18 April 2011

Belgian Nationality Law of 1984, French consolidated version of 24 July 2017

British Nationality Act 1981 (UK)

Immigration Rules, HC 1039, 6 April 2013 (UK)

Law on Bulgarian Citizenship, consolidated version as amended by Law of 19 February 2013

Law No. 141(I)/2002: The Civil Registry Law 2002 (Cyprus)

Act 186/2013 on Citizenship of the Czech Republic

Act no. 113 of 20 February 2003 on Danish Nationality, as amended by Act No. 311 of 5 May 2004

Citizenship Act 1995, consolidated version as amended by Act of 15 June 2006 (Estonia)

Expatriation Act of July 28, 1868, ch. 249, 15 Stat. 223, R.S. § 1999

359/2003 Nationality Act, consolidated version incorporating amendments up to and including Act 974/2007 (Finland)

French Law on Asylum no. 52-893 of 25 July 1952 (*Loi relative au droit d'asile n° 52-893 du 25 juillet 1952*)

French Civil Code, Book I, Title I bis on French Nationality, as amended by Act no. 2006-399 of 4 April 2006

French Code on the Entry and Stay of Foreigners and Right of Asylum (*Code de l'entrée et du séjour des étrangers et du droit d'asile*)

Greek Citizenship Code, Law 3284/2004, 10 November 2004

Royal Decree of 20 July 2001 no. 865, Regulation for the Recognition of the Status of Stateless 865/2001 (Spain)

Civil Code (nationality legislation) (as amended by Law 52/2007) (Spain)

Kingdom Act on Netherlands Nationality; consolidated version including amendment of 25/11/2013 (Netherlands)

Irish Nationality and Citizenship Acts 1956–2004, as amended by Act No. 38 of 2004

Act No. 100/1952 Icelandic Nationality Act, as amended by Act No. 40/2012

The Republic of Lithuania Law on Citizenship of 2 December 2010 – No XI-1196

Law on Citizenship 1994, as amended by Law of 9 May 2013 (Latvia)

Law of 25 April 1995 on Status of the Former USSR Citizens who do not have the Citizenship of Latvia or that of any other State (Latvia)

Law No. 200 of 16 July 2010 on Foreigners (Moldova)

German Act on Statelessness Reduction of 1977 (*Gesetz zur Verminderung der Staatenlosigkeit Vom 29. Juni 1977*, BGBl. I S. 1101)

Federal Law of 31 May 2002 № 62-FZ 'About Citizenship of the Russian Federation', consolidated version 2 November 2004 (Russian Federation)

Act No. 40/1993 Coll. on Citizenship of the Slovak Republic; consolidated English version as last amended by Act no. 250/2010 Coll. (Slovakia)

Act on the Citizenship of the Republic of Slovenia as amended by Amending Act, Official Gazette No. 127/2006 of 7 December 2006

Federal Law of 29 September 1952 on the acquisition and loss of Swiss nationality; consolidated version as amended 30 Sep 2011 (Switzerland)

Law 2001:82: Swedish Citizenship Act; consolidated version as last amended by Law 2006:222 (Sweden)

Law No. 403/1964 on Turkish Citizenship

Law No. 5901/2009 Turkish Citizenship Law

Law N 2235-III (2235-14) on the Citizenship of Ukraine, as amended by Law N 2663-IV (2663-15) of 16 June 2005

Law No. 8389 of 5 August 1998 on Albanian Citizenship, as amended by Law No. 8442 of 21 January 1999

Federal Law on Austrian Nationality 1985, consolidated version as amended by BGBl. I Nr 37/2006

Law of 27 July 1999 on Citizenship of Bosnia and Herzegovina, consolidated version 2003

Montenegrin Citizenship Act of 14 February 2008, Official Gazette of Montenegro, No. 13/08, 26 February 2008

Law No. 26 concerning Egyptian Nationality, 1975

Law No. 1017-XII of 20.12.91 of the Republic of Kazakhstan, On Citizenship of the Republic of Kazakhstan, last amended 2002, 1 March 1992

Law No 04/L-215 on Citizenship of Kosovo

Act of 4 January 1934 on the Acquisition and Loss of Citizenship, reissued in 1960 (Liechtenstein)

Law on Citizenship of the Republic of Macedonia 67/92, published Official Gazette on 3 November 1992

Maltese Citizenship Act as amended by Act XV of 2013

Nationality Act of 22 July 1913, Reich Law Gazette I p. 583 — Federal Law Gazette III 102-1 as last amended by Article 2 of the Act to Implement the EU Directive on Highly Qualified Workers of 1 June 2012, Federal Law Gazette I p. 1224

Act No. 51/2005 on Norwegian Citizenship, as amended by Act No. 36 of 30 June 2006

Organic Law 9/2015: 7th Amendment of the Law 37/81 of 3 October (Portugal)

Law on the citizenship of the Republic of Moldova, No. 1024-XIV of 2 June 2000, consolidated version as last amended by Law no. 232-XV of 5 June 2003

Law on Romanian Citizenship no. 21/1991, as amended by L. nr 112/2010, 17 June 2010

Law on citizenship of the Republic of Serbia of 20 December 2004

Law on Vietnamese Nationality, No. 24/2008/QH-12, 13 November 2008

Act LV of 1993 on Hungarian Nationality, version of 1 January 2009

Law-Decree 17 of 1982 on Civil Registration, Marriage and Names (Hungary)

Hungarian Act II of 2007 on the Admission and Right of Residence of Third-Country Nationals and the Government Decree 114/2007, V. 24

Presidential Decree no. 572 of 12th October 1993 (Italy)

Italian Civil Code (Royal Decree no. 262 of 16 March 1942)

Italian Nationality Act (Act No. 91/92, L. 5 February 1992, n. 91, as amended by Act No. 94/2009)

International Conventions

United Nations

Universal Declaration of Human Rights, adopted by General Assembly Resolution 217 A(III) on 10 December 1948 in Paris, 217 A (III)

Convention Relating to the Status of Refugees, done at Geneva on 28 July 1951 (UNTS, vol. 189, p. 137)

Convention Relating to the Status of Stateless Persons, adopted on 28 September 1954 by a Conference of Plenipotentiaries convened by Economic and Social Council resolution 526 A (XVII) of 26 April 1954, UNTS, vol. 360, p. 117

Convention on the Nationality of Married Women, opened for signature in New York on 20 February 1957, United Nations General Assembly, A/RES/1040

Convention on the Reduction of Statelessness, adopted on 30 August 1961 by a Conference of Plenipotentiaries in pursuance of General Assembly resolution no. 896 (IX) of 4 December 1954, UNTS, vol. 989, p. 175

International Convention on the Elimination of All Forms of Racial Discrimination opened for signatures in New York on 7 March 1966, UNTS, vol. 660, p. 195

International Covenant on Civil and Political Rights, opened for signature in New York on 19 December 1966, UNTS, vol. 999, p. 171

Vienna Convention on the Law of Treaties, done at Vienna on 23 May 1969, NTS, vol. 1155, p. 331

Convention on the Elimination of All Forms of Discrimination against Women, adopted in New York on 18 December 1979, United Nations General Assembly, UNTS, vol. 1249, p. 13

Convention Against Torture and Other Cruel, Inhuman or Degrading Treatment or Punishment adopted by the UN General Assembly on 10 December 1984, UNTS, vol. 1465, p. 85

Convention on the Rights of the Child, adopted and opened for signature, ratification and accession by General Assembly resolution 44/25 of 20 November 1989, UNTS, vol. 1577, p. 3

Rome Statute of the International Criminal Court, done at Rome on 17 July 1998, ISBN No. 92-9227-227-6

Convention on the Rights of Persons with Disabilities of 13 December 2006 (A/RES/61/106)

Council of Europe

European Convention on the Adoption of Children, done at Strasbourg, on 24 April 1967 (ETS No. 058)

European Convention on Nationality, signed in Strasbourg on 6 November 1997, Council of Europe, ETS No. 166

Council of Europe Convention on the Avoidance of Statelessness in relation to State Succession, Strasbourg, 19 May 2006, CETS no. 200

European Convention on the Adoption of Children (Revised), CETS No. 202

Other instruments

Convention on Certain Questions Relating to the Conflict of Nationality Law, signed on 13 April 1930 in the Hague, League of Nations Treaty Series, vol. 179, p. 89, No. 4137

American Convention on Human Rights, 'Pact of San José', signed at San José in Costa Rica on 22 November 1969, Treaty Series, No. 36, Organization of American States, 1969 (entry into force on 18 July 1978)

International Documents
United Nations

UNHCR, Handbook on Procedures and Criteria for Determining Refugee Status, Geneva 1992

Centre for Civil and Political Rights, *General Comment No. 17: Article 24 (Rights of the Child)*, 7 April 1989

OSCE and UNHCR, *Handbook on statelessness in the OSCE Area. International standards and good practices*, 28 February 2017

Resolution 116 (VI) D on Stateless Persons, Economic and Social Council, March 1948

Resolution 248 (IX) B, Economic and Social Council, August 1949

Resolution 526 A (XVII) of Economic and Social Council, 26 April 1954

Security Council Resolution 1373, 28 September 2001, S/RES/1373 (2001)

UNHCR, *Action to Address Statelessness. A Strategy Note*, March 2010

UNHCR, *Background Note on the Application of the Exclusion Clauses. Article 1F of the 1951 Convention relating to the Status of Refugees*, September 2003

UNHCR, *Citizenship and prevention of statelessness linked to the disintegration of the Socialist Federal Republic of Yugoslavia*, European series, vol. 3, No. 1. Geneva: June 1997

UNHCR, *Conclusions Adopted by the Executive Committee on the International Protection of Refugees 1975–2009 (Conclusion No. 1 - 109)*, December 2009

UNHCR, *Conclusion on Identification, Prevention and Reduction of Statelessness and Protection of Stateless Persons, No. 106: (LVII)*, October 2006

UNHCR, *Draft Articles on the Protection of Stateless Persons and the Facilities for their Naturalisation*, February 2017

UNHCR, *Ensuring birth registration for the prevention of statelessness*, Good Practices Paper - Action 7, November 2017

UNHCR, *Establishing statelessness determination procedures to protect stateless persons*, Good Practices Paper, Action 6

UNHCR, *Expert Meeting — Interpreting the 1961 Statelessness Convention and Avoiding Statelessness resulting from Loss and Deprivation of Nationality ('Tunis Conclusions')*, March 2014

UNHCR, *Expert Meeting — Interpreting the 1961 Statelessness Convention and Preventing Statelessness among Children ('Dakar Conclusions')*, September 2011

UNHCR, *Expert Meeting - The Concept of Stateless Persons under International Law ('Prato Conclusions')*, May 2010

UNHCR, *Global Trends. Forced Displacement in 2015*, annex 2, 20 June 2016

UNHCR, *Guidelines on International Protection No. 5: Application of the Exclusion Clauses. Article 1F of the 1951 Convention relating to the Status of Refugees*, 4 September 2003, HCR/GIP/03/05

UNHCR, *Guidelines on Statelessness no. 1: The definition of 'Stateless Person' in Article 1(1) of the 1954 Convention relating to the Status of Stateless Persons*, HCR/GS/12/01, 2012

UNHCR, *Guidelines on Statelessness no. 2: Procedures for Determining whether an Individual is a Stateless Person*, HCR/GS/12/02, 5 April 2012

UNHCR, *Guidelines on Statelessness no. 3: The Status of Stateless Persons at the National Level*, HRC/GS/12/03, 17 July 2012

UNHCR, *Guidelines on Statelessness No. 4: Ensuring Every Child's Right to Acquire a Nationality through Articles 1–4 of the 1961 Convention on the Reduction of Statelessness*, December 2012

UNHCR, *Handbook on Procedures and Criteria for Determining Refugee Status under the 1951 Convention and the 1967 Protocol relating to the Status of Refugees*, HCR/IP/4/Eng/REV.1 Reedited, Geneva, January 1992, 1979

UNHCR, *Handbook on Protection of Stateless Persons*, Geneva, 30 June 2014

UNHCR, *In Search of Solutions: Addressing Statelessness in the Middle East and North Africa*, September 2016

UNHCR, *Introductory Note by the Office of the UNHCR to the 1954 Convention*, Geneva 2014

UNHCR, *Mapping Statelessness in Finland*, November 2014

UNHCR, *Note on the Cancellation of Refugee Status*, 22 November 2004

UNHCR, *Note on UNHCR and Stateless Persons*, 2 June 1995, EC/1995/SCP/CRP.2

UNHCR, *Prevention and Reduction of Statelessness and the Protection of Stateless Persons*, No. 78 (XLVI) – 1995, 20 Executive Committee 46th session, Contained in United Nations General Assembly document A/AC.96/860 and document no. 12A (A/50/12/Add.1), 20 October 1995

UNHCR, *Text of the 1954 Convention relating to the Status of Stateless Persons with an Introductory Note by the Office of the United Nations High Commissioner for Refugees*, 2014

UNHCR, *The problem of statelessness in Ukraine and the ways of addressing it*, Kyiv 2014

UNHCR, *Woman Alone: The fight for survival by Syria's refugee women*, 2 July 2014

UNHCR & Plan, *Under the Radar and Under Protected. The Urgent Need to Address Stateless Children's Rights*, June 2012

United Nations, *A Study of Statelessness*, Lake Success–New York, August 1949, E/1112; E/1112/Add.1

United Nations, *Draft Articles on Diplomatic Protection with commentaries*, International Law Commission 2006

United Nations Conference on the Elimination or Reduction of Future Statelessness. Comments by Governments on the revised Draft Convention on the Elimination of Future Statelessness and the revised Draft Convention on the Reduction of Future Statelessness Prepared by the International Law Commission at its sixth session, A/CONF.9/5, 1959

Council of Europe

Committee of Experts on Nationality, Report on Conditions for the Acquisition and Loss of Nationality, Strasbourg, 14 January 2003

Explanatory memorandum of the Committee of Ministers to member states on the nationality of children, 9 May 2009, CM/Rec(2009)13

Explanatory Report to the European Convention on Nationality, European Treaty Series-No. 166, Strasbourg, 6.11.1997

Recommendation CM/Rec(2009)13 of the Committee of Ministers to member states on the nationality of children, adopted by the Committee of Ministers on 9 December 2009

Recommendation No. R (99) 18 of the Committee of Ministers to member States on the avoidance and reduction of statelessness, adopted by the Committee of Ministers on 15 September 1999

Recommendation CM/Rec(2009)13 and explanatory memorandum of the Committee of Ministers to member states on the nationality of children, 9 May 2009

Recommendation 1261 (1995) on the situation of immigrant women in Europe, adopted by the Committee of Ministers on 7 June 1995

Other documents

Ad-Hoc Query on Recognition of Stateless Persons, European Commission and European Migration Network, 4 May 2015

Article F4: La demande de reconnaissance du statut d'apatride [in:] *Manuel Asile et retour*, Département fédéral de justice et police, Secrétariat d'Etat aux migrations, https://www.sem.admin.ch/dam/data/sem/asyl/verfahren/hb/f/hb-f5-f.pdf

Auštrevičius proponuje nadać obywatelstwo Litwy Saakaszwilemu, ZW.lt, 28 July 2017

Estonian Government Easing Citizenship Laws For Children and Elderly, 2.10.2014, ERR news, https://news.err.ee/113784/estonian-government-easing-citizenship-laws-for-children-and-elderly

European Commission and European Migration Network, *Ad-Hoc Query on Recognition of Stateless Persons*, 4 May 2015

European Council on Refugees and Exiles, *Position on Exclusion from Refugee Status*, March 2004

Guide de Procedures de l'Ofpra, https://ofpra.gouv.fr/sites/default/files/atoms/files/161215_-_guide_de_procedures.pdf

International Law Association, 31st Conference report (1922)

International Law Association, 33rd Conference report (1924)

Saakashvili doesn't plan to seek Lithuanian citizenship, BC, Vilnius, 9.08.2017

Statelessness, Discrimination and Marginalisation of Roma in the Western Balkans and Ukraine, ERRC, ISI, ENS, Budapest, October 2017

Statelessness in the EU, European Migration Network, 11 November 2016

The World's Stateless Children, Institute on Statelessness and Inclusion, January 2017

Bibliography

Abel P., *Denationalization*, 6 Modern Law Review 1942–1943

Albarazi Z., *The Stateless Syrians*, 11 Tilburg Law School Research Paper 2013, 24 May 2013

Albarazi Z. and van Waas L., *Understanding statelessness in the Syria refugee context. Research Report*, Norwegian Refugee Council & Institute on Statelessness and Inclusion 2016

Batchelor C.A., *Statelessness and the problem of resolving nationality status*, 10(1/2) International Journal of Refugee Law 1998

Batchelor C.A., *The 1954 convention relating to the status of stateless persons. Implementation within the European Union member states and recommendation for harmonization*, 22(2) Refuge 2005

Bauböck R., Paskalev V., *Citizenship deprivation. A normative analysis*, 82 Centre of European Policy Studies. Papers in Liberty and Security March 2015

Bhabha J., *Children without a state. A global human rights challenge*, London 2011

Bianchini K., *A comparative analysis of statelessness determination procedures in 10 EU States*, 29(1) International Journal of Refugee Law 2017

Bianchini K., *Protecting stateless persons: The Implementation of the Convention Relating to the Status of Stateless Persons across EU States*, Leiden–Boston 2018

Bingham L., Harrington Reddy J. and Kohn S., *De jure statelessness in the real world: Applying the Prato summary conclusions*, New York 2011

Bliss M., *'Serious reasons for considering'. Minimum standards of procedural fairness in the application of the article 1 F exclusion clauses*, 12 International Journal of Refugee Law 2000, Special Supplementary Issue

Blitz B., *Statelessness, protection and equality*, Forced Migration Policy Briefing 3, Refugee Studies Centre, Oxford University, September 2009

Bond J., *Principled exclusions. A revised approach to article 1(F)(A) of the Refugee Convention*, 35(1) Michigan Journal of International Law 2013

Bredbenner C.L., *A nationality of her own. Women, marriage, and the law of citizenship*, Berkeley 1998

Bujalski R., *Angielsko-polski słownik orzecznictwa sądów europejskich* [*English-Polish dictionary of decisions of European courts*], Warszawa 2009

Chahrokh H., *Mapping Statelessness in Austria*, UNHCR Austria, January 2017

Chan J.M.M., *The Right to a Nationality as a Human Right. The Current Trend Towards Recognition*, 12(1–2) Human Rights Law Journal 1991

V. Poleshchuk (ed.), *Chance to Survive. Minority rights in Estonia and Latvia*, Tallin 2010

Chiurulli Ch., *La protection des apatrides. État des lieux*, Wavre 2014

Citizenship and prevention of statelessness linked to the disintegration of the Socialist Federal Republic of Yugoslavia, European series, Geneva, vol. 3, no.1, June 1997

Conklin W.E., *Statelessness. The enigma of an international community*, London 2014

Cott N.F., *Marriage and women's citizenship in the United States, 1830–1934*, 103(5) The American Historical Review, December 1998

Doek J., *The CRC and the right to acquire and to preserve a nationality*, 25(3) Refugee Survey Quarterly 2006

Džankić J., *Investment-based citizenship and residence programmes in the EU*, 8 European University Institute Working Paper RSCAS 2015

Edwards A. and van Waas L., *Introduction* [in:] A. Edwards and L. van Waas (eds.), *Nationality and Statelessness under International Law*, Cambridge 2014

Edwards A. and van Waas L., *Statelessness* [in:] G. Loescher, K. Long, N. Sigona and E. Fiddian-Qasmiyeh (eds.), *The Oxford Handbook of Refugee and Forced Migration Studies*, Oxford 2014.

Flauss J.-F., *L'influence du droit international des droits de l'homme sur la nationalité* [in:] Cadeau E. (ed.), *Perspectives du droit public. Études offertes á Jean-Claude Hélin*, Paris 2004

Foblets M.-C., Yanasmayan Z., Wautelet P., *Country report: Belgium*, 27 EUDO Citizenship Observatory 2013

Formal Renunciation of United States Citizenship to Avoid Criminal Liability under Selective Service Law Constitutes a Voluntary Relinquishment of Nationality within the Meaning of Afroyim v. Rusk, 71(8) Columbia Law Review, December 1971

Fox M., *Garry Davis, man of no nation who saw one world of no war, dies at 91*, The New York Times, 28 June 2013

Gajos-Kaniewska D., *Sukces HFPC: bezpaństwowa Viktoriia dostała polskie obywatelstwo* [*Success for HFHR: stateless Viktoriia gets Polish citizenship*], Rzeczpospolita, 19 July 2017

Gallagher A., *The international law of human trafficking*, Cambridge 2011

Gardocka T., *Przesłanki ekstradycyjne w prawie polskim* [*Extradition grounds in Polish law*], 60(2) Studia Prawnicze 1979

Gardocki L., *Zarys prawa karnego międzynarodowego* [*International criminal law: overview*], Warszawa 1985

Geoff G., *Exclusion and evidentiary assessment* [in:] Noll G. (ed.), *Proof, evidentiary assessment and credibility in asylum procedures*, Leiden–Boston 2005

Ginsburgs G., *The citizenship law of the USSR*, Hague–Boston 1983

Goldston J.A., *Holes in the rights framework. Racial discrimination, citizenship, and the rights of noncitizens*, 20(3) Ethics and International Affairs 2006

Goodwin-Gill G., *Convention relating to the status of stateless persons*, United Nations Audiovisual Library of International Law, United Nations 2010

Goodwin-Gill G., *The rights of refugees and stateless persons* [in:] Saksena K.P. (ed.), *Human rights perspective & challenges: in 1990 and beyond*, New Delhi 1994

Govil R., Edwards A., *Women, nationality and statelessness* [in:] Edwards A. and van Waas L. (eds.), *Nationality and Statelessness under International Law*, Cambridge 2014

Grahl-Madsen A., *The status of refugees in international law*, vol. 1, Leiden 1972

Graupner R., *Statelessness as a consequence of the change of sovereignty over territory after the last war* [in:] British Section of the World Jewish Congress, *The Problem of Statelessness*, London 1944

de Groot G.-R., *Children, their right to a nationality and child statelessness* [in:] Edwards A. and van Waas L. (eds.), *Nationality and Statelessness under International Law*, Cambridge 2014

de Groot G.-R, Luk N.C., *Twenty years of CJEU jurisprudence on citizenship*, 15(5) German Law Journal 2014

de Groot G.-R., Swider K., Vonk O., *Practices and approaches in EU member states to prevent and end statelessness*, Brussels: European Parliament 2015

de Groot G.-R., Vink M.P., *A comparative analysis of regulations on involuntary loss of nationality in the European Union*, 75 Centre of European Policy Studies. Paper in Liberty and Security in Europe, December 2014

de Groot G.-R., Vink M.P., *Birthright citizenship. Trends and regulations in Europe*, EUDO Citizenship Observatory, RSCAS/EUDO-CIT-Comp.2010/8, November 2010

de Groot G.-R., Vink M.P., *Loss of citizenship. Trends and regulations in Europe*, Comparative Report, 4 EUDO Citizenship Observatory, RSCAS/EUDO-CIT-Comp., June 2010

de Groot G.-R., Vonk O.W., Dumbrava C., Vink M.P., *'Benchmarking' legal protection against statelessness* [in:] L. van Waas and M.J. Khanna (eds.), *Solving statelessness*, Oisterwijk 2017

de Groot G.-R., Vonk O.W., Vink M.P., *Protection against statelessness. Trends and regulations in Europe*, 1 EUDO Citizenship Observatory 2013

Guerry L., *Married women's nationality in the international context (1918–1935)*, 1(43) "Clio. Women, Gender, History" 2016

Gyulai G., *Nationality unknown? An overview of the safeguards and gaps related to the prevention of statelessness at birth in Hungary*, Hungarian Helsinki Committee, Budapest 2014

Gyulai G., *Statelessness in Hungary. The protection of stateless persons and the prevention and reduction of statelessness*, Hungarian Helsinki Committee, Budapest 2010

Hanjian C., *The Sovrien. An exploration of the right to be stateless*, Massachusetts: Polyspire, 2003

Harvey A., *Recent developments on deprivation of nationality on grounds of national security and terrorism resulting in statelessness*, 28(4) Journal of Immigration, Asylum and Nationality Law 2014

Hathaway J.C., Foster M., *The law of refugee status*, Cambridge 2014

Henckaerts J.-M., *Mass expulsion in modern international law and practice*, Hague 1995

Hofmannová H., *Legal Status of Stateless Persons in the Czech Republic*, 3(1) The Lawyer Quarterly 2013

Hudson M.O., *The Hague Convention of 1930 and the nationality of women*, 27(1) The American Journal of International Law, January 1933

Ingraham B.L., Tokoro K., *Political crime in the United States and Japan. A comparative study*, 4(2) Issues in Criminology 1969

Ioannidis M., Koutnatzis S.-I.G., *Evolution and gestalt of the Greek State* [in:] S. Cassese, A. von Bogdandy and P.M. Huber (eds.), *The Max Planck handbooks in European public law*, vol. 1, *The administrative state*, Oxford 2017

Isaacson W., *Einstein. His life and universe*, transl. by J. Skowroński as *Einstein. Jego życie, jego wszechświat*, Warszawa 2010

Jagielski J., *Obywatelstwo polskie. Komentarz do ustawy* [*Polish citizenship. Commentary on the Act*], Warszawa 2016

Jagielski J., *Obywatelstwo polskie. Zagadnienia podstawowe* [*Polish citizenship. The basics*], Warszawa 1998

Jagielski J., Dąbrowski P., *Specjalny status prawny* [*Special legal status*] [in:] R. Hauser, Z. Niewiadomski and A. Wróbel (eds.), *System Prawa Administracyjnego* [*The system of administrative law*], vol. 7, *Prawo administracyjne materialne* [*Substantive administrative law*], Warszawa 2017

Jansen S., van Waas L., *Preventing childhood statelessness in Europe. Issues, gaps and good practices*, European Network on Statelessness 2014

Jayaraman S., *International terrorism and statelessness. Revoking the citizenship of ISIL foreign fighters*, 17(2) Chicago Journal of International Law 2016

Kadirbeyoglu Z., *Country Report: Turkey*, 31 EUDO Citizenship Observatory 2010

Kandalec P., *Naturalizace v České republice*, Praha 2018

Kardas P., *Przestępstwo polityczne w prawie polskim. Próba analizy teoretycznej na tle obowiązującego stanu prawnego [Political crime in Polish law. Attempt at theoretical analysis in the context of current legislation]*, 1–2 Czasopismo Prawa Karnego i Nauk Penalnych 1998

Kälin W., Künzli J., *Article 1F(b). Freedom fighters, terrorists, and the notion of serious non-political crimes*, 12 International Journal of Refugee Law 2000, Special Supplementary Issue

Kerber L., *Toward a history of statelessness in America*, 57(3) American Quarterly, September 2005

Kilner J., *Rostropovich, cellist who fought for artistic freedom*, Reuters, 28 April 2007

Knop K., Chinkin Ch., *Final report on women's equality and nationality in international law*, Committee on Feminism and International Law, International Law Association, London Conference 2000

Knop K., Chinkin Ch., *Remembering Chrystal MacMillan. Women's equality and nationality in international law*, 22(4) Michigan Journal of International Law 2001

Kostrubiec J., *Georg Jellinek — klasyk niemieckiej nauki o państwie (w 95. rocznicę śmierci) [Georg Jellinek — the classic of German science of the state (at the 95th anniversary of his death)]*, 7 Studia Iuridica Lublinensia 2006

Kruma K., *Country report on citizenship law: Latvia*, RSCAS/EUDO-CIT-CR 2015/6, January 2015

Kruma K., *EU Citizenship, nationality and migration status. An ongoing challenge*, Leiden–Boston 2014

Kwakwa E., *Article 1F(c). Acts contrary to the purposes and principles of the United Nations*, 12 International Journal of Refugee Law 2000, Special Supplementary Issue

Lawyers Committee for Human Rights, *Safeguarding the rights of refugees under the exclusion clauses. Summary findings of the Project and a Lawyers Committee for Human Rights Perspective*, 12 International Journal of Refugee Law 2000, Special Supplementary Issue

Lenard P.T., *The right to family. Protecting stateless children* [in:] T. Bloom, K. Tonkiss and P. Cole (eds.), *Understanding statelessness. Lives in Limbo*, New York 2017

Leo S., *Graphic detail: How UK government has used its powers of banishment*, The Bureau of Investigative Journalism, 27 February 2013

Levenson Th., *Einstein in Berlin*, New York 2003

Litwin J., *Pozbawienie obywatelstwa z przyczyn politycznych w ustawodawstwie powojennej Europy [Denationalization on political grounds in the legislations of post-war Europe]*, 9–10 Palestra 1934

Litwin J., *Prawo o aktach stanu cywilnego. Komentarz [Law on Civil Registration. Commentary]*, Warszawa 1961

Lynch M., Teff M., *Childhood Statelessness*, 32 Forced Migration Review 2009

Malinowski A., *Polski język prawny. Wybrane zagadnienia [Polish legal language. Selected topics]*, Warszawa 2006

Manly M., *UNHCR's mandate and activities to address statelessness* [in:] A. Edwards and L. van Waas (eds.), *Nationality and Statelessness under International Law*, Cambridge 2014

Mantu S., *Contingent citizenship. The law and practice of citizenship deprivation in international, European and national perspectives*, Leiden–Boston 2015

Mantu S., *'Terrorist' citizens and the human right to nationality*, 26(1) Journal of Contemporary European Studies 2018

Przybysławska K. (ed.), *Mapping statelessness in Poland*, UNHCR and The Halina Nieć Legal Aid Center, Kraków 2019 (in print)

Marin C., *Ending childhood statelessness. A study on Romania*, 1 European Network on Statelessness, Working Paper 2015

Massey H., *UNHCR and De Facto Statelessness*, UNHCR Geneva, LPPR/2010/01, April 2010

McKeever D., *Evolving interpretation of multilateral treaties. 'Acts contrary to the purposes and principles of the United Nations' in the Refugee Convention*, 64(2) International and Comparative Law Quarterly, April 2015

McKinsey K., *Lose a husband. Lose a country*, 147(3) Refugees Magazine 2007

Mendoza M., *Stateless in Slovakia: What if you renounce US citizenship...*, GlobalPostm 6 December 2011

Mik C., *Analiza stopnia implementacji postanowień konwencji dotyczących bezpaństwowców z 1954 r. i 1961 r. w prawie polskim [Analysis of the degree of implementation of the provisions of the 1954 and 1961 Conventions on statelessness in Polish law]*, 3(59) Zeszyty Prawnicze Biura Analiz Sejmowych 2018

Molnar T., *A fresh examination of facilitated naturalisation as a solution for stateless persons* [in:] L. van Waas and M.J. Khanna (eds.), *Solving statelessness*, Oisterwijk 2017

Mrekajova E., *Naturalization of stateless persons. Solution of statelessness?*, Tilburg 2012

Mutharika A.P., *The regulation of statelessness under international and national law*, New York 1989

Nguyen L., *Report on citizenship law: Vietnam*, RSCAS/GLOBALCIT-CR 2017/13, September 2017

Nyinah M.K., *Exclusion under article 1F. Some reflections on context, principles and practice*, 12 International Journal of Refugee Law, Issue suppl_1, July 2000

van Oers R., *Deserving citizenship. Citizenship tests in Germany, the Netherlands and the United Kingdom*, Leiden 2013

Oppenheim L.F., *International law. A treatise*, London–New York–Bombay 1905

D. Owen, *Citizenship and Human Rights* [in:] A. Shachar, R. Bauböck, I. Bloemraad and M. Vink (eds.), *The Oxford handbook of citizenship*, Oxford 2017

van Panhuys H.F., *The role of nationality in international law. An outline*, Leyden 1959

Pearce J., *Solzhenitsyn: A Soul in Exile*, transl. by W. Fladziński as *Dusza na wygnaniu*, Warszawa 2004

Perry J., Carey C., *Some aspects of statelessness since World War I*, 40(1) The American Political Science Review, February 1946

Poleshchuk V., *Chance to survive. Minority rights in Estonia and Latvia*, Foundation for Historical Outlook 2010

Poleshchuk V., *Naturalisation procedures for immigrants. Estonia*, 8 EUDO Citizenship Observatory, SCAS/EUDO- CIT-NP 2013

Połatyńska J., *Sukcesja państw a obywatelstwo osób fizycznych* [*Succession of states and the nationality of individuals*], Łódź 2013

Potyrała A., *Ochrona uchodźców w ustawodawstwie państw członkowskich Unii Europejskiej z Europy środkowej i wschodniej* [*Protection of refugees in the legislations of the European Union's member states from Central and Eastern Europe*], 1 Środkowoeuropejskie Studia Polityczne 2012

Preuss L., *International law and deprivation of nationality*, 23 Georgetown Law Journal 1934–1935

Przybysławska K., *Niepożądani uchodźcy. Granice ochrony i zasady wykluczenia w świetle prawa międzynarodowego* [*The unwanted refugees. Limits of protection and rules for exclusion in international law*], Warszawa 2009

Przybysławska K., Pilaszek A., *Ochrona bezpaństwowców przed arbitralną detencją w Polsce* (official English version exists as *Protecting Stateless Persons From Arbitrary Detention in Poland*), report by The Halina Nieć Legal Aid Center and the European Network on Statelessness, Kraków 2015

Pudzianowska, D., Korzec, P., *Citizenship 'on paper'. On the risk of statelessness of Polish children raised in same-sex unions abroad*, 16(2) National Taiwan University Law Review, 2021.

Pudzianowska D., *Obywatelstwo w procesie zmian* [*Citizenship in a process of change*], Warszawa 2013

Pudzianowska D., *„Opatrzność" czy „nieopatrzność" ustawodawcy? O ochronie bezpaństwowców w prawie polskim* [*The legislature's 'providence' or 'improvidence'? About the protection of stateless persons in Polish law*] [in:] Jagielski J. and Wierzbowski M. (eds.), *Prawo administracyjne dziś i jutro* [*Administrative law today and tomorrow*], Warszawa

Pudzianowska D., *Warunki nabycia i utraty obywatelstwa Unii Europejskiej. Czy dochodzi do autonomizacji pojęcia obywatelstwa Unii?* [*Conditions for the acquisition and loss of the citizenship of the European Union. Is there a need for an autonomous concept of EU citizenship?*] [in:] G. Baranowska, A. Gliszczyńska-Grabias and A. Bodnar (eds.), *Ochrona praw obywatelek i obywateli Unii Europejskiej. 20 lat — osiągnięcia i wyzwania na przyszłość* [*Protection of the rights of citizens of the European Union. 20 years — achievements and challenges for the future*], Warszawa 2015

Pudzianowska D., Szczepanik M., *Wokół problemu bezpaństwowości dzieci w Polsce* [*In the orbit of the problem of statelessnes of children in Poland*] [in:] D. Pudzianowska (ed.), *Status cudzoziemca w Polsce wobec współczesnych wyzwań międzynarodowych* [*The status of a foreigner in Poland in the face of modern international challenges*], Warszawa 2016

Rajan S., *International surrogacy arrangements and statelessness* [in:] *The world's stateless children*, Institute on Statelessness and Inclusion, January 2017

Ramus W., *Instytucje prawa o obywatelstwie polskim* [*Institutions of Polish citizenship law*], Warszawa 1980

Renucci J.F., *Droit européen des droits de l'Homme*, Paris 2002

Robinson N., *Convention relating to the status of stateless persons. Its history and interpretation. A commentary*, New York 1955, reprinted by the Division of International Protection of the UNHCR 1997

Roma Belong — Statelessness, discrimination and marginalisation of Roma in the Western Balkans and Ukraine, European Network on Statelessness, European Roma Rights Centre, The Institute on Statelessness and Inclusion, Budapest, October 2017

Ross J.I., *An introduction to political crime*, Bristol 2012

Rustom C., Schoonvae Q., *Mapping statelessness in Belgium*, UNHCR, October 2012

Wiliński P. (ed.), *Rzetelny proces karny w orzecznictwie sądów polskich i międzynarodowych* [Fair criminal trial in the decisions of Polish and international courts], Warszawa 2009

Samore W., *Statelessness as a consequence of the conflict of nationality laws*, 45(3) American Journal of International Law 1951

Scott J.B., *Unprogressive Codification of Nationality at The Hague*, 18 Women Lawyers' Journal 1930

Seckler-Hudson C., *Statelessness. With special reference to the United States*, Washington, D. C. 1934

Semjonov A., Karzetskaja J., Ezhova E., *Ending childhood statelessness. A study on Estonia*, ed. by L. van Waas, 4 European Network on Statelessness. Working Paper 2015

Shiblak A., *Stateless Palestinians*, 26 Forced Migration Review 2006

Sievers W., *A call to Kinship* [in:] R. Bauböck, B. Perching and W. Sievers (eds.), *Citizenship policies in the New Europe*, Amsterdam 2009

Smilevska M., *Ending childhood statelessness. A study on Macedonia*, 2 European Network on Statelessness, Working Paper 2015

Sochin D'Elia M., *Country report: Lichtenstein*, 29 RSCAS/EUDO-CIT-CR 2013

Spiro P.J., *A new international law of citizenship*, 105(4) The American Journal of International Law 2011

Spiro P., *Mandated membership, diluted identity. Citizenship, globalization, and international law* [in:] A. Brysk, G. and Shafir (eds.), *People out of place. Globalization, human rights, and the citizenship gap*, New York 2004.

Stiller M., *Statelessness in international law. A historic overview*, 3 Deutsch-Amerikanische Juristen-Vereinigung Newsletter 2012

Studer B., Sturge K., *Citizenship as contingent national belonging. Married women and foreigners in twentieth-century Switzerland*, 13(3) Gender & History, November 2001

Suchocka H., *Prawo do posiadania obywatelstwa* [*The right to nationality*] [in:] R. Wieruszewski (ed.), *Prawa człowieka. Model prawny* [*Human rights. Legal model*], Wrocław 1991

Swider K., *A rights-based approach to statelessness*, unpublished doctoral dissertation defended at the University of Amsterdam, 2018

Sword K., Davies N., Ciechanowski J., *The formation of the Polish community in Great Britain 1939-1950*, School of Slavonic and East European Studies, University of London, London 1989

Thomas R., *From 'Adversarial v. Inquisitorial' to 'Active, Enabling, and Investigative': Developments in UK Administrative Tribunals* [in:] L. Jacobs and S. Baglay (eds.), *The Nature of Inquisitorial Processes in Administrative Regimes: Global Perspectives*, London–New York 2016

Vichniac M., *Le statut international des apatrides*, Recueil des Cours 1933-I, de la Collection 1933/43

Volpp L., *Divesting citizenship. On Asian American history and the loss of citizenship through marriage*, 53 UCLA Law Review 405 (2005)

Volpp L., *Feminist, sexual and queer citizenship* [in:] A. Shachar, R. Bauböck, I. Bloemraad and M. Vink (eds.), *The Oxford handbook of citizenship*, Oxford 2017

Vonk O., *Nationality law in the Western Hemisphere. A study on grounds for acquisition and loss of citizenship in the Americas and the Caribbean*, Leiden–Boston 2015

van Waas L., *A Comparative Analysis of Nationality Laws in the MENA Region*, 9 September 2014

van Waas L., *Nationality Matters. Statelessness under International Law*, School of Human Rights Research Series, vol. 29, Intersentia 2008

Weis P., *Nationality and statelessness in international law*, London 1979

Weis P., *Statelessness as a legal-political problem* [in:] British Section of the World Jewish Congress, *The Problem of Statelessness*, London 1944

Weis P., *The United Nations Convention on the Reduction of Statelessness, 1961*, 11(4) The International and Comparative Law Quarterly October 1962

Wierzbicki B., *Pojęcie przestępstwa politycznego w prawie międzynarodowym* [*The notion of political crime in international law*], Warszawa 1979

Wihtol de Wenden C., *La question migratoire au XXI siècle. Migrants, réfugiés et relations internationales*, Paris 2017

Williams J.F., *Denationalization*, 8 British Year Book of International Law 1927

Ziembiński Z., *Logika praktyczna* [*Practical logic*], Warszawa 2000

Zimmermann A., Wennholz P., *Article 1F 1951 Convention* [in:] A. Zimmermann (ed.), *The 1951 Convention Relating to the Status of Refugees and its 1967 Protocol. A commentary*, Oxford 2011

Zincone G., Basili M., *Country report Italy. Country report*, 35 RSCAS/EUDO-CIT-CR 2010

Ius, Lex et Res Publica

Studies in Law, Philosophy and Political Cultures

Edited by
Anna Jaron

Vol. 1 Anna Jaron: Socio-Economic Constitutional Rights in Democratisation Processes. An Account of the Constitutional Dialogue Theory. 2012.

Vol. 2 Stanisław Filipowicz: Democracy – The Power of Illusion. 2013.

Vol. 3 Teresa Dukiet-Nagórska (ed.): The Postulates of Restorative Justice and the Continental Model of Criminal Law. As Illustrated by Polish Criminal Law 2014.

Vol. 4 Agnieszka Kupzok: Enforcement of Patents on Geographically Divisible Inventions. An Inquiry into the Standard of Substantive Patent Law Infringement in Cross-Border Constellations. 2015.

Vol. 5 Alicja Jagielska-Burduk / Wojciech Szafrański: Legal Issues in Cultural Heritage Management. A Polish Perspective. 2016.

Vol. 6 Maciej Mataczyński (ed.): The Takeover of Public Companies as a Mode of Exercising EU Treaty Freedoms. 2017.

Vol. 7 Maciej Barczewski (ed.): Value of Information. Intellectual Property, Privacy and Big Data. 2018.

Vol. 8 Pawel Smoleń, Marcin Burzec: Introduction to Polish Tax Law. 2018.

Vol. 9 Łukasz Pohl, Konrad Burdziak: Judicial Interpretation of the 1997 Criminal Code Provisions on Self-Defence. 2019.

Vol. 10 Adam Szot: Judicial Review of Administrative Discretion. The Influence of Court Decisions on Administrative Actions. 2019.

Vol. 11 Michał Peno / Konrad Burdziak (eds.): The Concept of Modern Law. Polish and Central European Tradition. 2019.

Vol. 12 Leszek Leszczyński / Bartosz Liżewski / Adam Szot (eds.): Potential of Precedent in the Statutory Legal Order. 2019.

Vol. 13 Łukasz Bolesta: In Search of a Model for the Legal Protection of a Whistleblower in the Workplace in Poland. A legal and comparative study. 2020.

Vol. 14 Paweł Chmielnicki / Adam Sulikowski (eds.): New Perspectives on Legislation. A Comparative Approach. 2020.

Vol. 15 Marcin Burzec / Beata Kucia-Guściora / Paweł Smoleń: Agricultural Activity in Poland: A Fiscal and Legal Study. 2020.

Vol. 16 Magdalena Półtorak / Ilona Topa (eds.): Women, Children and (Other) Vulnerable Groups. Standards of Protection and Challenges for International Law. 2021.

Vol. 17 Josef Albert Fox: Die polnische Verfassung vom 3. Mai 1791. Hintergründe der Entstehung und der Außerkraftsetzung. Stellung Polens im Zeitalter der Aufklärung. 2021.

Vol. 18 Barbara Janusz-Pohl (ed.): Juvenile Justice Systems: Poland-Brazil-Portugal. 2021.

Vol. 19 Leszek Leszczyński: General Reference Clauses in the Judicial Process. Context of Legislative Intentions Interpretative Discretion. 2021.

Vol. 20 Francisco J. Campos Zamora: Das Problem der Begründung richterlicher Entscheidungen. Eine Analyse auf der Grundlage der Theorie der juristischen Argumentation. 2021.

Ius, Lex et Res Publica

Studies in Law, Philosophy and Political Cultures

Edited by

Barbara Janusz-Pohl and Anna Jaron

Vol. 21 Aneta Skorupa-Wulczyńska: Language Rights of the Citizen of the European Union. 2022.

Vol. 22 Mateusz Osiecki: International Legal Aspects of Aerial Terrorism. Methods of Law Enforcement in Avia-tion. 2022.

Vol. 23 Vladimír Sharp / Gabriela Blahoudková / Jakub Handrlica (eds.): Law, Pandemics and Ownership Restrictions. 2022.

Vol. 24 Piotr Kasprzyk / Anna Konert: Drones – Future of Aviation Law? Interference of Public Law in Private Law. 2023.

Vol. 25 Szymon Pawelec (ed.): Consensual Procedures in Criminal Law – Comparative Perspective. 2023.

Vol. 26 Dorota Pudzianowska: Statelessness in Public Law. 2023.

www.peterlang.com

www.ingramcontent.com/pod-product-compliance
Ingram Content Group UK Ltd.
Pitfield, Milton Keynes, MK11 3LW, UK
UKHW011005120926
8556IPUK00027B/48

9 783631 860724